LANDING IN HELL

LANDING IN HELL

The Pyrrhic Victory of the First Marine
Division on Peleliu, 1944

PETER MARGARITIS

CASEMATE

Philadelphia & Oxford

Published in the United States of America and Great Britain in 2018 by
CASEMATE PUBLISHERS
1950 Lawrence Road, Havertown, PA 19083, USA
and
The Old Music Hall, 106–108 Cowley Road, Oxford OX4 1JE, UK

Hardback Edition: ISBN 978-1-61200-645-1
Digital Edition: ISBN 978-1-61200-646-8 (ePub)

A CIP record for this book is available from the British Library

Printed and bound in the United States of America

Typeset in India by Versatile PreMedia Services. www.versatilepremedia.com

For a complete list of Casemate titles, please contact:

CASEMATE PUBLISHERS (US)
Telephone (610) 853-9131
Fax (610) 853-9146
Email: casemate@casematepublishers.com
www.casematepublishers.com

CASEMATE PUBLISHERS (UK)
Telephone (01865) 241249
Fax (01865) 794449
Email: casemate-uk@casematepublishers.co.uk
www.casematepublishers.co.uk

Front cover: Men of the US 1st Marine Division fighting just beyond White Beach, Peleliu, 15 September 1944. (U.S. Marine corps photo)
Back cover: Landing craft (U.S. Marine corps photo) and First Marine Division patch.

Contents

This book is dedicated to the memory of my good friend, Sergeant George Peto, USMC, one of the "Old Breed," who went ashore in the first wave at Peleliu with the Third Battalion, 1st Marines, and who over seventy years later, collaborated closely with me on the original essay from which this book has been written.

List of Illustrations

Preface

As a writer of military history, I became aware in the spring of 2015 of an annual essay contest that was sponsored by the U.S. Naval Institute. That year's contest carried a first prize of $5,000. The essay could be no more than 3,000 words, and the topic was to be on some noteworthy U.S. Marine Corps event that had made a significant impact in American history. Having researched and written most of my career on either the American Civil War or the European Theater in World War II, I realized that writing about Marines would be a challenge. This would be a new avenue of historical investigation for me.

Unsure of what subject to write about, I consulted with a few of my American Legion cohorts who were Marine veterans. Their consensus was that I write about the controversial invasion of Peleliu that had taken place in September, 1944. They felt that the Marines that had landed had been needlessly wasted in that bloody operation, and that their story had never adequately been told. A Navy buddy of mine suggested that if I were to decide to write about Peleliu, that I should consult with an old World War II Marine veteran, one who lived relatively near me in central Ohio and who had been there. His name was George Peto. He was one of what they called the "Old Breed" and had actually participated in the Peleliu operation.

George and I first met on June 24, 2015 in a Bob Evans restaurant to discuss the idea. We immediately took a liking to each other, and I invited him to assist me with the essay. We felt that we would make a good team, since I was an experienced writer and researcher, and George had not only been there with the first wave, but had a remarkable memory about what he had experienced.

Our essay unfortunately did not win the contest, so George and I decided to expand our work and turn what we had written into a book. During the course of our endeavor though, as this exceptional old man told me more about his past, I listened, fascinated, marveling at his consistent, detailed memory of extraordinary things that had happened to him many decades ago. At last, I realized that a much better book to write would be about his life. I wanted to—I *had* to—write about him, to preserve his memories for everyone, especially his daughter Nancy, his son George Lee, and his friends. He good-naturedly agreed, and so we were off.

The result was an incredible story about a remarkable Marine. Published in late July, 2017 and entitled *Twenty-Two on Peleliu*, it detailed George's exploits, from a young boy growing up in the backwoods of southern Akron, Ohio, to the hot dry plains of Utah, working on soil conservation projects with the Civilian Conservation Corps, to his exploits as a Marine, and his life after the war. It follows his early career in the Marines, to the jungles of the Pacific in intensive Pacific campaigns, to his life back in Ohio.

I truly enjoyed co-writing about his exciting life, while at the same time, I was able to gather so much information from him and from our research about war in the Pacific. Unfortunately, just after our first draft was finished, George passed away. I had vowed to see the book published, and so I continued on, finishing the book, and securing a publisher.

As I awaited the book's release though, a nagging thought kept popping up in my mind. I had never followed through on our original project. I knew from my investigations and from my experiences with Mr. Peto exactly how brutal the Peleliu operation had been for the First Marine Division. And my research had uncovered a whole myriad of accounts that were either not true, imprecise, or never really studied. One such controversy, for instance, centered on the U.S. Navy's third and last day of intensive, pre-invasion bombardment. Some accounts claimed that it never happened. A few claim that it did, and was quite effective in achieving its objectives. I eventually discovered that the truth was somewhere in the middle.

These inaccuracies and the need to get a correct analysis out, along with a healthy dose of guilt for not having finished the narrative, led me to undertake the project once again. The original story that my friend George had provided so much detailed, first-hand information on before he passed away needed to be told.

The Peleliu operation, I found out, was considered a relatively small part of a much larger, global effort, and as such had been hurriedly planned, and only with "available" resources and supplies. The Marines who participated in the operation, after having had to live for months in primitive conditions on which to train and get ready, were transported to and landed onto what unexpectedly was discovered to be a veritable hornets' nest. There they had to fight a ferocious battle that they had not anticipated, nor for which they had been adequately been allowed to prepare.

Hence, this book. I hope that in many ways, it clears up most of the clouds that surround earlier historical accounts. The conclusions reached here, while under my pen, are mostly those agreed upon by those who had been there or had been in operational command at that time.

I would like to thank a couple people for helping me in my endeavor. My heartfelt appreciation goes to George Peto's daughter and son, Nancy and George Lee, for their continuing support in their father's initial project. I would like to offer my appreciation as well for the Marine Corps League, especially the Belleau Woods Detachment #508 in Columbus, Ohio, for their unswerving cooperation and assistance. Last, my deep gratitude to my wonderful wife Mindy, who continues for some reason to put up with my bizarre methods and eccentric moods.

Peter Margaritis

Introduction

On September 15, 1944, victory for the Allies had become a glowing light on the horizon. The United States, in its inexorable trek across the Pacific toward Japan, continued its drive with the invasion of a tiny island named Peleliu, the second southernmost of the Palau Island group. Securing the island was considered an important requirement as a prelude to the long-awaited invasion of the Philippines.

The main assault on Peleliu was to be made by the First Marine Division under the command of 55-year-old Major General William Rupertus. He had joined the division in March of 1942, and as the Assistant Division Officer (ADO), had fought with the division in the fierce Guadalcanal campaign.

After having studied the upcoming operation and after having been briefed by his staff, Rupertus concluded that this operation would only take three or four days, and that resistance would be initially moderate but brief. He boasted to his officers that, "We'll be through in three days. It might take two."

Some six long weeks later, having sustained terrific losses in fierce, nearly continuous combat, the last of his division was finally evacuated from the island. At that point, Phase 2 began, and the Army took over with the task of reducing and eliminating what was left of the hidden Japanese defensive positions. That took another four weeks.

The Marine division would be out of action for six months, its infantry regiments having averaged 50 percent casualties—the highest unit losses ever in Marine Corps history—that occurred in the three rifle assault regiments, the 1st, 5th, and 7th Marines. (Casualties in the division's other units, such as the 11th Marines (Artillery), the tank battalion, engineers, and medical battalion were not as severe.) While the Marines in the end had been triumphant, their victory was truly what would be called Pyrrhic.

The expression refers to a battlefield success, but one that inflicts such a devastating toll on the victor that having won is little better than having been defeated. The winner's losses are tremendous, usually almost as heavy as those of their enemy, thus in effect negating a true sense of achievement.

The term is derived from an ancient king of Epirus, a small 3rd-century BC Greek city-state country located in what today is the southern part of Albania and the northwestern part of Greece. Epirus at that time was a powerful Greek state, and King Pyrrhus, a second cousin of Alexander the Great, and was in his own right a formidable general. Thirty-eight-year-old Pyrrhus took his country to war in 280 BC against the Roman Republic to assist an ally, the Greek state of Tarentum in southern Italy. The Romans were trying to subdue all of the Greek states in Italy and Sicily. Tarentum, located in the Italian boot heel, would not be able to survive a direct Roman assault alone.

Pyrrhus put together a coalition army of about 27,000 and some 20 war elephants, loaned to him by his father-in-law, Ptolemy II of Egypt. He crossed the Ionian Sea in 280 BC and landed near Tarentum. The next spring, he invaded Apulia, a region at the tip of the Adriatic Sea, and, marching up Italy's eastern coast, he met the Roman army at the town of Asculum. After a ferocious, bloody two-day struggle in which the tide of battle turned several times, the Epirotes were finally victorious. Their army though, had been devastated by the battle, their casualties tremendous. Pyrrhus lost over a quarter of his army, and many good commanders, as well as veteran soldiers, had been killed or maimed, many of them irreplaceable. His losses were so great that he could no longer continue the offensive and had to prematurely go into winter quarters to rebuild his army. On the other hand, the losers, the Romans, were able to rapidly replace their losses, so the defeat did little to set them back.

Pyrrhus himself was disheartened by such a costly victory. The Greek essayist Plutarch later wrote that when one of his remaining commanders congratulated the king on his win, he looked at the man sourly and replied, "Yes, and if we are victorious in one more such battle with the Romans, we shall be utterly ruined."

There have been other similar examples in history where the winning side has suffered nearly as much as the enemy, either in casualties or in strategic losses. Napoleon's marginal victory at Borodino in September, 1812 left him in control of the battlefield, but his losses were some 30,000 men, a critical number for an army far from home; and soon he would face the terrible freezing Russian winter. The British won their battle over the American colonists at Bunker Hill in June, 1775, after three frontal charges up the hill, but they lost two and a half times more men than the colonists. The Americans' claim of a moral victory substantially furthered their cause for independence. British General Howe later shook his head and bemoaned the fact that his win had been "too dearly bought."

Lee suffered a similar victory at Chancellorsville, Virginia in May, 1863. In a daring piece of tactical brilliance, he narrowly defeated the twice-as-strong Union forces, losing some 13,000 men to the Union's 17,000. His losses though, in both men and matériel, would be harder to replace, and casualties were very costly in terms of the experienced fighters lost, including the death of his most trusted and capable general: Stonewall Jackson.

Then there were the bloody battles of World War I on the Western Front—the Somme, Verdun, and Passchendaele, not to mention the lesser campaigns where thousands were killed or maimed to gain a few hundred yards here or there.

Peleliu was no different in this regard. The Marines were eventually victorious over the Japanese that fall of 1944, but the cost to them was tremendous. So many hardened veterans and officers in the famed First Marine Division—the "Old Breed"—became casualties, and the rifle units suffered a higher percentage of losses than ever before (or since) in Marine Corps history. There are a number of reasons for this, including several mistakes that occurred. And the sad part about it is that in the end, taking that island proved unnecessary in winning the war. In fact, many argue that it should not have been undertaken.

This book analyzes why the casualties were so excessive, as well as clearing up a number of confusing issues previously recounted.

CHAPTER ONE

Target: Peleliu

Political Background

Along with the Marshall, Mariana, and Caroline islands, the Palaus (called "*Parao Shoto*" by the Japanese) just west of the Carolines, had been occupied by the Japanese for decades. After they had declared war on Germany in 1914, the Japanese Navy had sent a force to occupy the islands. After the peace treaty was signed, these annexed islands were awarded to Japan in 1920 as a mandate* by the newly formed League of Nations. Japan, in turn for being given wide-sweeping administrative powers, was tasked with "promoting to the utmost the natural and moral well-being and social progress" of the islanders. Since then, Japan had assumed all the land rights of the islands; the Palaus had been developed by the Japanese into a formidable base, with the island government located on the small island of Koror near the center of the chain.

Throughout the 1920s, Japan became increasingly fascist as dissent within the country was more and more suppressed. In September of 1931, Japan, now controlled by the military, initiated a bold expansionist plan by invading Manchuria. The League of Nations finally declared Japan the aggressor and demanded that occupied Manchuria be returned to China. Japan refused, and in late February of 1933, it withdrew its delegation from the League of Nations, but brazenly retained its island groups as the *de facto* sovereign. At the same time, it closed these mandates off to the rest of the world.

---

* Mandate is a term that refers to the 11 territories or protectorates surrendered by Germany and the Ottoman Empire at the end of World War I. The process was created by the League of Nations through Article 22 of its charter, whereby a territory was assigned to an Allied power (the "Mandatory"), ostensibly until the territory could govern itself. Nearly all mandates remained under the control of their Mandatory until after World War II.

In the early part of World War II, the Palaus became a forward staging area from which the now formidable Imperial Navy had furthered Japanese influence down into the Dutch East Indies and New Guinea. By 1944, they had further expanded the Palau island chain into a major supply center and had turned them into a Pacific main line of defense for the Japanese Home Islands.

Geography

The Palaus are a multifarious group of over a hundred tropical islands and islets of about 189 square miles of land. Located some 825 miles southwest of Guam and 2,000 miles south of Tokyo, they are oriented roughly north-northeast to south-southwest for about 80 miles. This remote tropical island group in the western part of Micronesia has its own language that includes several different dialects. Average rainfall is over 140 inches a year, mostly coming in the summer and early fall. Temperatures average in the 80s, although they frequently top 100°F (38°C). Humidity averages around 82 percent.

The five main islands in the cluster are, north to south: Babelthuap, Koror, Eli Malk, Peleliu, and Angaur. Babelthuap is by far the largest, about 125 square miles, and about ten miles wide. Nearly all of them are surrounded by an offshore barrier reef of coral. Most of the others are small islets or atolls, many just an acre or two in size. Just north of Babelthuap, between it and Ngajangel Island to the north, surrounded by broken reefs, is a large, triangular-shaped, natural, deep-water lagoon known as Kossol Passage. Some 12 miles wide, it has very few shoals and is large enough to be used as both a temporary anchorage and a seaplane operating area. Its only drawback is that, exposed on all sides, it offers no protection from the weather, with high winds resulting in large swells.

The southernmost island, Angaur, is about seven miles southwest of its nearest neighbor, Peleliu. It is shaped roughly like a crescent, somewhat like the top of a classic baby carriage, with the hood facing Peleliu to the east. Angaur is about two and a half miles long and less than two miles wide at its widest point. Its terrain is much flatter than Peleliu, with its high point only about 200 feet above sea level, although there are several wooded coral ridges at the northwestern corner. Like Peleliu, the island was mostly made up of thick jungle. The Japanese had over the years built a number of phosphate strip-mines on the island, interconnected by a narrow-gauge railroad. There were several wide beaches suitable for landings, although the most ideal were on the southwestern and northeastern shores.

The innocent-sounding Peleliu (called *"Periju"* by the Japanese) lies strategically some 450 miles east-southeast of the Philippines and 650 miles north of New Guinea. It is the second-to-last southernmost island, about 23 miles from the capital island of Koror in the center of the chain, and 27 miles from Babelthuap to its north, by far the largest and northernmost Palau island.

Peleliu is somewhat shaped like a lobster claw, which is why in the planning stages, the Americans often referred to it as "the lobster claw island." This small coral-limestone island is less than six miles long and a bit over two miles wide, measuring only about 6,400 acres in size. The eastern arm of the island is much shorter than the western one, which is about two miles long. Between them lay several marshes and mangrove swamps.

The geography of the island in 1944 was slightly different from its present shape, but its topography has essentially remained the same. Most of the island—barring the Umurbrogol massif northeast of the airfield—is level and except for the northern end, which was either open terrain or coconut groves, the island was either thick with jungle or wet with marshes and mangrove swamps. For most of the southern part, Peleliu is more or less flat, and, except for the beaches and the fairly large airfield, was originally covered with thick jungle, brush, scrub trees, and a variety of mangroves and swamps. There are no natural water sources on the island.

The beaches on the southwestern side of the island and on the southeastern tip were open, and could be considered possible landing areas. The beaches on the southwestern side totaled about 2,600 yards in length, with the southern end just 1,600 yards from the southern tip. Here the distance to the barrier reef ranged from 400 yards on the left, to 750 yards in the center, and 550 yards on the right. The beach at the southern end was much narrower, with a number of coral outcroppings along the edge. Each beach area was ringed by dense jungle, including a concentration of coconut, mango, and palm trees.

The airfield was located in open terrain just north of the southwestern beaches. It boasted two long runways, each about 50 feet wide. The longest, running parallel to the island's longitudinal axis, was 5,500 feet long, the other, perpendicular to it, was 3,800 feet long, and the topography was such that both could easily be extended for larger aircraft. The airfield also featured a hard surfaced, 2,700-foot taxiway that connected the runways, the turning circles, and the service aprons.

Begun in 1938, with some 3,000 Japanese and 500 Korean military personnel, the airfield included a large, cinderblock control headquarters, several metal buildings, and dozens of other structures, including a modest communication building, machine shops, quarters, fuel storage, and a small power plant. The airstrip was well developed and big enough to accommodate large strategic bombers. Thus, it was considered by the Allies as a strategically important objective for the entire maritime area, and therefore would be a major factor in the decision to invade the island.

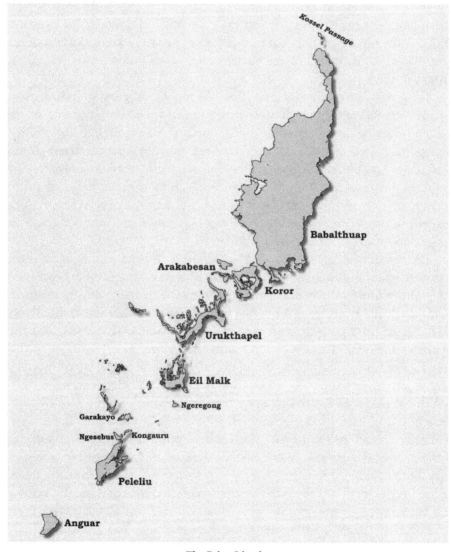

The Palau Islands.

At the time, Peleliu and Angaur combined carried a small population of about 300 natives. Unlike the tens of thousands on Koror with paved streets and electricity, these locals lived comparatively simple lives, subsisting on fishing, communal gardens and small livestock.

There are a number of coral-limestone hills located at the northwestern and eastern tips, and two promontories at the far southern end. Just northeast of the airfield though, is a feature strikingly different from the rest of the island's topography. This is a jagged cordillera that runs up the spine of the island for about three miles. The natives call it "*Umurbrogol*," the Japanese called it "*Momoji*," and the Marines would acrimoniously come to christen it "Bloody Nose Ridge." This small massif is a dense chain of pinnacles, treacherous ravines, ridges and defiles almost a thousand yards wide, with slopes that rise to 550 feet above sea level, well covered with brush and low vegetation along the sides and tops, and with thick jungle along the gulches. In among all this were countless numbers of caves, both natural and manmade, with many being old phosphate mines. The Japanese had engaged in a major defensive program to modify, expand and reinforce these, as well as create new ones that were often connected by narrow tunnels.

Peleliu is surrounded by an offshore coral barrier reef. In some areas such as the northeast, it has a steep gradient, while in some sections like the western side, it is broader. The distance between the reef and the shore varies, from 1,500 yards in the northeast, to almost a mile and a half in the north, to only 300–400 yards at the southern end.

The Decision to Invade

Since the United States' sudden, jarring entry into World War II in early December of 1941, the American plan for victory in the Pacific had naturally centered on capturing the Home Islands of Japan. This main objective had by the early months of 1942 resulted in a solid strategy by the Army and the Navy. Unlike the war against Germany, where several substantial Allied forces were involved, defeat of the Japanese would have to be almost exclusively conducted by the United States. As such, victory would entail by necessity a unique and new approach that had two goals.

The first was to stop the Japanese expansion in the Pacific. By the start of 1942, the Empire of Japan controlled a good part of China and Burma, all of Malaya (including Singapore), the Dutch East Indies, and Indochina. They had also fortified their mandates, the Mariana Islands, the Carolines, the Marshalls, and the Palaus. Their widespread offensive across the Pacific had seen the fall of Guam, Wake, the Gilberts, the Solomons, and finally, the Philippines. Malaya, French Indochina, and Dutch Borneo had fallen. New Zealand was threatened, and Australia had been bombed several times.

The second goal was, as much as anything, to break the stretched oceanic logistical lines that Japan had established years ago. The Japanese now required these vital sea lanes to both defend their empire and to protect the shipment of goods desperately needed to maintain vital war production.

For the U.S. to ultimately be able to defeat the Japanese by closing in on the homeland, it was determined necessary to commence a full-scale assault throughout the Pacific. The "island hopping strategy," as it became known, was the only realistic means to array the Allied forces close enough to the final objective of the Japanese mainland.

The Americans had in early May, 1942 scored a marginal naval victory at Coral Sea, thwarting a Japanese invasion of Port Moresby in New Guinea. Then, a month later, they won a decisive victory at Midway, though their efforts to move forward from there that summer were not exactly decisive in nature. A sort of stalemate developed in the Pacific. Neither side could effectively move against the other.

However, the industrial might of a resolute United States then began to come into play: factories were gearing up rapidly, and vast reservoirs of manpower were growing the armed forces at a breathless rate. Hundreds of thousands of men poured into and out of training centers, war matériel for land, sea, and air started to roll off the assembly lines toward the fronts.

Impasse notwithstanding, the Americans were ready to begin their grand strategy for victory. By now, the Americans and the British Commonwealth together were undertaking a maximum effort to neutralize Japanese strongholds and gain logistical support bases with which to expand the Pacific campaign. With the Commonwealth concentrating their efforts in India and Malaysia, the Americans moved westward across the Pacific. At the beginning of August, 1942 they initiated what would become the bitterly fought campaign to take Guadalcanal. Air, land and naval assets on both sides maneuvered and fought for the area. The Allies eventually prevailed, and 1943 saw a shift in momentum as they slowly, inexorably, began to push back. By the summer of 1944, with U.S. war production now in full swing, many of the Central and Southern Pacific island chains had been seized, while in the south, the Army was pushing up New Guinea.

The main American plan of advance had by now evolved into a two-prong thrust across the Pacific. The U.S. Navy under 59-year-old Admiral Chester

W. Nimitz, who commanded all Allied naval forces in the Pacific with the title of CinCPac, was to oversee the assault along the northern route across the Central Pacific. The second component was led by the Army, under 64-year-old General Douglas MacArthur, Supreme Commander, Allied Forces, Southwest Pacific Area (SWPA) whose objective was to directly assault the enemy through the Southwest Pacific.

By the spring of 1944, the Allied plan seemed to be working. Nimitz's naval forces in their westward trek had taken the Marshall Islands and were working on the Marianas. The successful implementation behind this advance was a coordinated, two-fisted Navy assault weapon.

The first of this one-two punch combination was a well-developed, massive naval force that centered on a fast carrier task force, a powerful surface attack group of battleships and cruisers, several large escort squadrons, and a virtual armada of support ships that included oilers, escort carriers, and supply vessels. This immense fleet, with all of its technologically updated might, could move across the Pacific at will and take on any naval force that the enemy could mount against it. As such, it posed a grave threat to the Japanese Navy.

The second fist was in the form of a large amphibious task force that could deliver a sturdy, effective landing force onto almost any island in the Pacific. This force had grown over the last two years and now included in its ground forces some five or six divisions, accompanied by a host of amphibious support units.

Working together, these two components made a winning combination. After the naval forces had pounded the target for days from the sea and the air, the Marine landing force, sailing in out of a sea of various types of transports and covered by an array of multi-caliber naval guns that pounded the beachhead areas mercilessly, would storm ashore, forge inland, and secure their objectives.

Naturally, Nimitz's forces needed adequate support, and the newly created Service Force that had been fashioned by Vice Admiral William L. Calhoun was quite up to the job. This massive, mobile, logistical group had, thanks to the industrial might of the United States, in its ranks vast numbers of supply, support, repair, and medical assets that could sustain both the naval and the amphibious fighting units across thousands of miles of ocean. They were often able to replenish fighting units while underway, able to repair disabled ships in small, setup harbors, and medically treat and evacuate the wounded in an efficient pattern of mobility and efficiency.

After hard fighting and substantial losses through the end of 1942, the Americans had won the air, sea, and land battles of Guadalcanal, and from

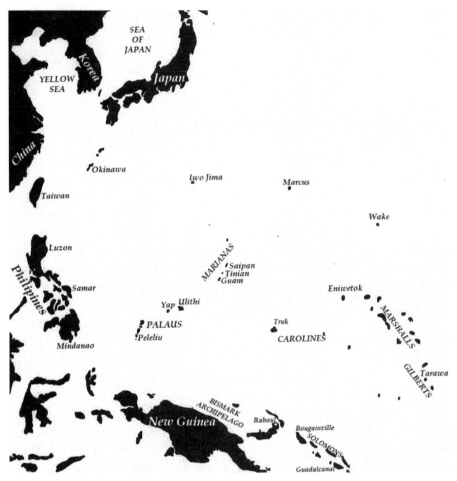

The Pacific theater of operations, 1944.

there, had moved onward to Bougainville, New Georgia, and nearly all of the Solomon Islands. While Nimitz's fleet pursued an island-hopping battle plan across the Central Pacific, in the south, General MacArthur and his Southwest Pacific Forces surged ahead, moving northwest up New Guinea, which was finally taken in the spring of 1944. Now the general was setting his sights on what for him had been his main objective and the center of his thrust: returning to and triumphantly liberating the Philippines. These were the islands that at the onset of the war, he had so rapidly lost in an embarrassing and unbecoming struggle, and from which he had had to evacuate in disgrace. MacArthur was now keen on getting payback.

In so many of the War Department's war-gaming strategies that had been developed over the years, even stretching back to before Pearl Harbor, it had been understood by American senior officers that control of the Philippines would ultimately be essential to any final victory in the Pacific, and as such, the Palaus figured prominently in its seizure.

First of all, the island group lay right in the path of what most plans determined would be one of, if not the Navy's main line of advancement to the Philippine islands in support of MacArthur to the south. The northernmost island, Babelthuap, had become a moderately sized base and staging area for the Japanese. At the other end, the southernmost island, Peleliu, boasted a large airfield located on a relatively flat plain. The Japanese had used it early on in the war as a refueling stop for aircraft coming from aircraft production plants on the Japanese Home Islands and flying on to the Solomons or New Guinea. If this airfield could be taken, it could be turned into a major airbase from which the Americans could mount a massive bomber offensive against the Japanese forces to the west. Conversely, if it was not taken but instead bypassed, it would be a major communications and logistical threat to the flanks of any coordinated thrust that was undertaken beyond it.

Throughout 1943, securing Peleliu had long been considered by MacArthur to be critical to his success, and as such it remained a milestone in his planning. Thus the Navy had automatically incorporated its seizure into the schedule, and in the fall of 1943, the planning for what was codenamed Operation *Stalemate*, the capture of the Marianas and the Palaus, was initiated. In this operation, Peleliu and Angaur Island would be assaulted by the First Marine Division and the Army 81st Infantry Division. The large, northern island of Babelthuap would be taken by the Army 27th Infantry Division.

Some nine months later though, the strategic picture had undergone several changes. Commitments to other operations into the Marianas and additional intelligence reports on the Palaus made changes to the operation necessary. The Saipan operation required the 27th Division's participation, and the invasion of Guam had become bogged down. Thus on July 7, the Navy Pacific High Command revised the Palaus campaign, now retitled the Palau invasion Operation *Stalemate II*. Planning was overseen by Marine Major General Julian Smith.

By the end of that year though, a strange, competitive inter-service rift in strategic planning had clearly emerged. The U.S. Navy, perhaps taking the Combined Chiefs of Staff strategic guideline given on December 3 of "obtaining bases from which the unconditional surrender of Japan can be forced" perhaps a bit too literally, was pushing to have its northern thrust become the focus of the war effort to take Japan.

The Army in contrast was insisting that the main focus should be to create these bases by taking the Palaus and going into the Philippines, then moving northeastward, up to the island of Formosa, and from there onto mainland China. Although the Chief of Naval Operations himself, Admiral Ernest J. King,* believed that both plans could be undertaken simultaneously, he clearly felt that the northern route would lead to a much quicker and less costly victory than by, as he put it, "battering our way through the Philippines," which is what the Japanese expected.

By the summer of 1944, with the second front in Europe having been opened and the subsequent ground war in France now at its height, on the other side of the world, the two strategies in the Pacific were openly clashing. The President of the United States and Commander-in Chief, 62-year-old Franklin Delano Roosevelt, found himself vexed by this nagging, distracting problem between these two services.

To make matters on this disagreement worse, the Japanese in May 1944 had started yet another counteroffensive in China, one that now threatened the areas that the U.S. Army had planned to initially use in its strategy. Just after a conference in London of senior British and American generals a week after D-Day, the U.S. Joint Chiefs of Staff opened up the idea of bypassing the Philippines altogether (and thus follow the Navy's plan).

The chairman of the joint chiefs of staff, 63-year-old U.S. Army general George C. Marshall, was himself at the time fully concentrated on the huge undertaking in the European theater. He did not want to get the Army embroiled in a large land campaign in the Philippines and China. He was therefore quite open to this proposal, especially since the brunt of the effort would be undertaken by the Navy (including the Marines), which he knew was now a powerhouse out there. MacArthur of course, was incensed by the whole idea of thrusting northeast, arguing several points why such a strategy would infuriate the Filipinos at having been abandoned. Clearly, the matter needed a resolution.

Finally, near the end of July, the president found time to take a break. In Europe, Operation *Cobra* had seen the American forces breaking out of

---

* King actually wore two hats: not only was he Chief of Naval Operations (CNO), but he also carried the lesser title of Commander-in-Chief, United States Fleet (COMINCH), which included all U.S. naval surface forces in the Atlantic and the Pacific, but did not include the Asiatic Fleet, nor naval land forces. The COMINCH billet was abolished in October, 1945 by King, who by then had been promoted to fleet admiral.

the Normandy pocket, and Patton starting his lightning dash across France. After being nominated for an unprecedented fourth term as president in the Democratic National Convention in Chicago on July 21, President Roosevelt turned his full attention to the Pacific dilemma. He ordered MacArthur and Nimitz to join him in a strategic summit conference in the Pacific, so that they could coordinate their plans and make a determination on the final strategy could be made once and for all. The orders went out, MacArthur getting his via Admiral Nimitz.

The president knew well that his joint chiefs were split in their theories on how to win the war in the Pacific, so partly for that reason, he deliberately left them in Washington. He was determined to hear both sides directly from MacArthur and Nimitz and then hopefully come up with a solution that would placate both of them. Accompanied by his personal chief of staff, Admiral William D. Leahy, Roosevelt crossed the country and sailed for Hawaii aboard the heavy cruiser USS *Baltimore*.* On the other side of the Pacific, MacArthur took off from Brisbane, Australia in a B-17 (aptly named "Bataan") and flew in from the east. By Wednesday afternoon, July 26, 1944, they had all arrived at the main naval base at Pearl Harbor.

The *Baltimore* reached Pearl Harbor just after 2 p.m., and after entering the harbor entrance, as it passed Fort Kamehaha on the right, the vessel stopped as a launch came out to meet it. The cruiser took aboard Admiral Nimitz and the 14th Naval District commandant, Vice Admiral R.L. Ghormley. The two had come out to personally meet the president. The cruiser got underway again, and as it came into the harbor, the president's flag flying under the national colors of the main mast, hundreds of sailors stood at attention in dress whites. The *Baltimore* finally docked at Pier 22-B at 3 p.m., having traveled 2,285 miles from San Diego.

As soon as the gangplank was secured, more senior officers came aboard to greet the president. Among them were Lieutenant General Robert C. Richardson, who was the military governor of Hawaii and senior army officer in the Central Pacific, and Rear Admiral William R. Furlong, the commanding officer of the Pearl Harbor Navy Yard. Right behind them came Ingram M. Stainback, the governor of the Hawaii Territory.

---

* USS *Baltimore* (CA-68, Capt. Walter C. Calhoun, commanding) was a heavy cruiser, the first of her class, commissioned in mid-April, 1943. At 13,600 tons, she was 674 feet long, 71 feet wide, and had a draft of 27 feet. With a crew of 1,200, she could make 33 knots. She was armed with nine 8-inch guns, 12 5-inch guns, 12 quad 40mm AA guns, and 24 20mm AA guns. In the course of the war, she earned nine battle stars.

MacArthur, who was well aware of the upcoming presidential election because he had recently himself been a candidate, now seemed convinced that the president was attending this conference in Hawaii mostly for political posturing. MacArthur had in the past had a number of run-ins with Roosevelt and had been keen to run against the established "Roosevelt Dynasty" for the presidency. The general after all was a Medal of Honor winner, as had been his father in World War I,* and now had won a string of victories in the South Pacific the last couple years. A respectable Republican and a war hero, he had been a natural candidate for the office of president, and up until the spring of 1944, several important leaders in the Republican Party had been convinced that the general would be the one to beat Roosevelt in the upcoming election. That included such important figures as newspaper tycoons William Randolph Hearst and Cissy Patterson.

As the campaign began though, MacArthur still remained keen on fulfilling his promised to return to liberate the Philippines, and when New York governor Thomas Dewey edged him out as the Republican frontrunner at the Republican Convention in late June, he returned to his war planning. Still, he continued carrying his distaste for Roosevelt. Now, a couple months later, quite suspicious that the president was just grandstanding by sailing across the Pacific to oversee this conference, the general deliberately made sure that he arrived in Hawaii before the president, but would upstage him by arriving late to meet him. Thus, although his B-17 landed some two hours before the *Baltimore* docked at 3 p.m., he deliberately put off the meeting. He chose instead to first go to his assigned quarters at Fort Shafter to freshen up.

As he entered the base though, he first went to the quarters of a subordinate there, the military governor of Hawaii and senior army officer in the Central Pacific, Lieutenant General Robert C. Richardson. The general though was not in, having chosen to go to the piers to meet the president after his cruiser

---

* General Arthur MacArthur Jr., as a lieutenant, was awarded America's top medal in 1890 for combat in the Civil War during the Chattanooga Campaign of 1863. As adjutant of the 24th Wisconsin, carrying the regimental colors, he charged up Missionary Ridge on November 25, 1863 at a critical point in the battle, yelling "On Wisconsin!" Arthur went on to fight in the Indian Wars, the Spanish-American War, and the Philippine-American War, eventually attaining the rank of lieutenant general. Douglas received his in 1942 for (today controversial to historians) defense of the Philippine Islands. This unique phenomenon of both father and son earning the Medal of Honor, the first time in history, would not be repeated until Theodore Roosevelt Jr. was so awarded for his actions in Normandy, following in the footsteps of his father, President Theodore Roosevelt, who earned the medal riding up San Juan Hill in the Spanish-American War (the president though, was only awarded the medal posthumously in 2001).

Admiral Chester W. Nimitz, Commander-in-Chief, Pacific Fleet (CinCPac). Seen here talking to General Rupertus.

General Douglas MacArthur, Commander, Southwest Pacific Area.

had docked. There at Richardson's quarters, MacArthur took his time chatting with some old army friends before taking a shower. Finally he departed in a large, open army limousine. MacArthur rode alone in the back, wearing a styled khaki-colored leather jacket, a crushed army officer's cap, and his trademark dark sunglasses. He and his motorcycle escort arrived at the dock with elaborate fanfare, which included sirens, whistles, and, of course, applause and cheers. His limo pulled up and MacArthur got out, stopping for two ovations before bounding up the gangplank and boarding the heavy cruiser at 3:45 p.m.

Admiral Leahy met him on deck and, with a smile, asked, "Douglas, why don't you wear the right clothes when you come to see us?"

Grimacing, MacArthur replied, "Well, you haven't been where I came from, and it's cold up there in the sky."

After a short meeting with the president and Admiral Nimitz (who was dressed as protocol required, in his starched regulation dress whites), they went on deck at 4:15 to do a photoshoot for the media photographers. They then each departed the ship around 4:30 for the night,* the president to his

---

* Interestingly, the only other time the president had ever visited Oahu was July 26, 1934, aboard the heavy cruiser USS *Houston* (CA 30). Just a year and a half into his presidency, having left Annapolis, Maryland on July 1, the ship pulled into Honolulu harbor on July 26, exactly ten years to the day before this conference.

assigned quarters at a lavish three-story Waikiki estate, just off Diamond Head on Kalaukau Avenue, overlooking the beach.* Admiral Nimitz returned to his quarters at 37 Makalapa Point in Pearl Harbor, and General MacArthur rode back to Fort Shafter. There he complained that evening to General Richardson about having to leave his headquarters for a photoshoot, especially when he had received an invitation from the president that evening to go on another publicity tour the next day.

The following morning, the general and the admiral met the president at his villa, and at 10:45 a.m., the three of them, accompanied by an entourage of various senior officers, began the day touring facilities on Oahu. They were accompanied by the media (MacArthur, on his way to see the president, had been quoted as being upset over being forced to leave his command for this "picture-taking junket.") With MacArthur sitting in the back between the president on the right and Nimitz on the left, they toured several military bases in a luxurious, bright-red 1941 Packard, owned by the Honolulu fire chief (Roosevelt later chuckled when he found out that only one other such vehicle was in Hawaii, and it was owned by the madam of Honolulu's largest house of ill repute; she had begged that they use her car, but it would have easily been recognized, and that would never do). Since the military had evoked a strict news blackout on this trip and the conference, few photos were taken, and there were absolutely no news reports sent. The conversation in the Packard mostly centered on politics and the upcoming presidential election in November.

The tour included visits to the Marine Corps air station at Ewa, the Navy ammunition depot at Lualualei, Schofield Barracks, Wheeler Field and the Post hospital in Honolulu, the Seabee camp at Moanalua Ridge, and finally the Marine Corps training center at Camp Catlin.

At 4:20, along with twenty-some senior officers and advisors, the VIPs were taken back to the president's quarters on Kalaukau Avenue. There, after cocktails they began a sumptuous prime-rib dinner at 7:30 p.m. About an hour later, the meeting began in an adjoining conference room. In addition to

---

* The estate had been owned by millionaire businessman Chris Holmes, heir to the Fleischmann yeast estate, a staunch Democrat, and owner of a major corporation on the islands, the Hawaiian Tuna Packers. When he died in February, 1944, the mansion, along with the rest of his estate, went into a trust, managed by the Hawaiian Trust Company. After the Roosevelt visit, to help the war effort, bunk beds were put into the upstairs rooms, and the mansion became a recreation center, first for Navy pilots, and later in the war, for other servicemen. The estate was purchased by the City of Honolulu in 1946 and turned into a popular nightclub, The Queen's Surf.

President Roosevelt was the senior Navy contingency, which included Admiral Leahy, Admiral Nimitz, and a number of his senior advisors. Representing the Army was just General MacArthur.

The president was sitting, wearing a white shirt with a dark bowtie with white spots, his glasses in their leather case in his shirt pocket. He began the meeting by taking a drafting T-square and, using it as a pointer, he turned his wheelchair around, to face a large map of the Pacific that had been mounted on board. Pointing to somewhere near the Philippine island of Mindanao, he then looked at General MacArthur on his right, and opened the conference by saying, "Well Douglas, where do we go from here?"

Returning to the Philippines had been a haunting obsession with MacArthur for almost two and a half years, ever since his combined forces had been defeated by the Japanese in December of 1941 in a humiliatingly swift campaign. Ordered to escape to Australia, he barely made it out, leaving in the dead of night of March 12 with an escort group of four PT boats. When he had finally arrived in Melbourne on March 21, he had made his stubbornly resolute promise statement to the islanders that "I came through and I shall return." That guarantee, now a fixation, had been the foremost objective in his strategy since then.

So now at this conference, MacArthur, wearing a light army jacket, looked defiantly at the commander-in-chief and replied, "Mindanao, Mr. President. Then Leyte and Luzon."

The president then turned to Nimitz and asked him what he thought. The admiral, already standing, took the T-square from the president and began his assessment. Pointing to the Philippines, he started by arguing not only against an invasion of the Palaus, but against an invasion of the Philippine islands as well, which, by extension, the Peleliu operation was designed to support. He spoke somewhat stiffly in a soft tone, and his remarks were simple and to the point.

Nimitz contended that they instead should concentrate on an alternate, two-prong drive to Japan. The southern prong would bypass a probably costly and lengthy invasion of the Philippines. Rather, they should concentrate on a drive to take Formosa (Taiwan), Iwo Jima, and Okinawa, in preparation for a direct assault on the Japanese main islands. The right-hand prong would be to attack them through an intensive strategic bombing campaign by moving up the Bonin Islands—an archipelago of some 30 islands 500–600 miles south of Japan—and securing them.

Then it was MacArthur's turn. He stood up, took the pointer from Admiral Nimitz, and began by countering that the main thrust instead should be

Strategic conference in Hawaii, evening, July 26, 1944. Admiral Nimitz (standing) outlines to (from left) General MacArthur, President Roosevelt, and Admiral Leahy the Navy's strategy to defeat Japan by taking the northern route. Unlike MacArthur, Nimitz recommended bypassing the Philippines (and thus, Peleliu) to drive straight to the Japanese Home Islands. The president ultimately rejected this plan and sided with the general. (U.S. Navy photo)

through the Philippines. His arguments were not so much military as they were political and ethical.

MacArthur tried to pressure the president into favoring his plan by reminding him of his iconic "I shall return" promise to the Philippine people back in March of 1942. His argument focused on the political implications (and perhaps subtly their ramifications in this an election year) of how fulfilling that pledge would benefit U.S.–Filipino relations. More damaging, MacArthur pointed out, would be the negative message to the rest of the Central Pacific. "Promises MUST be kept," he said pointedly, and to underscore his argument for maximum effect, his next sentences included the words "shame," "ethical," "unethical," and "virtue" several times.

The United States had after all, undergone a number of political struggles in the Philippines as the island state over the years at various times had tried to gain independence. The Filipinos, he argued, who in many respects looked upon America as their big brother or even their mother country, felt like they had been betrayed in early 1942. The Americans had blundered terribly and had failed them with not only its defective military strategy, but also (to them) its feckless lack of determination to aggressively defend their islands

If the Americans did not at this stage even try to liberate the Philippines, but rather blockaded and bypassed them, moving onward toward Japan, they would in essence allow the cruel Japanese occupation to continue persecuting the Filipinos, who in turn would be infuriated. Supplies on the islands, having already been short for months because of the American naval blockade, would become far more acute. In response, the Japanese would simply resort to taking more from the Filipinos, and, in doing so, subject them to further suffering, barbaric cruelty, and death. The islanders would feel betrayed and abandoned yet a second time. For the Americans to turn their backs on them now would no doubt give rise to a bitter sense of betrayal that would spark a new determination to break free of what would be seen as uncaring, American oppression. To them, this would be an outrage, one they would probably never forgive. It would be a stain on American honor that would come back to haunt them if (or more likely, when) the Philippines became their own nation sometime after the war. To worsen the effect, this unfaithful act of not fulfilling that pledge would have a negative impact in the eyes of other Far Eastern nations as well.

MacArthur concluded that therefore, the drive to take the Philippines had to be paramount. He then went into additional details of his strategy. To ensure the maximum chance of success in the campaign, as an integral part of his plan, they first needed to take Peleliu to cover his right flank, to provide a major airfield to support his forces, and to allow him to make his main assault unhindered. The Japanese airfields could be taken out from Mindanao, and as soon as U.S. airfields could be set up on Leyte or Mindoro, MacArthur could land at Lingayen Gulf and move to take Manila in a little over a month.

Here the president commented that the Philippines campaign might be too costly to undertake in terms of men and matériel. "To take Luzon would demand heavier losses than we can stand. It seems to me we MUST bypass it."

MacArthur assured him that their losses would not be heavy; at least, no more than they had been in the past. He added, "The days of the frontal attack are over. Modern infantry weapons are too deadly, and direct assault is no longer feasible." He paused and added, perhaps in an oblique inference to Nimitz's heavy losses in the Marianas, "Only mediocre commanders still use it. Your good commanders do not turn in heavy losses." In fact, he continued, taking Formosa would probably be more costly in losses. A landing there would be over a long supply line, and the troops coming ashore would not get any help from the local civilians, since Formosa had been under Japanese rule for half a century. MacArthur continued arguing the military positives of taking the Philippines. Unlike with Formosa, the Filipinos would doggedly support the American landings with strong guerrilla actions. Besides, he concluded, bypassing Luzon, like the strongholds at Rabaul and Wewak, was impractical because it was just too big a land mass—Leahy apparently concurred—and even if they could, the large Japanese forces based there would wreak havoc upon the left flank of any American advances to the north of them.

Although Nimitz's line of reasoning was itself solid, he had three factors that were working against him. First, as competent a leader as he was, Nimitz was for the most part not much of a dynamic speaker. Rather, he spoke in a soft tone, comparatively not nearly an eloquent a spokesman as the grandiloquent general. A subtle factor, granted; still, the arguments that he presented were not as persuading. Second, the idea of bypassing the Philippines (and thus, Peleliu) was actually the firm recommendation of his superior, Admiral Ernest King. Nimitz was just echoing those ideas. In fact, MacArthur later concurred with this statement, writing that Nimitz had not really agreed with King. Admiral Halsey's writings in 1947 also confirmed that statement. At the time, besides Nimitz, King's strategy was in reality questioned by a number of other senior admirals, among them Raymond Spruance, the hero of the battle of Midway.

The third factor working against Nimitz though, perhaps the strongest, was that he really had no viable argument, military or political, to counter MacArthur's heavily laid concerns about bypassing the Filipinos, and all that that would imply.

The high-level meeting went on for almost three hours until finally, around 10:30 p.m., the president, tired from the day's activities (and no doubt, as well as from MacArthur's arguments), declared, "Let's adjourn for now and get a good night's sleep." He paused and added, "We'll resume tomorrow morning at 10:30 for a final review, and then I'll give you my answer."

General MacArthur, according to his writings after the war, managed to get the president alone for some ten minutes after the meeting, just before Roosevelt had a chance to retire for the night. (One source—John Prados—claims that this occurred the next day, just before MacArthur departed for his flight.) MacArthur recapped one last time his ominous warning of going around the Philippines, now addressing the political repercussions of not going with his plan. He again brought up the upcoming general election in November: "I daresay that the American people would be so aroused that they would register most complete resentment against you at the polls this fall."

Roosevelt already had enough worries about defeating Thomas Dewey, who he pointed out was not only a well-liked Republican presidential candidate, but also widely popular as the governor of New York. Perhaps unspoken but nevertheless probably in the back of Roosevelt's mind was the fact that MacArthur himself had earlier been a Republican contender.

Just before going to bed, Roosevelt had a chat with his physician, Vice Admiral Ross McIntire. Then he took a couple aspirin and turned in.

The next morning, July 28, MacArthur and Nimitz arrived at the president's quarters at 10:15 a.m., and the conference started again, 15 minutes later as planned. Roosevelt, having pondered and then slept on the general's warnings, had already made up his mind on which strategy he was going to decide upon. Still, he politely listened for an hour and a half as both sides gave their final arguments, each reiterating the same contentions they had made the evening before.

MacArthur was on some sort of moral crusade, perhaps using the moral high ground because he had been awarded his Medal of Honor just two years ago for his defense of the Philippines. For whatever reasons, he was continuing that angle. At one point he said, "If the Philippines are left behind in the backwash of war, the Japanese army can live off the land, and will slaughter in revenge, thousands of prisoners, including women and children."

In the end, MacArthur was the more convincing. Roosevelt finally held up his hands for the discussion to end. He looked at his senior officers and told them that he was approving MacArthur's plan. They would go with an invasion of the Philippines—and thus, Peleliu. There was no visible reaction from either Nimitz or MacArthur. Admiral Nimitz, hearing the president's decision, accepted it with good grace, and told them that he would begin planning to support the campaign. A bit later, the president took MacArthur aside and told him with a smile, "Well Douglas, you win. But I'm going to have a helluva time over this with that old bear, Ernie King!"

The conference then continued as MacArthur voiced his concerns that the British, now that the naval war in Europe had been won, were plotting to expand their role in the Pacific and set up their own command in the Far East, which to him, would weaken U.S. influence across Asia.

The meeting broke up around noon, and as lunch was being prepared there at the president's quarters, a couple newspaper photographers were called in for a quick photoshoot. Afterwards, MacArthur, having won the strategic argument and perhaps having irritated the president for any number of reasons, stated that he was not staying to eat. His excuse to the president was that he had to get back to his headquarters immediately, grumbling, that he had "to resume fighting the war," and that his aircraft was already warming up at Hickam Field.

Nimitz stayed, and after MacArthur departed, he and the president had a sumptuous lunch, again heavily covered by the media. Nimitz then left for his quarters, and the president, accompanied by Admiral Leahy, General Richardson, and Admiral Ghormley, once again rode around Oahu, touring the island and the various units stationed there. He then returned to his quarters, had another lavish dinner (which included a 17-piece band for entertainment), and then went to bed around 10 p.m.

He continued touring Oahu on the 29th, including visits to the Army General Hospital, the Naval Air Station in Honolulu, Hickham Field again, and then the submarine base.

Then after a lunch, with about three dozen senior naval officers at Admiral Nimitz's quarters and another tour of the island, the president held a grand press briefing before his six-car motorcade drove to the pier. The president had a final chat with Nimitz, before his wheelchair was rolled up the gangplank to the USS *Baltimore*, boarding at about 7 p.m. The vessel departed Pearl Harbor a half hour later, headed for Adak Alaska in the Aleutians.*

Several historians have argued that Roosevelt decided to go with MacArthur's plan because, in the long run, MacArthur was right: it politically made sense. Advancing through the Philippines delivered the additional gift of placating MacArthur, who the president knew, could really give him all sorts of endless headaches back home. The general no doubt would not only have raised hell with both the conservatives who had supported him in his run for the White House, and with the Democrats supporting the president. The general would also have bemoaned the decision to other senior Army commanders and to the Department of War, complaining that this was just another effort by Roosevelt and Nimitz to allow the Navy to command the war in the Pacific and to glorify that service as being the foremost.

Some have criticized that the entire Philippine campaign that MacArthur had pushed so hard for was based upon his own egotistical obsession to fulfill his personal promise to the Filipino people. In retrospect, although taking the Philippines made more strategic sense than Formosa, MacArthur's campaign

---

* Most accounts of this conference state or imply that Roosevelt's stay in Hawaii was just from July 26 to July 27, that the conference began the evening of the 26th, and that Roosevelt left Hawaii the next day. Actually, as accounted here, the president arrived the afternoon of July 26, the conference did not begin until the evening of the 27th, and the president did not depart Pearl Harbor until the evening of July 29.

to clear every corner of the islands of its Japanese occupiers seemed to some later historians wasteful in time and resources.

With the conference ended, Nimitz resigned himself to the president's decision. After cocktails and dinner with his disappointed staff at his quarters that night, the admiral told his them that he had expected the decision, and that as far as he was concerned, they would carry it out in good spirit. He told them to fully cooperate with the field units to make it happen. Perhaps as an afterthought, a Navy captain later remarked to a *Newsweek* correspondent that Nimitz ordered a message be sent to the First Marine Division's headquarters, instructing that Operation *Stalemate* would proceed as planned.

True to his word, Nimitz began his strategic planning by first concentrating on the Peleliu operation. In his early developmental stages, Nimitz wrote that taking Peleliu would, "remove from MacArthur's right flank in this progress to the Southern Philippines, a definite threat of attack; second, secure for our forces a base from which to support MacArthur's operations."* Taking the Palaus would cover MacArthur's right flank as he moved on the Philippines, as well as outflanking the still formidable Japanese-held strategic port of Truk, which the Americans had decided to bypass.

The original tentative date that had been set for the Palaus operation was December 31, 1944. It had been moved up to September 8 because the U.S. westward advance had proved faster than expected. On July 7, it was concluded that the operation would take place on September 15th.

---

* From a letter written by Admiral Nimitz to Philip A. Crowl dd. October 5, 1949.

CHAPTER TWO

Planning

Initial Plans

Naval intelligence in late 1943 determined that the Japanese were fortifying the Palau Islands. Thus, an operation to take them all seemed out of the question. The first draft for the Palau operation called for an invasion of both Peleliu and Angaur in the south, and the distant atolls of Ulithi and Yap, northeast of the Palaus. After careful analysis though, Nimitz decided to modify the plan. Instead of invading the two farthest atolls, the largest, northernmost island of Babelthuap would be invaded, since, like Peleliu, it had an airfield that could be developed. Ulithi and Yap would be invaded following the seizure of Peleliu. The date for the invasion was set at September 15, to coincide with MacArthur's invasion of Morotai, some 480 miles to the southwest. Sixty-two-year-old Admiral William F. "Bull" Halsey, Commander, Western Pacific Theater and also Commander, Third Fleet, was to be the senior commander for this campaign.

However, extensive intelligence reconnaissance later led planners to decide that the Babelthuap airfield was not large enough and had limited potential for development. In contrast, the one down on Peleliu was found to be just the opposite. It was good-sized and lay on low, flat land. With some expansion, it could be used for large strategic bombers. To complicate matters was a critical factor that resources for this operation were scant with so many other operations either underway or looming, including the significant Philippines invasion. So the Navy finally decided to let Babelthuap go for later and to concentrate instead on Peleliu and Angaur. Thus, planning would have to be extensively changed, which in turn would cause some delays.

Another unexpected setback unfolded in the Pacific that critical summer of 1944. The Americans at the time were also concentrating their military efforts on the Marianas, some 800 miles northeast of the Palaus. In succession, they engaged the Japanese in a series of major operations, starting with the invasion of Saipan in mid-June, the Japanese counteroffensive which resulted in the battle of the Philippine Sea a few days later, the invasion of Guam on July 21, and of Tinian three days later on July 24.

The Americans had encountered stiff resistance in each amphibious operation, and taking the Marianas took a good deal longer and expended much more of an effort than had been planned. This resulted in more aerial operations, more delays, more casualties, and, most importantly, much higher expenditures in supplies and ammunition. American forces there were committed and had to remain *in situ* until the operations were finally completed, stretching well into August.

Despite these concerns, planning for the Peleliu campaign continued. The landing would be made by elements of the "Third Mac" (III Amphibious Corps, which had originally been I Amphibious Corps at Guadalcanal) under the command of Major General Roy Geiger, who was to take over from General Julian Smith on August 13, right after he had wrapped up in the Marianas. Geiger's background was mostly Marine aviation, but he had experience commanding large units, and his performance in the Marianas confirmed that. Nearly 60 years old, with a square jaw, a poker face, and piercing eyes that could cut right through a junior officer, and a cigar nearly always jutting out of his jaw, Geiger was the epitome of a tough Marine commander.

Under Geiger's command, two reinforced divisions would undertake the operation: the First Marine Division, and, temporarily attached to III Amphibious Corps, the Army's 81st "Wildcats" Infantry Division under Major General Paul J. Mueller.

Before all that could happen though, critical to the Marianas effort was the continued required presence of General Geiger, since at that time his corps command also included the Third Marine Division, which had taken part in the invasion of Guam, the largest island in the Marianas. Thus development of the Peleliu invasion had to take place without him until he could break loose to join the senior officers of his corps and the First Marine Division in their planning.

To make things worse, the division's commanding officer, General Rupertus, was absent as well. Right after he returned to the division in early May, his close personal friend and previous division commander, Lieutenant General Alexander Vandegrift, now the Marine Corps Commandant, ordered him to Washington to, of all things, sit in on the upcoming selection board for Marine lieutenant colonels and colonels. Although he had ordered Rupertus to the States for this innocuous task, in reality it was so that Rupertus would have a chance to see his second wife and new son. On May 9, a day after the division's new Assistant Division Officer (ADO), 50-year-old Brigadier General Oliver P. Smith, had reported aboard, Rupertus left Pavuvu where the division was located, bound on a PBY for the States, along with his chief of staff, Colonel John T. Selden. With provisional corps commander Julian Smith working out of Hawaii and also not in the area, the planning now fell upon ADO O. P. Smith and the rest of the division's staff. They would have to work out the details with the Navy on the upcoming operation.

O. P. Smith took on the task with typical Marine determination. In the six weeks Rupertus was away, he proactively oversaw the planning of the Peleliu operation, based upon guidelines coming down from Geiger stuck in the Marianas and from the Navy directives that were issued on June 2. When Rupertus finally returned on June 21 when a good part of the planning had already been done, he understandably found his officers distant and cool toward him. This only furthered his isolation, and added fuel to his dislike of his ADO.

The fact that the battle for the Marianas became more protracted than expected had several other critical consequences for the subsequent Peleliu operation besides Geiger's prolonged absence. First, additional resources that could otherwise have improved replenishment and rebuilding their components were given much less time to do so. Second, extended operations in the Marianas also cost the Americans preciously needed additional operational and logistical losses, which by necessity would have to cut into what was originally allocated for the Peleliu invasion. Third, more extensive planning for Peleliu had a lower priority than the actual Marianas operations that were ongoing far to the northeast.

Finally, on August 10, Guam was declared secure, and two days later, General Geiger and his staff flew out to join his units planning the Peleliu operation. He arrived on Guadalcanal on August 13, and was immediately flown to the nearby Russell Islands. There, he reported to Admiral Fort on his flagship, the USS *Mount McKinley** and immediately took over the operation

---

* USS *Mount McKinley* (AGC-7, Capt. Roy W. M. Graham commanding) was a specially designated U.S. amphibious flagship command vessel (A=auxiliary, G=general, C=command/control) specifically outfitted to carry a command staff to oversee amphibious operations. Originally built as the transport USS *Cyclone*, she was refitted in 1943 and recommissioned on May 1, 1944 as the *Mount McKinley*. At 12,550 gross tons, she was 460 feet long, 63 feet wide, and had a draft of 25 feet. She had a crew of 670 and could make 15 knots. Armament consisted of one 5⊠/38 gun and four twin-mounted 40mm AA guns. She had special berthing accommodations for senior officers. The vessel earned five battle stars during the war, another eight off Korea, and later three more off Vietnam. Also aboard were Rear Admiral Fort, and Vice Admiral Wilkinson. (Garand & Strobridge p. 278)

from General Julian Smith, who was still in Hawaii. Two days later, only a month before the scheduled invasion, Geiger arrived on Pavuvu and took over planning for the Marines, while Smith took over as the overall expeditionary force commander. The planners had finally decided to choose the western side of the island (the claw's base) for the landing. The main assault was to be made by General Rupertus's First Marine Division.

The first phase of the amphibious operation was the assault phase. Following several days of the Navy pounding the island defenses, the Marines, rested from their last operation at Cape Gloucester, would storm ashore on D-Day, secure a beachhead, and take the strategic airfield located at the western end of the island next to the beaches. The other division, the Army's 81st Infantry, would initially be held back, but once the beachhead was secure, it would invade the nearby islands of Angaur to the southwest and Ngesebus to the north. It would then later be used for the second phase, to take the northeastern parts of Peleliu.

The Navy had originally planned for Angaur to be invaded first, and then Peleliu. General Julian Smith though, objected strongly. If Angaur was assaulted first, he argued, the Japanese would have plenty of time to bring down reinforcements from Babelthuap and Koror to the north and move them through the nearby islands of Ngesebus and Kongauru. Taking or at least invading Peleliu first would prevent the enemy from reinforcing Angaur. Of course, the possibility of Peleliu getting reinforced remained a threat the planners would still have to deal with.

The landing on D-Day would be made by the Marines' three rifle regiments: the 1st Marines, the 5th Marines, and the 7th Marines.* Each regiment of about 3,240 men in turn would consist of three 930-man battalions, a 250-man headquarters battalion, and a 200-man heavy weapons battalion. The landing would not only be supported by corps-level units, but also by many additional support units directly attached to the division, including engineers, additional artillery, and amphibious assault support craft. Thus, this so-called reinforced First Marine Division comprised some 27,000 men (sources vary between 26,400 and 28,000), but only about 9,750 were combat riflemen who would have to do most of the fighting. The rest would function in support and other types of specialist assignments.

---

* Early on, it became a tradition that Marine regiments, regardless of their type, were referred to by their numerical designator and simply the word "Marines." Thus, the 5th Marine Regiment, which is a rifleman regiment, is referred to as "the 5th Marines," and the 11th Marine Regiment, an artillery unit, is similarly called "the 11th Marines." (Ross p. 21)

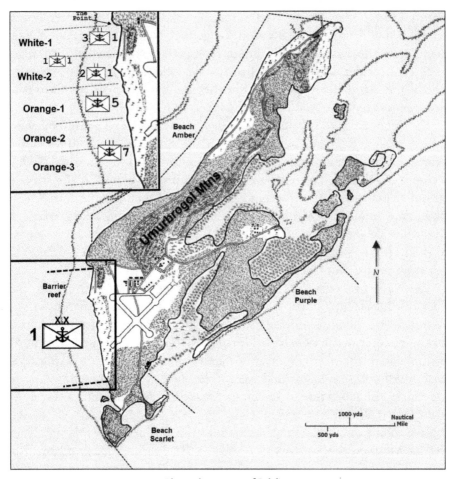

White-1

White-2

Orange-1

Orange-2

Orange-3

Beach Amber

Umurbrogol Mtns

Barrier reef

Beach Purple

Beach Scarlet

N

1000 yds   Nautical Mile
500 yds

Planned invasion of Peleliu.

Recon photos of several sections of the island were studied to determine the most ideal spots to land. A number of open, sandy shores were identified and considered. The planners though, found problems with each of the site areas.

The Purple Beach areas along the southeastern side of the island (along the bottom of the "lobster claw") provided an ideal beach that had wide, open areas for the landing craft, and the offshore reef was closer to the shoreline. This area though, had several drawbacks. For one thing, the Japanese had heavily reinforced the area with gun casements and several pillboxes, and while the beaches themselves offered wide areas for landing, they were surrounded by mangrove swamps, which would make swift advance difficult. Complicating

Major General Roy Geiger, Commanding Officer, III Amphibious Corps.

Major General William Rupertus, Commanding Officer, First Marine Division.

matters was that this section of the island narrowed into a small, critical piece of connecting land about 1,500 yards inland. That natural bottleneck and the marshes would provide the enemy an easy way to stop up the landing forces and contain them with minimal effort.

The two Amber Beach sections on the northwestern side of the island faced several concerns. First, this area was the farthest from the principal objective: seizure of the airfield. Second, the offshore reef here was wider, which would slow down the ferrying of men and supplies over it. Third, the beaches were only about 200–300 yards wide, and would be vulnerable to enemy resistance. A determined, flanking enemy thrust from Ngesebus Island to the left might prove devastating to the Marines struggling to get ashore. Later recon photos made this a greater concern. The images showed to some extent the true height of the Umurbrogol positions, as well as a number of defensive positions that were noted there. The possibility of the drive potentially getting bogged down by harassing enemy fire from these heights would leave the Marines exposed along an open, narrow beachhead, with little room to land supporting artillery. The Marines would have to attack up steep, sharp ridges to get to the distant objective, the airfield, and any enemy on those heights would be well dug in, staring down their throats.

The White and Orange beaches on the western side of the island seemed adequate for the job, and they were right next to the airfield. The beaches seemed easily attainable and the invaders would be able to move forward reasonably quickly over relatively low land to take the critical airfield. There was also enough space to allow supporting units such as the tanks and artillery to land and adequately deploy.

However, there was a real concern that bothered the Marine officers. The entire region was overseen by the Umurbrogol massif to the northeast. Enemy artillery and mortar positions almost certainly located there would command the area and could thus wreak havoc. The Marine officers though, agreed to take that risk, partly because the 7th Marines hopefully would be able to quickly outflank the positions. In addition, the planners were assured by their Navy counterparts that overwhelming firepower from the offshore warships, the supporting landing craft, and the wasp-like strikes of the tactical bombers from the carriers would be more than adequate to take out, or at least neutralize any enemy positions there.

The idea of a two-pronged landing was considered, with one element landing on the western side, and another coming in on the Scarlet Beach sections at the southern tip of the island; however, these sections at the southern tip were dismissed: there were sharp coral ledges that would slow down a quick advance inland. Moreover, the enemy had constructed several anti-invasion obstacles just offshore.

Eventually, only the western shore of the island was chosen. The Marines would land on what was marked as five beaches that ran north to south along the western coast. The beaches were steep, coarse, and comparatively rough, with coral chunks strewn about. Still, they could reliably take traffic, even when wet, so it was this area that the planners decided upon.

Enemy beach defenses, while detailed, were not too extensive. There were a number of tank obstacles such as metal tetrahedrons strung out just offshore, as well as several antitank ditches and trenches. There were also many sections of barbed wire, as well as a few hundred mines, from the beach itself to a couple hundred yards inland.

The shoreline that was chosen was broken up into sections. Starting with the left flank, the beaches were designated White-1, White-2, Orange-1, Orange-2, and Orange-3; overall, a strip totaling 2,400 yards in length. The Marines were to seize the western airfield and then drive directly across the center of the island to split the enemy forces in two.

The biggest concerns that the Marine planners had revolved around three questions that were on everyone's mind. How many Japanese troops were on the island, how adequate were their defenses, and how hard would they fight to defend the island?

Regarding the first question, the most conservative estimate put the number of enemy on Peleliu at over 9,000, although later, more accurate estimates put the number at over 10,000. Amphibious planning and experience had come up with a three-to-one rule of thumb. It would take at least three times the number of estimated enemy on the island to conduct a successful assault. The First Marine Division itself going into battle numbered 16,459 (843 officers and 15,616 enlisted but excluding a rear echelon left on Pavuvu of 103 officers and 1,668 enlisted). Heavily reinforced with artillery, engineers, and amphibious transport units, the division had about 25,000 men. However, as mentioned, only 10,000 or so made up the infantry that would carry the assault forward.

Regarding the enemy defenses, all intelligence was based either on nearly obsolete pre-war information, on recon photos taken by submarines offshore, or by naval aircraft involved in earlier airstrikes. All seemed to show a lack of any significant development, except of course, on the airfield. The photos did show a number of permanent installations located all over the island at visually advantageous positions. These included several pillboxes and reinforced casemates covering all potential beach sites, especially those around the southwestern beach areas. At least two antitank ditches were identified. In addition, areas of offshore obstacles and mines were noted.

The question of how hard and in what manner the enemy would conduct its defense was entirely based on previous island assaults. It was generally accepted that the Japanese would fight fanatically, often in suicidal fashion. The planners acknowledged that the airfield was the most strategic asset in the area, and consequently, the enemy would try to hold it at all costs. Since it was located right next to where the Marines would be landing, it was assumed the defense would hinge on two main factors: a series of concentrated fire from automatic weapons, mortars and artillery, and coordinated with several traditionally intense counterattacks in the *banzai* style that the Marines had come to experience at Guadalcanal and Cape Gloucester.

Rupertus's original (and highly optimistic) plan called for only the 1st and 5th Marines on the initial landing, and the 7th Marines kept back in reserve. However, General Julian Smith was not favorable to this, recommending that all three regiments land simultaneously, with an army *regimental combat team* (RCT) held in reserve, just in case. General Geiger, after he had arrived and had been briefed, agreed, overriding Rupertus's plan. He too felt that two regiments would not be enough. He therefore modified the plan to include the 7th Marines on the far right flank. The assault would now be made by all three Marine rifle regiments abreast onto the five beaches. The regiment on the right would turn, secure the southern promontories, and march up the right side of the island. The one landing in the center would move forward and take the airfield. The regiment on the left would turn north and advance up the ridge. Right after the landing, the Army's 81st Infantry Division would land on the smaller island of Angaur to the south and take it, after which one of its regiments would land on Ulithi atoll, some 350 miles northeast of Peleliu.

Renowned 46-year-old Colonel Lewis B. "Chesty" Puller's 1st Marines (codename "Team Spitfire") would land on the beachhead's left flank. His 3rd Battalion would land on the far left at Beach White-1 and the 2nd Battalion to their right on Beach White-2. The 1st Battalion, the 1st Marines' regimental reserve, would wait and then land behind them. The regiment had three tasks: to anchor the beachhead's left flank, to secure the area north of the airfield, and to then move forward onto the base of the Umurbrogol massif.

Colonel Harold "Bucky" Harris, the youngest of the regimental commanders at 41, would lead his 5th Marines (codename "Team Lonewolf") in the center. The 1st Battalion would land on Beach Orange-1 and the 3rd Battalion on Beach Orange-2. The 2nd Battalion would not go in initially and would be held as the regimental reserve. The 1st Battalion, after connecting to 2/1, was to join the 3rd Battalion, and the two were to strike inland and seize the island's most important target, its formidable airfield.

The 7th Marines (codename "Team Mustang") under 50-year-old Colonel Herman Hanneken would land at the beachhead's far right flank on Beach Orange-3. Because the regiment could only be assigned one beach, the two assaulting battalions would have to land in succession. The 3rd Battalion would go in first, followed by the 1st Battalion. After securing the flank, they were to then advance through the mangrove swamps across the end of the island and secure the open terrain at the southeastern end of the island, designated Scarlet Beach. The regiment's other unit, the 2nd Battalion, was designated as part of the division's reserve, and only be committed to the landing if, when, and where it might be needed.

It was clear to all that the 1st Marines on the left would have the toughest time of it, facing the difficult task of assaulting forward against entrenched enemy positions on the northeastern slopes. Puller though, had the utmost confidence in his men, and he was reassured that he would have full gunfire support from the warships offshore, as well as unremitting assistance from tactical bombers that would keep the enemy pinned down. The Shermans would come in with the fourth wave and provide armored assistance, and

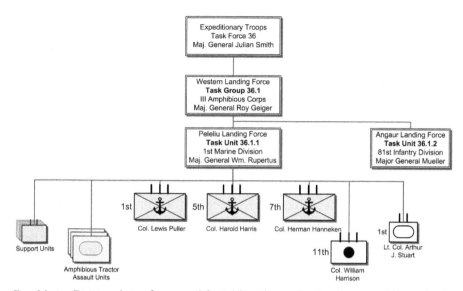

First Marine Division chain of command for Peleliu. The two landing forces would be under the overall command of Marine General Roy Geiger.

the artillery, once deployed would help as well. In the meantime, the 7th Marines on the other end of it would encounter little resistance and be able to quickly sweep across the island to outflank those Japanese positions on the ridges.

In addition to 2/7, Lieutenant Colonel Spencer S. Berger's reserve group would include a few tanks from the division's 1st Tank Battalion's Company C, the division's recon company, a JASCO company,* a platoon of engineers, and a small medical company. In addition to the division's reserve group, Colonel Arthur P. Watson's 323rd RCT from the 81st Infantry Division would also initially be kept on standby in case it too was needed.

The remainder of the Marine 1st Tank Battalion under Lieutenant Colonel Arthur J. Stuart would begin landing with the fourth wave on the Orange beaches. As the division's only armor, the Shermans would provide close-in mobile fire support for the riflemen.

An hour after the landing began, the Marine division's artillery unit, the 11th Marines under Colonel William Harrison, would start landing at beaches Orange-1 and Orange-2. They would immediately set up and begin

---

* Joint Assault Signal Company. Created in the fall of 1943, JASCO units were made up of a combination of Navy and Marine personnel. Their mission was to coordinate naval gunfire and tactical air support with the Marines on the beach, and to provide ship-to-shore communications.

Colonel Lewis "Chesty" Puller, Commanding Officer, 1st Marines.

Colonel Herman "Hard-Headed" Hanneken, Commanding Officer 7th Marines.

providing artillery support for the riflemen. They would also be reinforced with two 155mm artillery batteries from III Corps, the 3rd and the 8th Gun battalions.

Providing transportation for the actual landing would be a number of amphibious tractor battalions, and, additionally, supporting the rifle regiments would be scores of auxiliary and specialized battalions, including engineers, service groups, and medical units.

Offshore from the targeted beaches, the coral barrier reef that surrounds the island averaged around 500 yards out, with only a light to moderate surf. To get ashore, the Marines would approach the landing area from the west in eight waves. They would draw near the shore in special floating assault vehicles classified as LVTs (Landing Vehicle, Tracked). The officers referred to them as amtracs (short for amphibious tractors), although many of the men nicknamed them "water buffaloes" or "alligators."

The LVTs would be transported to Peleliu mostly in 30 specially designed shallow draft vessels known as LSTs (Landing Ship, Tank), although the men sarcastically referred to the acronym definition as "large slow target"). These vessels were about 330 feet long and 50 feet wide. Fully loaded, they displaced almost 4,000 tons, but still only had a maximum draft of about eight feet (only three and a half at the bow). Powered by two GM diesel engines, they could make up to 12 knots in calm waters, but averaged on a combat run only about seven or eight knots. Crew complement was eight or ten officers and crew of 100 enlisted. Most craft were lightly armed, typically with mounted antiaircraft guns.

Colonel Harold "Bucky" Harris, Commanding Officer, 7th Marines.

General Oliver Prince ("O. P.") Smith, Assistant Division Officer, First Marine Division. Here shown at his CP on Peleliu.

First created by the British early in the war and then later put into mass production by the United States, they were designed to give the Allies the capability to move and land men, equipment, vehicles, and supplies across an ocean and land them onto irregular shores. To do this, the LST featured a large set of two bow doors that opened horizontally to allow a third, inner door to be lowered and act as a ramp to allow the unloading of trucks and mechanized vehicles.*

The LVTs that would ride in the LSTs were essentially watertight tracked armored personnel carriers that could move through water using specially designed treads, somewhat similar in theory to Mississippi River side-wheel paddleboats. Whenever they came to an underwater barrier like a coral reef, these same treads were durable enough to allow the vehicle to crawl over the coral until they were clear of the reef and then able to continue. In a similar fashion, once these vehicles reached the beaches, they could crawl up onto the shore before the men had to exit, giving those aboard longer protection from enemy fire. The LVTs could chug toward the beach at up to 4½ knots; it was estimated that the trip ashore would be about half an hour, 15 minutes from the transfer point (the reef).

---

* During the war, many LSTs were converted for other functions such as repair, medical, or transportation of large equipment, including, in some cases, crated light reconnaissance aircraft that were loaded and unloaded by cranes. The U.S. eventually constructed about a thousand LSTs. Most that survived the war were later either scrapped or put into mothballs.

The older LVTs (LVT-1 or LVT-2 models) could carry some 18 men, and some mounted one or two .50-caliber machine guns near the front. The newer models such as the LVT-4s were larger and could carry up to 30 men. They also featured a rear exit ramp that allowed personnel to disembark while not being exposed to direct enemy fire.

While LVTs were first used in a combat role at Tarawa to provide close-in fire support to the men that were landing, this would be the first time the First Marine Division would use this technique in an amphibious assault to cross over a water barrier on its way to the beaches.

Preceding these LVTs would be a wave of newer support fire models, designated LVT-2A and LVT-4A. These craft were modified to carry heavier weapons mounted in front for more firepower, including a turreted 37mm gun or even a 75mm howitzer. They would go in first to provide firepower for the riflemen coming in behind them. In addition, they had been provided with some additional (thin) armor. All these units would go in first to provide cover fire for the following LVTs. Additionally, over a dozen LCIs* were being loaded with 4.5-inch rocket launchers to provide close support.

The follow-up waves with additional riflemen, munitions and critical front-line supplies were scheduled to land in five-minute increments, coming ashore in DUKWs† or else to be brought to the barrier reef in

---

* *Landing Craft Infantry*, nicknamed "Elsie Items," was a medium-sized, ocean-going troop transport specifically designed for amphibious operations to debark up to 200 infantry directly onto a beach. Over 900 were built in World War II. Averaging 250 tons (380 fully loaded), they were 160 feet long and 24 feet wide, with a draft of about six feet. Top speed was 15 knots, and each carried a complement of 24. Armament normally consisted of just four 20mm guns. All LCIs were constructed in the classic LCI model and classified as LCI(L) (large). They were tasked only with unloading troops. Many were later modified for special purposes, mostly for close-in support fire. The LCI(G) (gunboat) carried a 40mm gun, extra 20mm guns and a half dozen .50-cal. machine guns. Some also carried rockets. The LCI(R) (rocket) was more designed for that mission, carrying a half dozen 5-inch rocket launchers permanently attached to the deck. Thus, aiming them entailed turning the ship to the desired bearing, and when the rockets were fired crewmen had to move away from the launchers. The LCI(M) (mortar) mounted three or four 4.2-inch heavy mortars to provide close indirect support to the landing troops. A few LCIs were modified to become LCI(A) (ammunition carriers) expressly to bring extra ammunition ashore.

† Pronounced "ducks." Also referred to as Higgins boats, named after Higgins Industries (Andrew Jackson Higgins, president), the company that originated the design and manufactured most of the craft. These were 6½-ton, 8-foot-wide amphibious transports that could make 6 knots to the shore and then drive up onto the beach. Each could land 24 men or 2½ tons of supplies. They were not armored and thus unsuitable against a well-defended beachhead. The term is from the original coding of the manufacturer (General Motors Corporation): **D** because the model was a

LCVPs* and then transferred to the landing amtracs by amphibious cranes affixed to nine pontoon barges. Three barges were to be loaded up with drums of gasoline and lubricating oil; marked with signs that read "Gas," they were to be available just off the reef for LVTs to refuel. Yet another dozen barges were to be used as floating dumps for provisions at night, when the transports had moved away to safer areas. Additionally, specially fitted large amphibious trailers of supplies would be towed to the barrier reef by LCVPs, hitched to amtracs on the other side of the reef, dragged across it, and then towed ashore.

Each LST would provide a column of five Shermans and at the front of the vessel, one LVT to act as pilot. This innovation had first been learned in the Marianas. The Navy was able to adequately waterproof the Shermans in the tank battalion. However, while the Shermans had been specially modified, including the installation of what were termed "deep water fording kits," it was still a slim remedy at best. It would only take a Sherman stumbling into an underwater crater or pit to turn it into a 35-ton anchor. They just could not be made buoyant. So the Navy decided to ferry them close enough inshore where the tanks could crawl along on the seabed. The amtrac, which was fully watertight and floated as it moved through the water, would disembark first and lead the column, followed by the five Shermans. The amtrac would steer the column safely onto the reef and then to the beachhead, avoiding craters, obstacles, and mines.

There were two sets of vessels for this purpose. The tanks themselves would travel in an amphibious craft designated LCTs. These vessels were relatively small at only 375 tons. Each was about 117 feet long (Mk V), could make 8 knots, and carry up to five Sherman tanks. The LCTs in turn would be transported in vessels designated as LSDs (Landing Ship, Dock). LSDs were comparatively larger 4,000-ton vessels, used to launch full -loaded smaller landing craft such as LCTs by means of a large well deck in the stern. The deck could be raised for travel and lowered to launch the craft within. LSDs were generally more seaworthy than LSTs, and much faster, able to make

---

1942 design, **U** for utility use, **K** to indicate all-wheel drive, and **W** because this 6-wheel vehicle had dual rear axles. (Moran & Rottman, p.40, Sloan p. 355 endnote)

* *Landing Craft Vehicles and Personnel* were small, 11-foot wide, flat-bottomed landing craft that could make up to 12 knots. With a shallow 3-foot draft, and using a bow ramp, they could ferry to and from shore up to 36 men or four tons of cargo and/or vehicles. They were also called "Higgins Boats."

17 knots, as compared to the slower LSTs at only 12 knots. An LSD had a crew complement of 250 men and could carry and unload up to four LCTs at a time.

Thus, the tanks would crawl onto LCTs which in turn were to be steered into the LSDs. The well deck would be raised, so that the LCTs could travel dry and be easily serviced. Once an LSD was in position offshore, it would flood its well deck again and then lower its stern gate. The now-floating LCTs would make their way out of the ship and then continue on to ferry the tanks up to the coral reef, where they would then unload them. These Shermans, like the LVTs, having already been made semi-watertight, would be equipped with specially fitted treads to be able to crawl across the water and overcome the reef. From there, they would each be able to make a run to the beach, creeping along the bottom. The tanks would thus move forward in columns, with an LVT at the head of each column to act as a navigational pilot. If the LVT moved into deep water and began to float, it would stop and turn to find another way in for its column. Once ashore, the Shermans could operate normally as tanks and provide fire support for the rifle companies. The corps and division artillery units would come in later waves, to be transported in DUKWs launched from LSTs.

Plans were also finalized for evacuating the wounded until the point was reached in the operation where adequate medical facilities could safely be set up on the beaches. The injured would be loaded onto amtracs (preferably, the later models that featured the rear access door) and slowly transported to the barrier reef. Once there, they would be transferred to small boats or DUKWs and taken out to the two hospital ships or to troop transports, since the majority of them had medical facilities on board for about two dozen wounded. Those that still had capacity would fly the "Mike" signal flag, so that the approaching coxswains would know where to bring their casualties.

General Rupertus finally returned to Pavuvu on June 21 and was briefed on the planning, including General Geiger's major modification of adding the third regiment in the initial landing. The division's strategy, detailed in a top-secret, five-page letter from Rupertus to the expeditionary force commander, General Julian Smith, called for the Marines to take the island and then turn it over to the Army for occupation and expansion, so that the Marines could leave and recover, in preparation for another operation.

General Smith approved his plan, but also recommended that at least one regiment of the 81st Infantry Division be attached to the Marines as a reserve—just in case. Rupertus responded that this would not be necessary, writing: "I do not consider this attachment to be necessary. I assure you that there is little chance of the division needing it." Citing that the operation would not even need a division reserve, he added: "I do not think that it will be necessary for me to commit this battalion … in the action on island P."

Smith wrote back that he concurred with Rupertus's conclusion. Neither of them knew how wrong they would be. The plan was finalized and Rupertus approved it on August 15.

The Navy Contingent

For this part of the Pacific campaign, Admiral Halsey had decided to split his large fleet into two components: The Cover and Support Group, and the Joint Expeditionary Force, which would undertake the landings.

The first group would provide air and surface cover for the Joint Expeditionary Force, and would remain under Halsey's direct command. It centered on the fast carriers in Task Force 38,* commanded by Vice Admiral Marc A. Mitscher. His carriers in turn included four carrier task groups:

- TG-38.1 (Vice Admiral John S. McCain): two carriers, two light carriers, three heavy cruisers, three light cruisers, and 11 destroyers. This group was to cover MacArthur's assault on Morotai to the south.
- TG-38.2 (Rear Admiral Gerald F. Bogan): two carriers, two light carriers, two battleships, four heavy cruisers, one light cruisers, and 17 destroyers.
- TG-38.3 (Rear Admiral Frederic C. Sherman): two carriers, two light carriers, five battleships, four light cruisers, and 18 destroyers. This group would remain part of Halsey's strike force.
- TG-38.4 (Rear Admiral Ralph E. Davidson): two carriers, two light carriers, one heavy cruiser, one light cruiser, and 12 destroyers.

The Cover and Support Group also included Halsey's main battle fleet. This consisted of two task forces:

---

* Naval units were organized in a similar fashion to Army ground units. A fleet was broken down into task forces (TFs), the first number designating the parent fleet (e.g. TF-31 was in Halsey's Third Fleet). A task force in turn was broken down into smaller task forces and/or task groups (TGs), sequentially identified by a decimal and its identifier. A task group was, similarly further broken into task units (TUs).

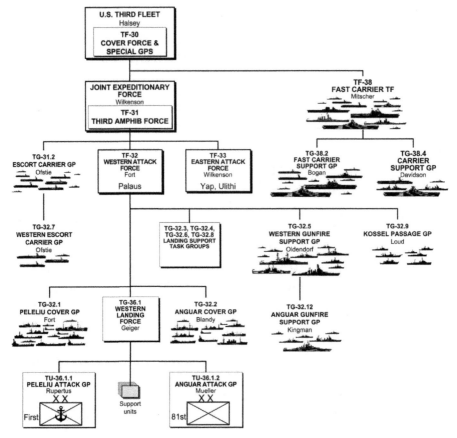

Naval order of battle for the Peleliu campaign. While Admiral Halsey was the overall commander, the senior operational naval officer for the campaign would be Admiral Fort.

- Task Force 34 Heavy Surface Striking Force (Vice Admiral Willis A. Lee, Jr.): six battleships, two heavy cruisers, six light cruisers, and 11 destroyers.*
- Task Force 35 Light Surface Striking Force (Rear Admiral Walden L. Ainsworth): four light cruisers and nine destroyers.

All of the amphibious groups together, collectively labeled the Joint Expeditionary Force and designated Task Force 31, would be under the

---

* The battleships (BATDIVs 7, 8, and 9) and the destroyers (DESDIV 99) were normally part of TG-38.2 and TG-38.3. When detached for an independent mission, they were redesignated *in toto* as TG-38.5 (also under VADM Lee), now assigned to TF-34.

command of Vice Admiral Theodore S. Wilkinson.* His armada would in turn be divided up into three forces:

- TG-31.2: Escort Carrier Group (Rear Admiral Ralph A. Ofstie, flagship USS *Kinkun Bay*), consisting of eleven escort carriers and 12 destroyers. This force included the Western Escort Carrier Group, designated, TG-32.7, which consisted of ten escort carriers and thirteen destroyers. They would provide close air cover for the landing forces.
- TF-32: Western Attack Force (Rear Admiral George H. Fort, flagship USS *Mount McKinley*) would consist of the amphibious forces tasked with taking Peleliu and Angaur.
- TF-33: Eastern Attack Force (Vice Admiral Theodore S. Wilkinson, flagship USS *Mount McKinley*) would consist of the amphibious forces tasked with taking Yap and Ulithi.

Admiral Fort's Task Force 32 would in turn consist of several main subcomponents:

- TG-32.1: Peleliu Amphibious Attack Group (Rear Admiral George H. Fort, flagship USS *Mount McKinley*).
- TG-36.1 (Under TG-32.1): Western Landing Force (Major General Roy Geiger, flagship USS *Mount McKinley*), consisting of the First Marine Division, designated TU-36.1.1 (Major General William H. Rupertus, flagship USS *DuPage*) for Peleliu, and the 81st Infantry Division, designated TU-36.1.2 (Major General Paul J. Mueller, flagship USS *Fremont*).
- TG-32.2: Angaur Cover Group (Rear Admiral William H. P. Blandy, flagship USS *Fremont*).
- TG-32.3: Peleliu Transportation Group 3 (Under TG-32.1, Captain P. Buchanan, flagship USS *DuPage*), which consisted of all the transports, LSTs, and LCIs that would be carrying the First Marine Division and supporting units to the invasion site, escorted by seven destroyers.

---

* Senior naval officers commanding the various groups for the Peleliu operation wore many hats. For instance, Admiral Wilkinson commanded not only TF-31, but also TF-33 under it. Oldendorf commanded TG-32.5, but also TU-32.5.1, TU-32.5.3, and Cruiser Division 4. Admiral Ainsworth commanded Task Force 35, TU-32.5.2, and Cruiser Division 9. Several commanders used for their flagship or command ship the same vessel. For example, Admiral Fort and General Geiger carried their flag aboard the USS *Mount McKinley*. Captain Buchanan (CTG-32.3) and General Rupertus used as their command ship the USS *DuPage*.

- TG-32.4: Angaur Transport Group (Rear Admiral William H. P. Blandy, flagship USS *Fremont*).
- TG-32.5: Western Gunfire Support Group (Rear Admiral Jesse B. Oldendorf, flagship USS *Louisville*), consisting of five battleships, four heavy cruisers (Cruiser divisions 4 and 11), four light cruisers (Cruiser divisions 9 and 12), and a force of 14 destroyers as escort. TG-32.5 was broken down into three groups:
  - Fire Support Unit Able (TU-32.5.2, Rear Admiral Ainsworth), consisting of Battleship Division 4 (the battleships Maryland and Pennsylvania), heavy cruiser Indianapolis, light cruiser Honolulu, and four destroyers.
  - Fire Support Unit Baker (TU-32.5.3, Rear Admiral Oldendorf), consisting of Battleship Division 3 (battleships Idaho and Mississippi), heavy cruisers Louisville and Portland, and five destroyers.
  - TG-32.12, (Rear Admiral Howard F. Kingman, flagship USS Tennessee),[*] the gunfire support groups for the Angaur landing, consisting of Battleship Division 2 (the battleships Tennessee and California), heavy cruiser Minneapolis, light cruisers Cleveland, Denver, and Columbia,[†] and five destroyers.
- TG-32.6: Angaur Tractor Group (Captain Seay, flagship USS *Bailey*).
- TG-32.9: Kossel Passage Group (Commander Wayne R. Loud), which consisted of six destroyer-minesweepers, two minesweepers, a minelayer, and six repair vessels. This unit would mine-sweep and secure the Kossol Passage below Babelthuap to the north, organize it into a safe anchorage for the surface forces, and secure a seaplane base there.
- TG-32.13: Peleliu Tractor Group (Captain Robertson, flagship USS *Hazelwood*), consisting of 30 LSTs, a repair vessel, 18 LCI(G)s, and four LCI(M)s.

---

[*] Admiral Nimitz's war diary for September, 1944, mistakenly lists TG-32.12 under the command of Rear Admiral Theodore E. Chandler. However, Chandler at the time was involved in the Atlantic as part of the invasion of Southern France, and did not report aboard in the Pacific until October 2, 1944.

[†] Some sources (e.g., Ross p. 135, Moran & Rottman p. 29) mistakenly identified the heavy cruiser USS *Columbus* (CA-74) as being present. However, the *Columbus* would not be commissioned until the end of November, 1944, two and a half months after Peleliu began. Rather, the vessel that was present was USS *Columbia* (CL-56), in commission since late July, 1942. It is an understandable mistake.

Naval Fire Support

Rear Admiral Jesse Oldendorf commanded TG-32.5, the Western Gunfire Support Group, which would be providing naval gunfire support (NGS) for the invasion. The mission of these warships would be to take out the main defensive positions on the island before the Marines stormed ashore. They were to pound the island before, during, and after the landing.

Oldendorf's main battle force centered around six old battleships, or OBBs.* Four of them were Pearl Harbor veterans: the USS *Pennsylvania*, *Maryland*, *California*, and the *Tennessee*. Added to these pre-World War II battlewagons were the USS *Idaho* and *Mississippi*. In addition, there were four heavy cruisers (CA)† present: the *Indianapolis*, *Louisville* (Oldendorf's flagship), *Minneapolis*, and the *Portland*. Additionally there were four light cruisers (CL): the *Columbia*, *Cleveland*, *Denver*, and the *Honolulu*. Providing escort and close-range shore bombardment was a screen of 14 destroyers.

On August 2, the naval commander overseeing the entire invasion, Rear Admiral George Fort, commanding the Western Attack Force (TF-32), arrived at Pavuvu to begin developing the details of the operation with the Marines. Six days later, the Navy and Marine Corps staffs formally began planning conferences, deciding on the pressing issues, such as negotiating the barrier reef, creating logistical schedules, and finalizing the naval support that would be provided. This last subject was naturally of particular importance to the Marines.

On August 10, Captain P. Buchanan, who was to command the Peleliu Transport Group from his flagship, the USS *DuPage*, arrived on the island,‡ and planning for the transportation began. The vulnerable troop transports

---

* The term Old Battleship (OBB) was used by the U. S. Navy to describe their prewar dreadnought battleships. Those still in service in 1944 ranged from the training ship USS *Wyoming* (BB-32), commissioned in 1912, to the USS *West Virginia* (BB-48), commissioned in 1923. While these vessels were significantly inferior to those constructed during the war, they still made excellent gun platforms for gunfire against approaching vessels (as attested in the night battle of Surigao Straits on October 25, 1944, when six of these vessels under Admiral Oldendorf decimated a large Japanese surface force), or in providing support during amphibious landings. As such, especially after being refitted, they played an essential role as primary naval gunfire support in all of the Allied amphibious operations, both in the Pacific and the Atlantic.

† The CA code originally stood for "cruiser, armored," but was changed in 1931 to "cruiser, heavy." Similarly, the aircraft carrier hull classification of CV stood for "carrier, *voler*," the latter word French for "to fly."

‡ Captain Buchanan subsequently became ill and was replaced in late August by Captain H. R. Brittain as CTG-32.3, in addition to his duties as commander of Transport Division 24.

carrying the later waves would not be able to get closer to the beaches than nine nautical miles until all of the enemy shore batteries were taken out. The LSTs carrying the first eight waves would be able to get closer inshore, and the designated LST launching line where the amtracs would be embarked was established at about three nautical miles out. The amtracs would move in, rendezvous, and organize into assault waves at the line of departure, about two nautical miles (4,000 yards) out. Then they would move in at about three knots toward the beaches, a travel time of about a half hour.

All of this of course, would be critically dependent on and vulnerable to how fiercely the enemy batteries would respond to the approaching craft. To cover this threat, the original naval plan had called for a preliminary bombardment period of three days, followed by the pre-landing shelling on the early morning of D-Day. However, at that time, because it was involved in a number of operations that were either ongoing or being planned simultaneously, the Navy was spread thin. Because of that, the fleets were experiencing shortage issues. Thus, back on August 8, at a briefing held at Pavuvu, Rear Admiral Fort told General Geiger right up front: "You're not going to get all the gunfire support here that you got in Guam. I don't have the ships, and we don't have the ammunition."

This was a serious change from recent operations in the Marianas. At Guam, for instance, because of the recent American victory in the Philippine Sea, the Navy had fired off at the enemy a steady, 13-day preliminary bombardment before the invasion. This one though was only going to get two days, to begin on D-2.

The admiral's reasons for the Navy's reluctance to conduct a longer barrage were actually varied. One factor again was the generally accepted consensus that this was not going to be a heavily contested island. Based on reconnaissance and the fact that the isolated island chain had been bombed several times, naval planners accepted that Peleliu was probably going to be a relatively small operation, the widespread belief throughout the high command.

However, Fort's main concerns mostly stemmed from the two reasons he had given General Geiger, serious problems that his forces were at the time undergoing. The first was simply a lack of warships to commit to the bombardment because of operations elsewhere. More importantly though was a shortage of large- and medium-caliber naval gun ammunition, for which there would not be enough time to adequately replenish. Even more importantly, large quantities of all types would be critically needed for MacArthur's top priority, the upcoming Philippines invasion.

There was yet a last issue as well, one that was as critically important and tethered to the others. The Navy knew from experience that additional or extended shelling increased the deterioration of the barrels and breeches of the large main guns on the battleships and cruisers. The admirals were concerned that firing them too much would wear down the bores, especially on the larger-caliber guns, such as the main batteries of 14-inch 50-caliber guns on the older *Mississippi, Idaho, California,* and the *Tennessee.*˙

Nor was wear and tear limited to the barrels. The gun breeches themselves would suffer additionally from thermal stress, chemical corrosion, and mechanical wear down, eventually to the point where special, extensive maintenance was required. This cumulative effect would slowly render the gun unreliable for its purpose. As more shells were fired, the faster the deterioration rate would be as the barrels abraded and the breeches degraded.

Here, critical performance factors would eventually become serious concerns. First, the gun's muzzle velocity would decrease. Since there would be more blowby along the sides of the shell from the barrel's increasing inner diameter due to wear, the shell velocity would be lower. Thus, because of this, the shell would not be propelled as far. The ballistics of the projectile would change slightly with each round fired, as its range would be lessening. If the wear on the bore became too great, the shell might even jam in the barrel and, worse, explode in the tube. At a certain point then, one or more of the barrels in a turret would require repair.

This was not be a minor job. They would have to either be relined or replaced, a time-consuming undertaking that would have to be done in a fully equipped port facility. This of course would necessitate taking the warship out of action for a while. Naturally, this type of service delay to MacArthur's plans would no doubt result in serious repercussions coming from Washington.

Nor was this problem limited to the larger-caliber guns, although the wear on them progressed faster, and the concern for them was the most pressing. The smaller-caliber guns suffered from this problem as well. The USS *Mississippi* noted in its action report on Peleliu: "The six 5"/51-caliber guns of this vessel

---

˙ According to naval engineering sources (e.g., NavWeaps.com), most of the 14-inch guns fired at Peleliu had a barrel life of 200–250 rounds. That would give their main armament (12 guns in four turrets) a life of 3,000 rounds before requiring maintenance. The later improved version of the 16-inch gun on the *Colorado* class (here, the *USS Maryland*) had chromium plating, which extended its barrel life to about 395 rounds. Heavy cruiser 8-inch guns had an average life of 715 rounds, and light cruiser 6-inch guns had an average life of 750 to 1,000 rounds, depending on the model.

expended approximately 540 rounds each. This amounts to about 70 percent of the life of these guns."

The Marines though, had little sympathy for the Navy's problems, especially Smith and Geiger.* Geiger in particular worried that a dug-in enemy would be waiting for him on the island. He had originally recommended at least four days' preliminary bombardment before his men landed, so at that mid-August briefing he became considerably distressed to hear that he was only getting two. Sensing the danger this might present to his men coming ashore, he insisted in no uncertain terms to admirals Fort and Wilkinson that they get more than just two days' bombardment. Finally the Navy reluctantly acquiesced and made a compromise, agreeing to three days: the six battleships, eight cruisers, many destroyers, destroyer escorts, and support landing craft hopefully would be able to take out the enemy positions in that timeframe. Two days later, on August 10, General Geiger issued Operation Order 1–44 for the invasion. Five days later, after extensively going over the orders with him, General Rupertus issued the order to the division.

Unfortunately, two serious problems that directly affected the plan arose after these meetings. Because the Marianas operations had taken longer than expected, ammunition replenishment for the warships remained behind schedule. There might not be enough shells available to take on a three-day preliminary bombardment and provide call fire mission support after the landing. This was especially true since the Navy had to amass enough shells to carry out their role in MacArthur's upcoming invasion of the Philippines. The admirals decided that if shortages deemed it so, the originally scheduled two-day amount of ordnance would just have to be stretched over three days. This would hopefully work out well, since the enemy positions identified on the island were not extensive, and it was expected that the enemy would not put up extensive resistance. And anyway, it went against naval doctrine to simply pound a target for no reason.

The second problem occurred a couple weeks later. Having blasted the Japanese positions on Tinian and Guam from July 18 to August 9, the USS

---

* According to Dick Camp (p. 59), supposedly at one of the briefings, the naval officers had droned on several times at how each of their warships would move in as close as possible to the beachhead to provide cover, since their armor would be adequate to meet the incoming enemy counterfire (6,000 yards for the battleships, 4,000 yards for the cruisers, etc.), General Julian Smith finally heard enough. He reportedly stood up from his chair, stared at the naval officers, and said in a subdued tone, "Gentlemen, when the Marines meet the enemy at bayonet point, the only armor a Marine will have is his khaki shirt." However, this incident has been corroborated as having actually occurred before the Tarawa invasion back in November, 1943.

California and her sister ship, the USS *Tennessee* began heading south to put into Espiritu Santo for maintenance and replenishment before taking part in the upcoming Peleliu operation. On August 23, about 330 miles southeast of Guadalcanal, as the *California* was maneuvering to stay clear of a task unit, the *Tennessee* collided with her, smashing into her port bow. The damage to the *Tennessee* was not too bad, but that to the *California* was severe. Both vessels were able to continue to Espiritu Santo, where they immediately put in for repairs. The *Tennessee* would be patched up and ready for the Peleliu operation, but the *California* had to go into drydock. Estimates were that she would be out for a month. She would not be able to take part in the operation, and no other battleship was considered to replace her. *California* was to have taken part in shelling Angaur. Now the *Pennsylvania* would have to take her place. Thus, in one afternoon, the Peleliu operation had lost a sixth of the capital ships scheduled to bombard the island.

Pavuvu

A considerable reason that the Peleliu operation was going to be more difficult for the Marines was that training conditions before the campaign—and to a certain extent afterwards—were downright miserable.

At the end of April, the First Marine Division was tired from having fought the rain, the Japanese, and the jungles of Cape Gloucester. They were looking forward to some rest and relaxation. They had landed on New Britain back on Christmas Day, having just finished up three and a half months of combat operations. Many had come down with malaria. Those that had not been wounded and evacuated were tired and worn out. They had operated during the rainy season, and their equipment was dirty, mud-soaked, and smelly. What clothes they had left that had not rotted away on them from the soaking environment or was not in need of replacement was badly in need of cleaning. The men knew full well how the Corps operated, and that they would get at least a few months in a nice environment to recuperate and to prepare for wherever the hell they were going to fight next. So their hopes were high on where that recovery location would be. The last time it had been Melbourne, Australia. Maybe—hopefully—they would return there again, or at least to some other city in that country, where Americans were loved and appreciated.

General Geiger himself had selected the island of Pavuvu in the Russell Islands for the division to recuperate back in April. About ten miles long and six miles wide, it was just 40 miles northwest of the tip of Guadalcanal, it was close enough to the main hub of operations in the area, but still isolated from the air and sea traffic patterns. His staff had surveyed Pavuvu from the air, and as he saw the photos of lush vegetation, he was told of the nice gentle shores and the lovely palm trees. From the aerial photos, it looked like a tropical paradise. He concluded that this would be a good, remote spot for his men to rest and train. The island was isolated, and, unlike Guadalcanal, the men would avoid having to endure endless island work details, a fate that the Third Marine Division was now suffering there after their campaign on Bougainville in December, 1943. By avoiding having to provide hundreds of men every day for work details, the First would not suffer that fate, and therefore be better able to recover from the Cape Gloucester operation and get ready for the upcoming campaign. Besides, the general was assured that a Navy Seabee battalion would go in beforehand and spruce an area for the Marines to live and train in.

As it often turned out though, images from the air of an isolated, tropical island can be quite deceiving. Pavuvu had once, decades ago, boasted successful coconut plantations, but these had not been worked for years. Now the overabundance of these untended groves that had not been harvested since the war began had created thousands of rotting coconuts strewn all over the ground, a condition which naturally had contributed to the fecund populations of insects, vermin, and other crawly creatures that might thrive on such an overabundant food supply. The couple rough roads were mere dirt trails, and there were no housing facilities to speak of. To make matters worse, the ground was rich with ferns over a carpet of decayed coral, which did not absorb water too well. Thus, the topsoil was generally soft and moist in nature, and because there was no drainage and little rainwater absorption, it quickly turned to thick mud when walked upon, or driven over.

The Marines began arriving on the island in late April. The rainy season was supposedly over, but still lingered with occasional heavy showers. The island looked pleasant to the men coming in on the ships (as it had from the air), with simple piers, nice-looking shores, and lovely palm trees swaying in the soft breeze. Morale though, soon took a dive when the men came ashore and saw how primitive the conditions were. The Seabees 15th Battalion had just finished building the 1,300-bed hospital on nearby Banika Island near the end of March, and so by the time they were transported over to Pavuvu, they had been given very little time to clear any areas there, much less set up any facilities. Thus, instead of a place to rest and refit themselves from their recent combat on Cape Gloucester, the weary Marines were forced to develop their own rest and training areas. Setting up camp was a challenge, because of the high water level. And the best way to get around was barefoot. Tents unpacked were often old and sometimes rotting. The men often had to just resort to throwing their ponchos over their mosquito nets to stay dry at night.

Thus, the construction and work details that the general had hoped they would avoid on Guadalcanal ended up being even more vigorous on Pavuvu. It became quite the effort to clean up the area enough just to set up a decent training camp. The Marines had to spend weeks clearing away the jungle thick underbrush and removing seemingly endless masses of smelly, rotting coconuts, some six hundred acres of them; this was the most common detail to be on (not an easy task, especially if the stinking things broke apart as you were loading them and splashed their foul contents all over your trousers).

Life on Pavuvu was taxing. Work details were tasked with creating walkways, drainage ditches, showers, and latrines, and it all had to be set up in a humid, tropical climate. A shortage of lumber exacerbated construction difficulties. Wells had to be dug, and the water they eventually hit tasted terrible, flavored by juices from the rotting coconuts saturated into the ground. Compounding the problem was the fact that many of the men had come down with malaria in the last campaign, and doing hard labor like this, in sweltering heat, did little to improve their health.

There initially were no restrooms or shower facilities, so taking a shave or washing up involved the use of one's helmet, all of which were left outside so that whenever it rained the helmets would fill with rainwater. Likewise, taking a shower meant removing one's clothes and leaving one's tent naked with a bar of soap whenever it rained.

Even just "taking a dump," as the men called it, was a challenge. The latrine ditches dug for that purpose were too wide for one to straddle, and so one had to answer the call of nature perched over the edge.

Chowtime was certainly nothing to write home about. For the first couple months, there was no mess hall, so you had to take your meal back to your tent. Even standing in the chow line meant standing in mud, and the making the trip back to your tent through the muddy coral with your food and filled canteen cup, even in the daytime, was a challenge. Decent cooking facilities had to be set up.

Food provisions, like other supplies to the island, were simple and sometimes limited to just rations. Fresh food was never in any abundance. Division staff had planned on receiving fresh provisions regularly, and had even built some storage units for them. They were mostly empty. For breakfast, something that was supposed to pass for French toast was served, with limited supplies of diluted syrup, sometimes served with powdered eggs (getting the real

Sea of mud: Pavuvu in the spring of 1944. When the Marines arrived they were in for a rude shock: what looked like a tropical paradise from the air and from the ocean was actually a smelly, muddy, primitive hellhole. (USMC photo)

things was almost impossible). Occasionally soggy cornflakes and diluted canned milk were available. Lunch usually consisted of occasional spam and C-rations, with dehydrated potatoes and carrots, both of which mostly tasted like cardboard. Beverages consisted of coffee or a sort of lemony fruit drink that tasted more like battery acid. For dinner, one could look forward to a sort of corn beef hash dish that the men referred to as corned willy cakes (a pejorative term borrowed from the trenches of World War I), or possibly some canned Vienna sausage, and more cardboard vegetables. Fresh meat came over about once a week, but since there were few reefers to store it, the supplies did not last too long. There had been a number of stray cows on the island when the men arrived, but they belonged to the previous Australian plantation owners, and the Australians quickly put the cows off limits to the Marines after a few strays disappeared.

Unsurprisingly, given the naturally innovating nature of Marines, several of them took it upon themselves to undertake imaginative enterprises to supplement their meals with some of the natural fish and game on the island, but the fish were hard to catch, and the game was usually were too dangerous in nature to warrant even tacit hunting approval by command. Alligator steaks for instance, although certainly no match for beef, were nevertheless pursued by some adventurers. These efforts were soon forbidden when one or two raiders disappeared one night; on a couple of occasions a few others lost their way in the darkness and ended up taking a few potshots right next to some tent areas. Using hand grenades or explosives to go 'gator hunting or fishing was stopped after a couple men injured themselves in the process. Large clams were sometimes caught, but the resulting meal was considered only nominally better than the issued rations. Beer supplies were rare, and spirits were of course out of the question. Entertainment consisted of some old B-grade movies or newsreels, and of course, there were absolutely no women on the island. The only entertainment along those lines became those talented enough to be imaginative storytellers, recalling with relish (often many times) exploits of earlier years, or Australia in '43.

There was no recreational building, and for several weeks, there was really nothing to do before lights out, a phrase that was used in name only because at first there was no electricity on the island, even for divisional headquarters. The limited power that later was provided by a few generators was only used for high-level administrative functions. Still, some men made do by "borrowing" a little gasoline and fashioning a wick out of rope for crude lanterns to write home by. Mail call for the men became a desperately important function, because the letters and photos from home were their only lifeline to the outside world. Any man lucky enough to get a small care package from his family instantly became the most popular man in his platoon, especially since protocol dictated that the lucky fellow share the prize with his cohorts.

Near the end of May, a sort of crude amphitheater was set up so the men could see a movie in the evening. Usually they were old B-movies from the Thirties, but watching them became the only and thus most important social function for the Marines.

Nighttime was almost as bad as working in the day, especially in the beginning when the men essentially had to sleep on muddy ground or to string hammocks until their quarters were established. After one turned in, it was difficult to sleep. Squadrons of flying insects, including malaria-carrying mosquitoes, attacked from the air, while all manner of inquisitive bugs explored along the ground. A bigger problem than the insects were the battalions of slimy coconut crabs that emerged after dark, looking for food. With bodies about the size of a man's hand, and bristling with sharp spines, they would crawl into shoes, containers, and any type of opening. Sometimes on a Sunday, a few units would declare war on these crustaceans and aggressively hunt them all over the tent areas, usually taking out a few thousand.

There were other animals on the island that bothered the men, including iguanas, frogs, and of course, the alligators. The worst infestations were the rats. At night, they crept over the ground, the tents, and the ropes. They would come into the sleeping areas, looking for food, sometimes gnawing through one's mosquito net to join a man who happened to have food on his cot. Like the crabs, they crawled into cots, seabags, and crates. Frustration led to efforts of fighting back with various types of snares, explosive booby traps and flamethrowers, but slaughtering a few hundred a night did little to diminish their numbers, even though they were also easy prey for the bats that lived in the palm trees.

Morning sick call, as expected, brought out many more patients than there were corpsmen and doctors to attend to them, and as a result, those standing in line, barefoot and usually butt-naked, often had to treat each other for a whole host of maladies, from jungle rot, to ringworm, to cuts, bruises, fevers, and bites. Even the island hospital was a dump, nothing more than a tent with cots that sat on the ground. There was something about that tent that seemed to retarded one's healing, and the men avoided it if at all possible.

Perhaps summing up the mood of his comrades, one Marine supposedly one night, in purely bitter frustration, ran out of his tent at dusk and began to pound his fists against a coconut tree, sobbing angrily, "I hate you, gawddammit, I HATE you!"

There was only one reaction to this outburst from the men. After a moment, a growled reply came from a nearby tent: "Hit it once for me."

One depressing rumor that had been around for weeks was that no one would be transferred or rotated back to the States before the next operation, including those who had been in the division for two years now. This rumor was verified by a staff officer from III Amphibious Corps, who essentially told the division officers that there were just not enough men in the Corps to allow that. He stated, "Your people have got to stick it out, at least for the next operation."

While he was in Washington though, General Rupertus and his chief of staff insisted that the older veterans be rotated, and finally the Marine Corps high command consented; however, morale did not improve much when the first of nearly 4,900 replacements started arriving. The new arrivals did not enjoy their new training location at all. At the same time, the same number of veterans who had endured operations first on Guadalcanal, then Finchhaven, and finally Cape Gloucester began to get rotated out of what the men referred to as the Pavuvu stink hole for return to the States. While their own spirits rose substantially, they were still filled with a sense of guilt, because they were leaving good friends who would now bear the brunt of the next campaign without them. Their comrades they were leaving behind became even more morose, especially those who had served in all the campaigns but were considered too essential to be rotated out. Needless to say, the departing send-off did nothing to buoy the spirits of those left behind.

As if their conditions and their friends leaving were not bad enough, there was another issue that became a constant irritation. What had initially been just a rumor—that the men on Banika and over on Guadalcanal had much better living conditions—was soon confirmed by those enlisted fortunate enough to get over there on official business. There was only one boat that went across daily, an LCM, and guards made sure only authorized personnel could get aboard. Those who returned to Pavuvu confirmed the rumors: the men over on Banika ate much better, lived in adequate, comfortable quarters, and often had access to alcohol. They had electricity, and PXs, where they could get chocolate, and cigarettes, or cigars. As important as anything though, the hospital staff included a couple hundred female nurses and Red Cross volunteers, and although enlisted fraternization with them was strictly against regulations, the thought of an American female just a very short island hop away was enough to set one's mind in motion. Getting there though, was a privilege strictly limited to the very sick, those on official business, or to senior officers, and even then restrictions were considerable (One battalion commander was even relieved for overstaying a one-day pass.) Understandably, officers pulling rank to get what the men were starting to feel was, in relative terms, fun city, were deeply resented.

In mid-1944, while they were on Pavuvu, as part of the training syllabus, a new Marine Corps unit reorganization, created in Washington and entitled "F-Series," was implemented. The modifications, based on studies conducted during operations undertaken in the war thus far, were designed to improve a Marine battalion's mobility and to give each rifle company better firepower, as well as allow better coordination of the heavy mortars. The redesign also included changes to the makeup of the rifle squads and the platoon headquarters. Each of the three battalion heavy weapons companies was disbanded: D Company in 1st Battalion, H Company in 2nd Battalion, and M Company in 3rd Battalion. The 81mm heavy mortar platoons went to the 213-man battalion headquarters company, and the machine-gun platoons were redistributed among the rifle companies, along with the light 60mm mortars. This theme would remain for the G-Series reorganization in May 1945.*

---

* The concept of the battalion heavy weapons company though, would be restored a few years after the war.

As the division trained and slowly built up its strength with the arrival of new replacements from the States, the deplorable, primitive conditions on Pavuvu continued to stifle morale. Equipment shortages were commonplace. One problem was the basic rifle itself. It had been concluded that the M-1 carbine, while considered a good substitute for a pistol, was nevertheless not an adequate substitution for the heavier Garand rifle. The Marine units were now trying to replace them wherever possible, except for specialized units, such as antiaircraft or maintenance. Unfortunately, adequate supplies of the Garand were not readily available, nor were Thompson sub-machine guns.

Even when the men had equipment to practice with, training was difficult. The island was way too small to allow a division to camp, train, and maneuver, and provided very few facilities or open areas to train the replacements. Hiking to get in shape was often reduced to marching around the same open ground over and over. Artillery practice consisted of firing rounds into the ocean, with naval spotters offshore to observe accuracy. It was often difficult to find enough open space to conduct coordinated exercises with the Shermans, and so practice sessions had to fit into a tight schedule. Nor did facilities allow the experienced men to brush up on their skills. One account described these conditions well:

> Company streets were the only areas where men could engage in mock attacks. It was routine to see one outfit charging full-tilt between rows of tents into other troops in formations standing at rigid attention for rifle inspection, or other units practicing close-order drill ...
>
> A primitive rifle range was set up at the edge of one of the palm groves. It was largely ineffective ... No conventional bull's-eye targets were available, so the men took potshots at coconuts lined up on sand bags.
>
> Whenever tanks and infantry attempted joint maneuvers in the jungle the lumbering Shermans rapidly bogged down in the quicksand. Artillery batteries fired at imaginary targets in the hills, but it was impossible to determine the accuracy of their shelling. Mortar and machine gun crews were rusty from lack of activity. Flamethrower and demolition teams could only hold dry runs; there simply was no place for them to use their equipment without endangering other Marines.

Other problems arose in the maintenance of the weapons and ammunition. Some of the new gear proved to be so in name only, and not in condition. The webbing on ammo belts was often rotting, the fine grain explosive on the compressed powder rings on many mortar shells was crumbling, the outer casings on a number of bullets were corroding, and wooden components were sometimes found to be decaying.

During these weeks of preparation, the Marines tried out a few new weapons. One of these was the new Navy Mark I Ronco flamethrower, which the Seabees had developed back at Pearl Harbor. This weapon could shoot a stream of fiery napalm a distance of up to 150 yards. The division was given three in July, as well as three new LVT-4s on which to mount them (a fourth was used to carry additional napalm). The Marines practiced using them against mock pillboxes on the beaches. They did not realize at the time that in actual combat they would be better employed against enemy caves.

Another new piece of equipment was a recently developed shoulder-fired mortar, the 60mm T20. Purported to be more effective than the bazooka, it fired a standard HE mortar shell, with an effective range of about 600 yards, and could be fired more or less horizontally. The Marines were given about a hundred of them to try in combat. One was given to each rifle platoon, with the last 20 or so kept as spare. The Marines practiced carrying around the T20, and even though it was much heavier than the bazooka, it was felt that it still might come in handy against pillboxes and fortified positions.

Slowly, as living conditions became more bearable and replacements were assimilated into the units, morale gradually improved.

Hope

There was little that the command could do to bolster the spirits of the men, other than improving their living areas and continuing training. On the Fourth of July, the division held relay races and various sports activities, such as baseball, but the relaxational benefits of such events were fleeting.

A popular rumor that began going around was that the Japanese were not well prepared for them, and that the operation, while rough, would not be prolonged, like it had been at Guadalcanal, or Cape Gloucester. General Rupertus himself espoused that the operation would be a "short one; a quickie."

Undoubtedly though, the high point of the division's time on Pavuvu came in early August. Touring the South Pacific at that time was Bob Hope's USO troupe. A show had been scheduled to be held in the area—on nearby Banika Island, naturally. On the afternoon of Saturday, August 5, the entertainment group landed on Banika to entertain those in the hospital, and the Navy's 4th Base Depot. Tagging along with Bob was thick-mustached comedian Jerry Colonna, popular 31-year-old singer and actress Frances Langford, attractive 22-year-old dancer Patty Thomas, well-known announcer and comedian Bill Goodwin, guitarist and singer Tony Romano, jokes and skits writer Barney Dean, and bandleader Stan Kenton. The troupe had arrived on the island to do a show for the wounded and sick at the hospital.

The next morning, before the show began, the First Marine Division's recreations officer, who had found out about the upcoming show, took the ferry over to Banika, found the entertainment troupe, and approached Mr. Hope privately to make a special request. Bob later recalled what happened:

> A Special Service marine officer came to see me. "We've got the First Marine Division stashed on a little island called Pavuvu, about 20 miles from here," he said. "They're training for the invasion of Peleliu. Nobody knows this but the men themselves. They haven't had any entertainment for nine months. If you would come over with your troupe, it would be wonderful."
>
> "How do we get there?" I asked.
>
> "I think you ought to know there're no runways on Pavuvu," he said. You'll have to go in Cubs; one of you to each Cub. You land on a road."
>
> "We'll be ready tomorrow," I said. "I'll check with my people, but I'm sure they'll want to go."

The Marine officer was thrilled, and left to give the command on Pavuvu advanced notice. Bob turned out to be right. All of the show members agreed to go. They had never turned down a performance anywhere, and this was most definitely not going to be an exception. They did their show on Banika that day, and the next morning, Monday August 7, they took off for Pavuvu:

> Each of us was in a Cub with a pilot. When we reached Pavuvu, more than 15,000 guys were standing on the baseball field, waiting for us. Looking down, I realized that 15,000 faces pointed at the sky is a lot of faces. As we flew over, they let out a yell. It felt as if it lifted our Cubs up into the air.
>
> We did a show for them. While we were doing it, we knew that many of the men we were entertaining would never see the States again. If we hadn't felt the drama in that thought, we'd have been pretty thick-skinned. We weren't that thick-skinned.

The show was performed on a small stage in a large open area next to the piers, with most of the division camped out to watch the show. The smash opening was of course was "Bob 'Mosquito Network' Hope" doing his opening monologue. He joked about the area, his flight, and other current topics. He brought the house down though, when he referenced one of the island's biggest pains.

"I noticed your land crabs," he said dryly. "They reminded me of Crosby's horses because they all run sideways."

Patty Thomas gave a few of them dancing lessons, Tony Romano sang, and then Bob and Jerry Colonna traded jokes, such as:

"So Jerry, how'd you like the trip over from Banika?"

"Tough sledding."

"Why"

"No snow."

The show was a great success, and the men really appreciated the extra effort that they went to for them.

> When we got into the Cubs to go back to Banika, all 15,000 of those Marines lined each side of the road and cheered each Cub as it took off. If I never get another thrill in my life, that one will last me.

Bob later recalled after hearing later that some 60 percent of the division had been casualties on Peleliu, that entertaining for them was "one of the most emotional shows I've ever done."

As July turned into August, and with conditions on the island now at least tolerable, the men on Pavuvu began to again cohere into the élite fighting unit they had once been. The replacements were blended into their units and trained alongside the veterans. Everyone almost by instinct took to the job of preparing for the next operation, and the concept of fighting for each other gave them a renewed sense of pride and dedication to the upcoming tasks at hand. The Marines took to their training with renewed energy, and slowly began to prepare for whatever was coming next.

The Marines Leave for War

The First Marine Division, having completed those landing exercises at Guadalcanal, received their embarkation orders on August 5; five days later, the transport staff arrived on Pavuvu to coordinate with the units. The division began embarking equipment onto the arriving vessels as early as August 11, while the infantry units did not start boarding the transports until the middle of the month.

On August 27 and 29, the division took part in two large successful landing rehearsals at Guadalcanal, around Cape Esperance. There was no coral reef to deal with in conducting these landings, but a transfer line was simulated to reflect one. With the second rehearsal, the landing's cover group, Admiral Fort's Task Group 32.1, coordinated with the landing. The Navy stood offshore and practiced landing support (although no shots were fired). A few issues were addressed, including some radio communication problems, but nothing serious.

After the training exercises, the division was allowed to go ashore one more time before boarding the transports for the trip. The last of the units came aboard on August 31.

On September 4, the slower LSTs that were carrying the forward assault units left for the Palaus, averaging a sluggish 7.7 knots. Four days later, on the 8th, the LSDs and the faster transports left Guadalcanal. The entire set of convoys totaling 868 vessels, starting from several different areas, began to make their way to Peleliu, some 2,100 miles away.

The ledger for the 1st Battalion, 1st Marines records the following for September 8:

> 8 Sept 44: Under way at about 0640, no more fooling, we are headed for the real thing, Peleliu Is in the Palau group. Lectures being held in the mess hall on intelligence and naval and air support. Troop and inspection held in the hold. Morale of troops good, chow still in insufficient quantities, no condition red.

The slower convoys averaged almost 13 knots, along with other surface and auxiliary units. All the convoys moved northwestward through the Solomons and up past the northern coast of New Guinea. They included Admiral Fort's Task Group 32.1, the amphibious cover force, and Rupertus's landing group TG-36.1.1. Ferrying the Marines was a force of 30 LSTs, 18 transports, and two LSDs carrying Sherman tanks. Both sets of convoys would meet just before D-Day near the target area.

The weather was fair, and the Navy fed everyone well as the convoy made good progress sailing northwestward. The men rested, wrote letters home, read paperbacks, or sometimes just went on deck and looked at the ocean. The ledger for the 1st Battalion, 1st Marines records the following for September 11:

> 11 Sept 44: Ships routine at sea. Debarkation drill held in morning. Weather getting hotter, morale of troops still good. Health good, malaria has been cut down, everybody receiving 3 atabrines a day. No condition red.

Onboard the transports, the Marines were given more lectures and carried out more exercises. All 770 landing craft in the convoys were given final inspections and fueled in preparation for the landing.

The Preliminaries

Back in early March, July, and again in August, tactical aircraft from Davidson's Task Group 38.4 and Ofstie's escort carriers of TG-32.7 had bombed various targets over the Palau Islands, both by day and by night.

On September 7, TG-39.2, under the command of Rear Admiral F. E. M. Whiting, consisting of Cruiser Division 14, consisting of the light cruisers USS *Houston*,[*] *Vincennes* (flagship), and the *Miami*, and the four destroyers of

---

[*] The USS *Houston* (CL-81), a Cleveland-class light cruiser, was originally slated as the USS *Vicksburg*. However, when the heavy cruiser USS *Houston* (CA-30) was sunk on March 1, 1942

Destroyer Division 100—USS *Capertown* (DD-650, flagship), USS *Cogswell* (DD-651), USS *Ingersoll* (DD-642), and USS *Knapp* (DD-653)—commenced a two-day shelling of Peleliu and Angaur islands. With the cruisers each expending about 1,500 6-inch and 5-inch shells, firing from the northern side of the islands, these eight warships took out a number of buildings and defensive points near the shoreline and around the airfield, including communication facilities on Peleliu and supply points on Angaur, while carrier-based planes hit a number of supply facilities.

At the same time, on September 6, 8 and 9, the aircraft from Davidson's and Ofstie's carriers attacked again, bombing and firing rockets at various targets in the Palaus. Then again on September 10 and 11, TG-38.4's aircraft made several additional raiding missions on the Palaus, especially Peleliu and Angaur.

Three days before the Marines departed Guadalcanal, Rear Admiral Jesse B. Oldendorf's Task Group 32.5, the Western Gunfire Support Group for the invasion, arrived off Peleliu and set up positions to begin softening up the island's defenses in preparation for the landing. Just before dawn on Tuesday, September 12, three days before the landing was to begin, TG-32.5 was ready to begin its scheduled bombardment.

Coordinating with the Peleliu bombardment group again was Rear Admiral Ralph Ofstie's TG-32.7 of (initially) four escort carriers that were tasked with providing tactical air support. These four escort carriers were later to be joined by six more escort carriers from his other task group, TG-31.2. In addition to this force, three wolfpacks of submarines were to form a screen around the surface forces to report any interference from the Japanese Navy, and, if possible, to engage and destroy them.

The landing operations would be coordinated through General Geiger's command ship, the USS *Mount McKinley*, about a mile and a half offshore. Rupertus and his staff would be on the attack transport USS *DuPage*, which would anchor another quarter mile closer to the beach. O. P. Smith and his staff, including Colonel Joseph Hankins, commanding of the division's headquarters company, would work off the USS *Elmore*, which would anchor about a half mile out from the barrier reef, in the center of the landing area.

---

in the in the battle of Sunda Strait, and 100 new recruits from the namesake city (penned by the media as the "Houston Volunteers") came forward in May, the name of the new light cruiser under construction was, by President Roosevelt's direction, renamed the USS *Houston* to honor the crew and vessel that had so recently been lost. She was commissioned on December 20, 1943. In that same month, a new light cruiser, originally slated as the USS *Cheyenne*, was commissioned as the USS *Vicksburg* (CL-86).

At 0530 on September 12, Oldendorf's battle force began what was to be the planned three-day bombardment of Peleliu using four of his five prewar battleships, three of the four heavy cruisers, one of the four light cruisers, and about half of the destroyers. Additionally, aircraft from Davidson's Task Group 38.4 conducted yet more bombing raids over the island. At the same time, minesweepers began clearing mines around the approaches to Angaur Island and the western approaches to Peleliu, while demolition teams began clearing the approach lanes to the White and Orange beaches.

Not surprisingly perhaps, the makeup and the actions of Oldendorf's Fire Support Group vary from one source to the next. Most accounts of Peleliu indicate that all five of Oldendorf's OBBs were present, and many of these document that they took part in the island's shelling. Several sources though, correctly claim that there were only four battleships that actually took part in the Peleliu bombardment, leaving out the *Tennessee*, which was indeed in the area. She instead had been detached from Oldendorf's TG-32.5, along with the heavy cruiser *Minneapolis*, the light cruisers *Columbia*, *Denver*, and *Cleveland*, and six destroyers. This group became Admiral Kingman's TG-32.12, detached from the main body on September 11 for the Angaur component of the operation, scheduled to begin September 17.

As Oldendorf's vessels began pounding Peleliu on the morning of September 12, intermittently joined by Ofstie's carrier planes making attack runs, the *Tennessee* task group also began their own pre-landing bombardment. Their target though, was Angaur, some seven miles to the southwest, a secondary target that was to be assaulted by the Army after the Marines had landed. Thus, the *Tennessee* force did not actually participate in the Peleliu bombardment, although it was on standby for a naval gunfire support fire mission if needed. Kingman's TG-32.12 continued the Angaur pre-landing bombardment and then the naval gunfire support clear through the Army's landing there two days later. Thus, this much smaller and less heavily defended island was to receive a total of five days' bombardment, compared to the three scheduled for Peleliu, although the latter NGS group under Oldendorf was much more formidable.

Interestingly, several sources indicate the additional presence in the area of the USS *Iowa* (BB-61). Several Marines were sure that they had recognized the one-year-old battleship, watching her fire 16-inch shells that whooshed overhead and exploded inland (except for the USS *Maryland*, the other OBBs only had 14-inch guns, but none of the Marines would know that). These Marines might have on September 17 spotted instead the one-year-old USS *New Jersey* (BB-62, the second *Iowa*-class battleship

Admiral William "Bull" Halsey Jr., Commander, Third Fleet. At the last minute, he decided that Peleliu was not necessary, and radioed Nimitz a recommendation that it be canceled. (Official U.S. Navy photo)

Rear Admiral Jesse B. Oldendorf, Commander, TG-32.5. Although destined to be the hero of Leyte Gulf just six weeks later, his command at Peleliu is controversial. (Official U.S. Navy photo).

built), which Third Fleet commander Admiral Halsey had made his flagship less than a month before. However, the battleship did not take part in any shelling of the island.

Organizationally as a part of the Third Fleet, the *New Jersey* and the *Iowa* together made up Battleship Division 7, which was attached to Task Group 38.2 (Rear Admiral Gerald F. Bogan, commanding), which in turn was providing air support for the landings. One source indicated that the two vessels were actually together to receive mail the day before on the 16th. However, USS *Iowa*'s war diary shows the battleship on D-Day to be some 200 miles northwest of Peleliu, and it never came closer to the island than 65 miles in the few days after that.

All through the day, Admiral Oldendorf aboard his flagship, the heavy cruiser USS *Louisville*, himself observed the naval bombardment and aircraft strikes, along with rear admirals Ainsworth and Kingman.* The shelling continued into sunset, after which the warships retired to refuel and regroup.

---

* The USS *Louisville* (CA-28), the third U.S. vessel with that name, was a Northampton-class cruiser, commissioned on January 15, 1931. Initially classified as a light cruiser because her armor was much thinner than normal for such a large vessel, she was later reclassified a heavy cruiser because of her heavy armament. With a crew of 690, she displaced 9,200 tons, was 600 feet long and 66 feet wide, carried a draft of 23 feet, and could make 33 knots off her four screws. Armament

Naval gunfire support in action. Taken around September 12 off Peleliu from the heavy cruiser USS *Portland*, this photo shows in the foreground Admiral Oldendorf's flagship, the USS *Louisville*. The USS *Mississippi* is in the middle, and the USS *Idaho* is in the background. (National Archives photo).

At the end of that first day of shelling, bomb damage assessment photos were delivered to Oldendorf's staff. A good deal had been accomplished. He went to bed, satisfied that the pre-invasion preliminaries were off to a good start.

In the early morning of September 13, it began again. The four battleships and two cruisers of TG-32.5.1 sailed back to positions off to the northwest and south of the island, and at 0500, almost an hour before sunrise, the capital ships launched their spotting aircraft, and, a half hour later, Fire Support Unit Baker—consisting of the old battleships *Idaho* and *Mississippi*, heavy cruisers *Louisville* and *Portland*, and destroyers *Richard P. Leary*, *Robinson*, *Ross*, *Albert W. Grant*, and *Bryant*—commenced shelling the island. The other group, Fire Support Unit Able, had to withhold their fire for a few hours because of poor visibility. At this time, Kingman's TG-32.12 recommended the shelling of Angaur. About 45 minutes later, the first airstrike came in over Peleliu while the UDTs (Underwater Demolition Teams) continued their task of clearing the obstacles offshore.

So it went throughout the 13th. The task group intermittently continued firing all day long. The warships pounded predetermined areas on the island, pausing whenever tactical bombers roamed the skies overhead, selecting their targets. A good deal of the island's vegetation was devastated by the explosions,

consisted of three 8-inch triple-gun turrets, four 5-inch dual-purpose guns, two 3-pounder saluting guns, six torpedo tubes, seven quad-40mm antiaircraft guns, and 28 20mm Oerlikon guns. The *Louisville* earned 13 battle stars during the war, and was put into mothballs in 1946, and sold for scrap in 1959.

and large areas once covered in jungle were laid open. Any visible structures were targeted and pummeled.

Again, no appreciable return fire was noted coming from the island. The only casualty was a destroyer-minesweeper, the USS *Perry* (DMS-17), which struck a mine in the early afternoon and sank.

At 1800, just three minutes before sunset, Fire Support Unit Able ceased fire, and the warships again retired to a safe area to replenish.

That evening, after the two days of intensive shelling, Admiral Oldendorf, assessing the damage reports with his staff, was again satisfied at the progress of the pre-landing bombardment. Observations from the vessels, coupled to aerial recon photos, showed that the entire area had been plastered. The buildings and structures around the airfield were broken and in shambles, and the airfield was pockmarked with countless numbers of craters. His staff also noted that large areas of foliage had been taken out by the shelling. Areas along the spine of the island had been exposed, the ridges looking to be more rugged and steeper than had been originally interpreted.

Still, all the designated targets had been thoroughly shelled, and during the two days of massive bombardment, there had been no notable Japanese return fire. In fact, very little enemy activity could be seen at all, and, coupled to the original, basic belief that this would be a quick operation, Oldendorf was reassured that the bombardment had more than accomplished its mission, although he was worried about the lack of response from the enemy. Some sources record that to save ammunition, he wanted to cancel the third day's shelling that had been scheduled for the 14th and promised to the Marines. In any case though, his ships would still provide a heavy preliminary bombardment the morning of D-Day before the landing craft went in.

The Marine officers though, knew that if Oldendorf were to cancel the third day of shelling and several primary undisclosed targets remained, this decision would no doubt prove very costly for their men coming ashore.

True to his word though, in the early morning hours of the last pre-bombardment day, September 14, D-1, after having again withdrawn in the night to regroup and replenish, Oldendorf's Naval Support Group once more sailed back to the operations area (the *Honolulu* and *Indianapolis*, along with seven destroyers, had stayed off Peleliu all night to support UDT tasks). Going through the channel between Peleliu and Angaur, they formed a battle line with the vessels that had remained on station and, for the third day, began launching spotter aircraft. At 0545, about five minutes before dawn, they once again began shelling Peleliu.

Still, no return fire came from the island, except for a few instances of sporadic machine-gun fire directed at the UDTs, or at a few escort vessels providing cover for them close to shore. The island was ominously silent, except for thunderous explosions as Navy shells slammed into the ground, or the occasional drone of carrier planes as they made runs on various targets. There were no other indications that the Japanese were even there.

Except for one notable exception. It was a minor incident in and of itself, but if analyzed carefully, it would have shed critically significant light on the enemy's defensive layout and strategy for defending the island.

About 0915 hours,* the gunnery officer of the heavy cruiser *Portland*, nicknamed the "Sweet Pea," spotted a large column of water rising about a quarter mile off the port side of the ship's stern. An enemy artillery piece was returning fire. One of the ship's alert observers had discovered the spot where the shell had come from and had pointed it out to the gunnery officer. The shell had been fired from a 75mm artillery piece position in front of a cave at the base of the island's mountain ridge.

A few moments later, the enemy gun crew was seen furiously wheeling the artillery piece back into the cave and out of sight as a steel door closed in front of it. At that moment, the ship's 8-inch 50-caliber aft turret swung toward the target. The guns let loose, and the three 260-lb HE shells flew off at 2,800 feet/second toward the target and exploded around the target. Four more times, the Portland fired a salvo at the cave, and each time, the shells smashed into the target area.

As the gunnery officer assessed the damage through his binoculars, he became upset when he spotted the enemy gun crew once again wheel out the piece, aim and fire it, and then quickly wheel it back out of sight. He growled in frustration, "You can put all the steel in Pittsburgh on that thing, and still not get it."

The shelling of Peleliu continued, with fire support units Able and Baker taking turns in the process. The warships would temporarily cease fire whenever an airstrike began, so that the shells would not hit the tactical aircraft. Then they would resume fire.

At around 1800, three minutes before sunset, Fire Support Unit Able, the only force still shelling the island, ceased fire. With the *Honolulu* and two destroyers remaining behind, the NGS group sailed out of the area to reorganize and prepare for D-Day the following morning.

---

* The time for this incident is uncertain. One source even claims this happened on D-Day.

Admiral Oldendorf was satisfied that he had blasted the hell out of the island, and that all the enemy targets had been destroyed. He even sent out a message to that effect to Admiral Halsey, stating that he had "run out of targets," and that "the best that can be done is to blast away at suspected positions and hope for the best."

He firmly felt that—and his officers agreed—that tomorrow, after a thunderous, intensive, and spectacular pre-landing bombardment by all his ships, the Marines should be able to land and begin a quick and easy operation to take the island.

CHAPTER THREE

Invasion

D-Day

The LSDs and the faster attack transports caught up with the slower LSTs nearing Peleliu during the daylight hours of September 14. The convoys reorganized into landing formations as they slowly approached the area. After nightfall, the Marines made their final preparations to embark the next morning and after a nice meal and church service, they turned in early.

General Rupertus, having studied the upcoming operation, had concluded that this operation would only take three or four days, and that resistance would be initially moderate but brief. In this spirit of this unbridled optimism, he briefed his units before the assault, telling them that this operation would be "a real quickie," and that they would "be in and out in two days, three days at the most." Overly confident, he later repeated this opinion to his senior officers. He told them, "We're going to have some casualties, but let me assure you this is going to be a short one; a quickie. Rough, but fast. We'll be through in three days. It might take two." This opinion was of a pattern he had persisted with since his return from the States. He firmly did not believe that his men would encounter any enemy soldiers when they came ashore. Once, with typical bluster, he rumbled, "Somebody bring me the Jap commander's dress sword." He seemed to have a fixation about capturing some significant war trophy of an enemy commander. On New Britain, he had tasked the 1st Marines with bringing him the chair that his rival, Major General Iwao Matsuda, had used, so that he could boast of his prize to the media.

As a follow-up to his confident presumption, sealed instructions from the general had been distributed aboard several transports to all the news reporters and to each of his regimental commanding officers after they had sailed for the target area. The envelopes came with specific instructions that they were not to be opened until the day before the landing. On the morning of September 14

(D-1), the seals were broken and the envelopes were opened. The document inside (to the surprise of many) stated that the invasion would be intense, but the island would be taken in four days or less. Many who read the document considered this to be some sort of upbeat reassurance, and several individuals took it at face value. Some of the officers though, were not so sure. One of them was Lewis Puller, commanding the 1st Marines.

On the morning of D-Day, Friday, September 15, under beautifully clear skies, the invasion of Peleliu commenced. Reveille for the Marines came at 0300, and a half hour later, the Navy gave them the traditional pre-landing sendoff of grilled steak and eggs. At 0500, they began loading into the landing craft.

At 0530, with dawn only 22 minutes away, Admiral Oldendorf gave the command for the surface support force to once again open fire and commence their pre-landing bombardment of the island. In the next few minutes, several warships opened up, including the battleships *Maryland* and *Pennsylvania*. Once more, shells of all sizes began to slam into the island. Some 15 minutes later, the battleships *Idaho* and *Mississippi* joined in, and around 0700, the four cruisers of Cruiser Division 4 opened up as well.

In addition to the bombardment, as the shelling temporarily slacked off around 0750 (but still continued), about 50 tactical bombers from Davidson's Task Group 38.4 began making bombing runs overhead.

With a couple officers of his headquarters unit aboard his command ship, the attack transport the USS *Crescent City*,* Colonel Puller watched the island getting shelled. His concerns of a fierce response to the landing from hidden enemy positions had worried him all through the night. Now, a few hours before embarking the vessel for the landing, he walked up to the bridge to thank the vessel's commanding officer, Captain Lionel L. Rowe, for having treated his Marines so well on the journey over. The ship's captain, confident from his own observations of the intense bombardment and the lack of any enemy response, was convinced that the Navy had blasted what he thought were only a few Japanese positions in front of them. He asked Puller somewhat jokingly if he was going to return to the ship that evening for dinner. Puller looked at him in amazement.

---

* The *Crescent City*, APA-21, was launched in February, 1940 as the SS *Del Orleans* at Sparrows Point, MD and was recommissioned as the USS *Crescent City*, AP-40 on October 10, 1941. Modified at the end of 1942, she was recommissioned as an attack transport, APA-21 on February 1, 1943. She took on the 1st Marines at Pavuvu Island on August 18 and 19, at which time Colonel Puller came aboard and designated her as his command ship. (Crescent City Log)

Seeing the look on Puller's face, he became serious. "Everything's done over there," Rowe reassured him. "You'll walk in."

Puller of course was doubtful and replied dryly, "Sir, if you think it's that easy, why don't you come on the beach at 5 o'clock, have supper with me, and pick up a few souvenirs?"

The captain smiled and told him that he would not be able to do that: he would be too busy overseeing the landing of supplies for the Marines. After a moment, he added, "Puller, you won't find anything to stop you over there. Nothing could have lived through that hammering."

Puller gazed at the captain with obvious disbelief and then turned toward the island. After a few moments, he replied, "Well sir, all I can see is dust. I doubt if you've cleaned it out. For instance, I know they have underground oil dumps for that airfield. We haven't seen that blow ..."

When he was told that they were either dry or had already been destroyed by previous airstrikes the month before, Puller replied, "I've been boning over those maps for weeks, and I believe they'll have pillbox stuff; fortifications like we've never seen before. They've been at it for years."

The two officers talked a bit more as the amtracs carrying the first wave of Puller's regiment began forming up into a line. Puller turned to Rowe and told him, "We won't find little log barricades, like they had on Tarawa. We're going to catch some real fire."

Finally, Puller thanked the captain again and turned to leave the bridge. As he did, he said, "You watch me in the third wave, and see what happens to those amtracs at the beach."

Rowe replied, "Good luck, Puller. We'll expect you for dinner this evening."

Puller frowned and replied, "If we get out of this one, you'll be back in Hawaii long before we're through the job."

Puller returned to his staff and told them what Rowe had said. He divided his headquarters staff into two sections to minimize the risk of losing them all. He would lead the first section. They would go in on the third wave, along with a couple dozen riflemen and machine-gunners. The second section would be led by the 1st Marines executive officer, Lieutenant Colonel Richard P. "Bunny" Ross, Jr.

Later, as they prepared to board their amtrac, Puller apocalyptically confessed to his personnel officer, First Lieutenant Frank C. Sheppard,* "We'll catch hell is my guess. One of these days we're going to be ... driven into the sea."

---

* Not to be confused with Major General Lemuel C. Shepherd Jr., who had been the First Marine Division's Assistant Division Commander on Guadalcanal in 1943.

Clearly, Puller did not believe that they would have the good fortune they had experienced that first day at Guadalcanal or Cape Gloucester.

The Landing

The Navy continued to shell the island, with special targeting given to the designated landing beaches and the areas next to them. After about an hour of bombardment, the dust and smoke from the explosions on the island had become so thick that visibility for the fire control teams on the warships was next to nothing. Still, the ships kept up the fire.

As the Navy's bombardment group continued to heavily shell the island, the Marines in their transports finalized their preparations for the landing. They began loading just before 0500, and, by 0600, most of the men were down into the landing craft. At 0730, the amphibious landing began as the landing craft began to organize their groups.

A half hour later, with the initial LVT waves formed up, the first wave of the landing force crossed their line of departure and began heading for the beach. The NGS warships now undertook one more fire mission, all opening up against the coastline. From battleships down to destroyers, down to amphibious ships, they all laid down an intensive cover barrage of the beaches and surrounding areas to kill or at least pin down the Japanese as the first wave of Marines surged forward. The shelling of the forward areas increased in intensity while tactical bombers continued their sweeps over the area.

As the LVTs and DUKWs approached the barrier reef, the Navy's direct support fire kept up its intensity as the patterns were moved away from the beaches and back toward the surrounding areas. At the same time, several destroyers began lobbing a smoke screen of white phosphorus (WP) shells* onto inland targets in the foothills of the Umurbrogol to block the vision of enemy artillery observers who might spot the approach of the LVTs.

Around 0815, the 18 LCI gunboats in Group 9 and Group 39, each specially fitted with 42 4.5-inch rocket launchers in 12 racks, having closed to about a half mile offshore, began firing their volleys toward the enemy. They

---

* White phosphorus (later in Vietnam nicknamed "Willie Peter," derived from its military phonetic designation) is a tactical chemical weapon mostly used to either illuminate a target if exploded in the air, or to provide smoke cover to hide movement or visibility if exploded on the ground. The chemical spontaneously ignites when exposed to oxygen, giving off intense heat and dense white smoke as it quickly burns. It also makes an effective incendiary, because it burns as long as it is in contact with air. Smouldering fragments cause terrible, intensive burns on the human body.

sent hundreds of rockets streaming off to targets surrounding the beaches. Another four LCI-Ms—LCI(M) 739 through 742—that had been fitted with permanently mounted 4.2-inch heavy mortars began lobbing shells inland as well from 2,000 yards off.

As the Marines approached the reef, they could see that the Navy's shelling had taken out a good bit of vegetation along the shore, and many of the rugged features of the terrain, never discerned in the recon photos, were now visible, although barely, because there was a thick pall of heavy smoke over the island. Some of it had drifted seaward, making it difficult to get a clear image of what lay ahead.

The first amtracs were nearing the coral barrier when, unexpectedly, enemy artillery and mortar fire started coming down around them, as the fire quickly began ranging in on the approaching landing craft. The Alligators began reaching the reef, and slowly struggled to crawl over it, their wide snouts rising in the air as the tracks dug into the coral and the enemy shells increased in intensity. One by one, as their center of balance changed, each vehicle crashed down onto the coral, lumbered over the reef, cleared it, and then continued toward the beachhead, with the Navy's supporting fire undiminished. The DUKWs had an even harder time getting over the reef.

Some LVTs got hung up on the coral and were quickly zeroed in on by enemy gunners. Those that cleared the reef were targeted at the shoreline. Despite the intense enemy mortar fire, the LVTs continued to close onto the beachhead as airstrikes pounded the enemy.

A chaplain later recalled:

> How we got through the murderous mortar fire which the Japs were laying down on the reef we'll never know. The bursts were everywhere and our men were being hit, left and right.

As the LVTs approached the shore, the Navy began slacking off with the shelling. The main batteries ceased fire as the LVTs approached 500 yards from the beach, and the secondary 5-inch guns ceased fire when the first wave was about 300 yards off, although a few fired air bursts over the beaches to discourage enemy artillery observers and snipers.

With the temperature ashore already nearly 100°F, the 1st Marines on the left flank were the first to hit shore: the first LVTs to hit sand were from 3/1 on the left, coming ashore at precisely 0832, just two minutes behind the scheduled H-Hour. LVTs from 2/1 landed to their right less than a half minute later. They were followed shortly by the 5th Marines in the center, and the 7th Marines on the right flank. In response to the landing the cruisers ceased firing and waited for call fire missions from shore.

D-Day, on Peleliu, September 15, 1944, looking north-northeast. In the center heading toward the Peleliu beachhead are LVT-4As, armed with 75mm guns for fire support. At top left, an LCI(R) fires rockets toward the enemy. (Official U.S. Marine Corps photo).

Enemy fire on the Marines disembarking was intense. The Japanese had accurately surveyed the approaches in the months before the landing and had created precise grid maps for offshore fields of fire. Now their preparations were paying off. In the first ten minutes of the landing, over two dozen LVTs suffered direct hits, with most of these destroyed. According to the war diary of the USS *Mississippi*:

> During the approach, many landing craft were observed to have been hit by return fire from beach areas, and frequent splashes were seen among the landing parties. Numerous landing craft, tanks, and tractors were set ablaze.

On the left flank, enemy fire was coming from the Marines' left, and from areas to the north and northeast of the beachhead. On the right flank, incoming fire was coming from areas around the unnamed island to the southeast. According to a report later put out by Nimitz's headquarters:

> The enemy had a gun estimated to be a 3-inch, concealed behind the unnamed island to the south of ORANGE Beach. This gun could not be seen, except from an airplane. Within the hour following the landing, this gun with accurate deadly aim, knocked out about ten Alligators and DUKWS. The beach appeared littered with burning vehicles.

Further exacerbating visibility was a faint offshore breeze wafting seaward. As a result, the smokescreen that had been created by the pre-landing shelling was now having the reverse effect. As the heavy clouds and haze from the bombardment and the white phosphorus began to slowly dissipate, the light wind moved the murkiness out over the water. So now it was those aboard the American vessels who now could not see the landing too well.

To make the situation even worse, because the smoky haze was clearing from the enemy's view, one significant result of the three-day bombardment came into play. The shelling had taken out hundreds of trees and blocking foliage. The Japanese now had a clear vision of the amtracs approaching the beaches. Having scoped out the distances in the weeks before, their artillery and mortar shells on these pre-plotted approaches were often precisely on target. The smoke from their strikes also drifted out to sea and lent to the heavy haze that was hampering the American naval gunners.

Accurate as the incoming enemy artillery and mortar fire was though, it was fortunately not nearly as heavy in intensity or tonnage as the outgoing offshore shelling had been, so the overall, thick haze began to slowly dissipate. As visibility gradually began to improve for those offshore, the images presented them were alarming. Even though most of the LVTs were making it to the beaches, those observers aboard ship were starting to see that dozens of amtracs and DUKWs had been knocked out, many of them now burning hulks. A total of 26 would be totally destroyed that first day. The division's new logistical officer, Lieutenant Colonel. Harvey Tschirgi, finally able to see the beach from the USS *DuPage*, commented in an interview years later: "I'd never seen combat before, and the first thing that struck me was that this was a helluva way to treat $40,000 equipment."

In addition to being subject to indirect enemy mortar and artillery rounds, the entire area was now taking heavy direct fire, especially on the White beaches. Some of it was coming from a low, previously undetected ridge 100 yards in front. The most murderous fire though, seemed to be emanating from concealed positions on the 30-foot promontory to the left, a position that was quickly dubbed "The Point." More flanking fire was coming from another smaller, less pronounced point of land near the right side of Beach White-2. 1/1 was scheduled to follow its two sister battalions at 0930. Colonel Puller came in on the third wave, just to the left of that point. As his amtrac neared the shore, he yelled above the motor, "When we beach, get the hell off here. We'll be a big target!"

He jumped out of his LVT as soon as it crunched onto the sand and, running forward, immediately established his command post in the remnants of what had once been a coconut grove. As additional waves came ashore in five-minute intervals, the pinned-down 1st Marines on the left struggled to

D-Day, approaching the shore. Taken from a supporting warship, the second wave of amtracs (LVTs) approach the beachhead. The one at bottom with the .50-cal. gunner waving is an LVT-2. (Marine Corps Archives)

get off the beach to move inland. The enemy fire was just too heavy, from the ridge in front of them, from hidden artillery back in the Umurbrogols, and especially enfilading from The Point. Casualties quickly began to mount. Clearly, the naval bombardment had not had much effect.

The unexpectedly fierce enemy fire onto all the landing zones was now intense, accurate, and deadly, and dozens of men were hit. Those that had made it ashore struggled to get away from the beach, take cover, dig in, and regroup while machine-gun bullets, mortar shells, and various caliber artillery fire from batteries inland all rained down upon them. This incoming fire was effectively tearing up the shoreline, incoming supplies, and Marines struggling to move inland.

One of the few combat reporters who had decided to go in was with the 3rd Battalion, 7th Marines. *Life* magazine's Tom Lea, coming ashore in the third wave near the right flank at Beach Orange-3, watched spellbound as the riflemen disembarked the amtracs and came under heavy fire. He later described the chaos:

> Mortar shells swished and whopped through the air over our heads ... They hit without apparent pattern on the beach and in the reef at our backs. Turning my head seaward, I saw a direct center hit on an amtrac. Pieces of iron and men seemed to sail slow-motion into the air.

As bursts began to creep steadily from the reef in toward the beach, the shells from one mortar rustled through the air directly over our heads at intervals of a few seconds, bursting closer and closer ...

As I looked over my shoulder, a burst smashed into a file of Marines wading toward our beach from a smoking amtrac. Jap machine guns lashed the reef with white lines, and Marines fell with bloody splashes into the green water. The survivors seemed so slow and small ...

Almost immediately after the first wave had landed, the division's ADO, Brigadier General O. P. Smith, started to worry about the situation ashore. Aboard his own command ship, the USS *Elmore*, like Rupertus he was disturbed about the sudden heavy fire that was coming in from the enemy, and from what he could see offshore, a few amtracs were burning. He sensed from several brief and sometimes conflicting reports that things were not at all going well on the beach. Something was wrong.

Anyway, he had planned on hitting the beach himself sometime in the morning to set up the divisional CP,* so less than half an hour after the first wave had hit the beach, he made up his mind that it was time for him to go ashore. He took a part of his staff and his radioman and, piling into a DUKW, left the ship for the eight-mile run to the reef.

When they arrived at the transfer line, there were no DUKWs available to take them the last 2,000 yards to the beach. So after milling about for a bit, they finally spotted the nearby landing control vessel for the area, the USS *Hazelwood*,† and headed for it to wait for one. There, Smith saw firsthand how intense and effective the indirect enemy fire was on the incoming waves, especially after seeing several amtracs burning on the beach. Clearly going ashore in an armored amtrac would be safer than trying to make the trip in a DUKW, especially since the amtracs could clear the coral reef much quicker. Many of these vehicles though had already been knocked out in the initial

---

* Command post: the field headquarters for a unit, where the unit commander oversees the operations of his men, coordinates their activities, and acts as a link between the unit, other field units, and support assets. The typical CP includes selected staff members who operationally assist the commanding officer. In comparison, observation posts (OPs) are each manned by a component of the main unit and are established forward for observation, spotting, and other recon-related activities.

† USS *Hazelwood* (DD-531) was a Fletcher-class destroyer named after a famous commodore in the Revolutionary War. Commissioned June 18, 1943, she displaced 2,924 tons, was 377 feet long, 40 feet wide, and had a draft of 18 feet. With a crew of 275, she could make 35 knots. Armament included five single-turret 5-inch guns, six 40mm AA cannon, ten 20mm AA guns, two sets of five torpedo tubes, and a host of depth charges. Some seven months later, her commanding officer, Commander Volckert Petrus Douw, was killed along with 67 crewmen when a Japanese kamikaze struck the forward stack and bridge on April 29, 1945 off Okinawa. *Hazelwood* was repaired and survived the war, receiving a total of ten battle stars.

landing, and those left were busy landing new waves. It was not until after 1100 that Smith managed to get an amtrac to take his party ashore.

Climbing aboard, Smith directed the young coxswain to take them to a spot off to the right, somewhere between Orange-2 and Orange-3. The inexperienced driver though, despite having already made three trips to the shore already, was nervous, especially with mortar shells starting to land all around. They hit the barrier reef with a jarring thud that knocked all the staff officers off their feet. Clearing the reef, and with the shells landing ever closer, the coxswain began steering the vehicle to the left of where the general had specified. Trying to avoid some barbed wire at the halfway point, he skewed the craft even more, now heading northeast.

Getting anxious, the general leaned over and told the lad, "Look son, you're gonna run out of beach pretty soon, and we've got to move in here and now."

The coxswain finally set them down on Beach White-2, some distance north of their original intended spot, and just a few hundred yards from the tip of the airfield's east–west runway. Smith and his staff went down the rear ramp and waded ashore. After two of his men scouted the area, they all moved southward down the beach. Smith decided to establish the command post in an antitank trap some 50 yards inland from Beach Orange-2. After notifying the *DuPage* of their landing, they set up their CP. After two wiremen located the beach's shore party line, they spliced a phone line into it: the CP was ready for business shortly after 1130 hours.

Smith immediately established contact with the 5th and 7th Marines, but could not raise the 1st. Colonel Harris from the 5th Marines CP, at 1300, gave him a simple "So far, so good." Now beginning to get a clearer picture of what was going on, Smith would remain ashore throughout the day and all through that first grave night, commanding the division from his CP. His understanding of what was going on by then was considerable.

When he radioed a situation report to Rupertus on his command ship, the USS *DuPage*, the general became even more impatient, desperately wanting to go ashore himself. His chief of staff, Colonel Selden, tried to talk him out of it, telling him, "General, if you go ashore, you'll know less than you do now." He added that the messages coming from the ADO ashore were as detailed as they could be, so the situation ashore was still very fluid. Selden later recalled that, "It was all I could do to keep him from going in immediately." Rupertus then told Selden to take the divisional command staff ashore himself.

Selden explained to the general that the situation was still intense, and if the division's staff were taken out on that contested beachhead, it would be catastrophic. Also, bringing the general's large staff ashore would overburden the remaining amtracs feverishly trying to bring the successive waves of Marines ashore, along with high-priority supplies and ammo. The two officers got into a brief debate before Rupertus grudgingly acquiesced. What Selden could never tell the general was that Smith had a better instinct for handling any crisis ashore than he did.

The corps commander, General Geiger, was no less impatient than Rupertus or Smith, and so he decided in typical Marine style to come ashore that morning. Early in the afternoon, impatient with the conflicting information that he was getting from the shore, he walked down the accommodation ladder on the side of his command vessel, the USS *Mount McKinley*, calmly hailed a landing craft going by and along with his aide, hitched a ride to the beachhead.

On the ride in, he observed the heavy incoming enemy fire and, as O. P. Smith had done earlier, he noted with concern the burning hulks of several landing craft on or next to the beach. The number of those knocked out had by now become alarming. By 1000, that number of damaged amtracs by one report had risen to sixty. Many could be repaired, but a disturbing and growing number of them were total write-offs, especially those caught near or on the barrier reef.

Getting ashore in the center of the beachhead, General Geiger beheld an incredible sight. Here and there were burnt-out amtracs and DUKWs. Incoming supplies were strewn all over in sloppy piles, along with opened boxes, ammo crates, hastily unloaded drums, shattered trunks and logs, men being evacuated. As incoming waves brought more men and supplies onto the beach, men already ashore were either digging foxholes or laying in them. Here and there were scattered a number of bodies or body parts.

Geiger later noted earnestly that from a meteorological standpoint (temperature) as well as a military one (enemy fire) he had come ashore on "one helluva hot beach."

Geiger and his aide began moving around, asking questions of the units they came across, trying to find out why so many of the LVTs were either knocked out or disabled. Finally, around 1300, having been told roughly where the division's combat headquarters was, they approached the tank trap where General Smith had set up his command post.* He noted the bodies that the Graves Registration unit had already begun to stack in rows, as well as the pungent, putrefying odor of death that the hot, tropical air was intensifying.

The ADC looked up and, despite a number of mortar shells falling here and there, he saw the corps commander himself approaching. Geiger walked up to him, slid down into the tank trap, and asked how it was going.

---

* O. P. Smith records the commanding general walking up to the CP at about 1300 hours. However, Fort's war diary records him leaving the *Mount McKinley* at 1410 hours.

D-Day, Beach White-2. The 1st Marines, flanked on the left by hidden Japanese pillboxes and facing more in front, try to survive. (Marine Corps Archives).

O.P. Smith, surprised to see him, just shook his head and said jokingly with half a smile, "Look here, General, according to the book, you're not supposed to be here at this time."

Geiger replied, "Well, I wanted to see why the hell all those amtracs were burning. Plus, I'd like to see the airfield."

Smith shrugged, pointing up toward the ridge in front of them, and said, "That's simple—all you have to do is climb up this bank, and there it is."

Geiger looked where he was pointing, nodded, and began moving forward with his bodyguards to better see what was going on. As he crawled up the rise, a large-caliber shell whizzed close by, nearly taking his head off. Geiger slid back down the side of the embankment, stunned by the experience.

Smith asked him if he had seen the airfield. Shaken, he replied he had. Then he asked Smith where the division commander was. Smith answered, "He's still out on the *DuPage* with his broken ankle."

Geiger (probably gritting his teeth), replied, "Like I said before. If I'd know that before, I'd have relieved him."

Geiger then announced that he was leaving to head north and find Puller's CP. Smith though, thought that was a bad idea at that stage of the landing and had no problems telling the general so. "Now look, General," he said,

D-Day, Beach Orange-1. The 5th Marines struggle to find cover. (Marine Corps Archives).

pointing to their left. There's a gap of 800 yards above here, and we don't know who's in there, and you just shouldn't go up there."

Geiger was insistent though, and it was only after Smith insisted that he reluctantly changed his mind. Determined though, to get a better picture of what was going on, he left the CP with his aide and began moving southward down the beach to find first the 5th Marines' CP, and then that of the 7th.

The Point

By 0930, the 1st Marines on the left had suffered an hour of, in addition to the deadly mortar and artillery rounds dropping in, withering enemy machine-gun and small-arms fire from three sides: enfilading fire from The Point, direct fire sloping down from the ridge ahead, and more flanking fire from the small promontory on their right, far down near the right side of Beach White-2. Understandably, as the Marines desperately sought cover from the fierce, heavy, and accurate fire of all sizes and calibers, their advance had quickly stalled and had stayed bogged down. Only through exhaustive fighting and return fire, as they took alarmingly severe casualties, did they manage to move forward.

Their most critical objective was to take out the bunkers on The Point that had been hurling withering crossfire, raking the entire beachhead. Direct assault would be suicidal at best. Clearly, a unit would have to outflank it to take it. The 235 men of Captain George Hunt's K Company, 3rd Battalion, because of where they had landed on the extreme left, were given this thankless task.

Japanese coral pillbox. This enemy position, located over the water, blasted out of the coral, was positioned to outflank the beach next to it. (Marine Corps Archives).

Captain Hunt described their objective:

> The Point, rising thirty feet above the water's edge, was of solid, jagged coral, a rocky mass of sharp pinnacles, deep crevasses, and tremendous boulders. Pillboxes, reinforced with steel and concrete, had been dug or blasted in the base of the perpendicular drop to the beach. Others, with coral and concrete piled six feet on top were constructed above, and spiderholes were blasted around them for protecting infantry. It surpassed by far anything we had conceived of when we studied the aerial photographs.

This area had evidently been given little attention or no damage in the hours of shelling by the Navy, despite Colonel Puller's requests and so consequently it had not suffered any appreciable damage.

It was this location that the Japanese island commander, Colonel Kunio Nakagawa, by now an experienced, capable tactician, had anticipated a landing along Peleliu's western beaches and had made sure that The Point bristled with fortified positions to take advantage of its flanking position. Kunio had thus overseen the construction of the promontory's main features: five thick-walled concrete and steel pillboxes, each manned by a dozen

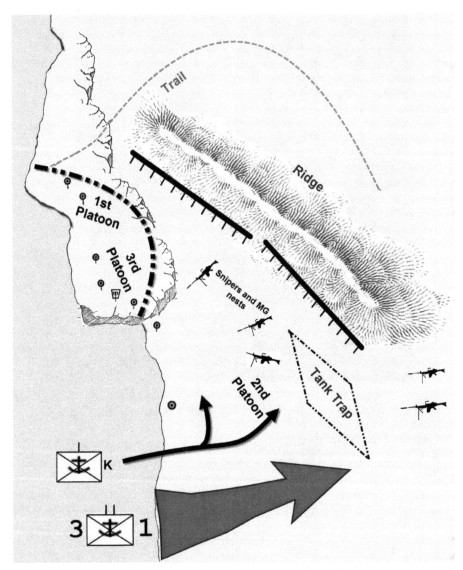

The struggle for The Point. While K Company was able to outflank the Japanese positions and take the area on September 15, they became isolated for the next 48 hours.

soldiers, and each covered on either side by light machine-gun nests and riflemen lying in depressions dug out of the coral, or in spiderholes (shallow sangars designed as one-man machine-gun defensive positions). Four of these reinforced bunkers contained a Mark-1 20mm cannon, which could fire over 500 rounds a minute.

The last, most fortified position was a massive, concrete and steel-girdered casemate that housed a Japanese 47mm Type 1 (1941) antitank gun. This weapon that could fire up to 15 shells a minute to a range of over four miles. This was the bunker causing the Marines such angst, the one forcing K Company to resolve to take out its anti-boat gun.*

Hunt, in order to stand any kind of chance in taking The Point, had to implement two details: first, the entire company, including the 1st Platoon, the reserve, would have to make the assault. Second, to be most effective, they would have to work their way around the base of the promontory and attack from the landward, or eastern side. Unfortunately, the entire company was not available to Hunt for the assault. He later wrote:

> About a hundred and fifty yards in from the beach, most of the 2nd Platoon had been caught in a tank trap, and on trying to assault out of it, had been terribly shot up. The trap was nearly fifteen yards wide, ten feet deep and extended parallel to the shore line for several hundred yards. It was a mammoth trench, with sloping sides of loose coral sand, hidden in the torn and uprooted underbrush of the coconut grove. It was raked by machine guns from the sides and from the precipitous coral ridge to its front, where pillboxes had been blasted in the rock.

The 2nd Platoon, trapped and trying desperately to lay low from the fire coming down from the ridge in front of them and from machine-gun nests on each side, were too pinned down to be of any help.

Nevertheless, 1st and 3rd platoons started their approach around the point, and then, when they were ready, the Marines darted forward and began to systematically take out the Japanese spiderholes and pillboxes. For nearly an hour and a half, Hunt's men, now isolated from the rest of 3rd Battalion which had moved off to their right and was under almost constant fire, methodically attacked each spot.

The anti-boat gun bunker was taken after one Marine dropped a smoke grenade from above and a second fired a rifle grenade that ignited explosives inside. The Japanese within, screaming as the ammo on their belts began

---

* The term anti-boat gun generally refers to a breech-loading artillery piece mounted on a small vessel or, more commonly, ashore in a bunker, and used against small vessels and landing craft. The term was primarily used in World War II in the Pacific theater to describe any one of a number of Japanese ordnance pieces mounted in island coastal positions. Their primary mission was to repel Allied landings by destroying incoming landing craft and small vessels. Most had two other roles as well: against attacking aircraft (AA), or as an antitank weapon against enemy armor. Anti-boat guns were invariably single guns typically emplaced in concealed fortified defensive bunkers. Ranging in calibre from 37mm to 200mm, most were Japanese field pieces or guns removed from the turrets of lost or older vessels.

exploding from the heat, fled the bunker and in so doing were immediately cut down by Marines waiting near the rear entrance.

After several savage assaults and heavy casualties, K Company finally took the anti-boat gun bunker. They secured The Point at 1015 hours and reported it taken to Colonel Fuller 15 minutes later. However, continuing fire from other enemy positions inland made further advancement slow and dangerous.

K Company struggled on.

The Right and the Center

At the extreme right of the beachhead, "Hard Headed" Hanneken's 7th Marines had come ashore at the narrowest part of the beachhead and were struggling across the southwestern end of the island. Fortunately, beach obstacles along the entire landing area were few, and the UDTs had been able to clear most of them. Although the Japanese had laid many mines in the beach area (in some places 100 yards deep), many of them fortunately malfunctioned. In addition, many did not explode because they simply had not been armed. This was primarily because these mines had been hurriedly planted one or two nights before by special Japanese swimmers, but in their haste, or ignorance, they forgot or did not know to pull the arming pins.

Lieutenant Colonel William E. Benedict, the division's D-1 (personnel officer), wrote after the war: "Had these mines been effective, the results would have been disastrous."

Other mine devices though, took a toll on the Marines, including a number of aircraft bombs positioned vertically in the ground with ad hoc firing pins to their bases.

Although they were not nearly as bad off as the 1st Marines on the left, the 7th Marines on the right flank had their own problems. It was along this part of the landing area that the Japanese defenses on the beach were the most concentrated, and the fire coming from their right was accurate and deadly. As the battalions were landing in confused succession on Beach Orange-3 at the southern end of the beachhead, Hanneken endeavored to set up his CP in a foxhole as intense machine-gun crossfire coming from their right swept across his troops.

Some of the fire was coming from where the southern tip of Peleliu bulged out into an unnamed tied island.* Like The Point at the other end, this islet also flanked the beaches, and although it was not as heavily fortified as The Point at the other end of the beachhead, it was manned by a number of heavy

---

* An islet connected to the mainland by a *tombolo*, a narrow spit or bar.

machine guns that now tore into the Marines as they strove to get ashore and move inland. In addition, there were a few mortar crews and at least one anti-boat gun on the islet that was busy taking out several landing craft. More crossfire was coming from a series of hidden positions on Ngarmoked Island, just south of the unnamed islet.

Over 20 years later, in a letter to the Marine Corps Historical Branch, dated June 12, 1966, the 5th Marines commander, Bucky Harris, by then a brigadier general, wrote:

> While the Naval Gunfire Support plan was under discussion, I strongly urged heavy caliber fire on the unnamed island just south of Orange 3, both in the pre-landing and assault phases. This island was a "natural" for enfilading the reef and Orange Beaches. During the ship-to-shore move I did not see a single indication of friendly fire on this target.

In fairness to the Navy, the unnamed island (identified as such on all of the disseminated grid maps within gunfire grid 122, squares A-B-F-G-K) was shelled on several occasions before the landing. The light cruiser USS *Honolulu*, for instance, had fired 13 four-gun salvos at the island on the morning of September 13. Now on D-Day, several aircraft made strafing runs on the island at 0937, and, at 1040, an LCI(G) approached the island and fired several dozen rockets at it. In addition, a half dozen LVT-4A amtracs mounting 75mm howitzers came down the beach, firing at anything that fired back. Thereafter, firing from the small islet was sporadic until it was later taken.

In the middle of the beachhead, the 5th Marines were lucky enough to avoid must of the deadly crossfire that the 1st Marines were getting pelted with on the left and the 7th Marines were taking on the right. In front of them though, was the vast open area of the airfield, which, they soon found out, was accurately covered by enemy mortars and artillery on the high ridges to their left. Even so, the men were able to slowly fight their way onto the airfield. Colonel Bucky Harris directed their assaults from his CP on Beach Orange-2.

The division's only armor support, the 30 M4 Shermans of Lieutenant Colonel Stuart's 1st Tank Battalion that had been transported from Pavuvu, approached the beach in the fourth wave. Chugging in six columns, five tanks per column, they approached the reef. As planned, each column was led by an LVT assigned to navigate the water ahead to be sure that the Shermans did not get entangled in any offshore obstacles, or venture into depths too deep for the tanks to traverse.

Enemy artillery and mortar fire became intense at this point as the tanks struggled to get over the reef. In the ten minutes it took to cross and clear it, over half of the Shermans suffered one or more hits. Fortunately, because of their armor, only three of them were totally disabled. Only a few more actually became stuck on the reef, thanks to the good work the UDTs had done in the two days before clearing most of the obstacles along the reef. Another factor was the fact that, even while clearing the reefs, the lower portion of the tanks were immersed in water, which had the effect of shielding the lower suspension and tracks from explosions. Otherwise, several more tanks would have been disabled.

Clearing the reef at last, the three tank columns of Company A headed for the White beaches to support the 1st Marines, and the other three moved toward the Orange Beaches. The riflemen ashore now at least had some armor support to be able to advance inland. Even so, six more tanks were knocked out after the landing, and by the end of D+1, only five of the original 30 would still be operating.

The 7th Marines on the right end of the beachhead had slightly better luck than the 1st Marines. After having reorganized, they took out the Japanese positions that were enfilading them from the right. They had then been able to steadily advance and move inland across the southern part of the island. However, they had moved forward slowly against stiff resistance.

Just to the left of the center, Puller's 2nd Battalion under Lieutenant Colonel R. E. Honsowetz had made relatively more progress than the 3rd Battalion stalled on their left. The 2nd had managed to probe forward a few hundred yards, moving slowly from crater to crater, taking out enemy spiderholes, and traversing strands of barbed wire. Later that afternoon, they were ordered to move back to the edge of the airfield and to dig in.

The 5th Marines, to their right and in the center of the American landings, had been able to push out the farthest, and by the late afternoon, they had actually started across the airfield. Then increasing enemy mortar and artillery fire began to concentrate on the western edge and in the center of the airfield. Clearly the enemy was up to something. Like 2/1 next to them, 1/5 and 2/5 pulled back to the edge of the airfield and dug in, while 3/5 on their right struggled on, trying to advance into the woods.

Sure enough, around 1530, some movement was seen along the northeast edge of the airfield, just past the barracks off in the distance. As this movement was being observed, the Japanese began a heavy preliminary mortar and artillery barrage. Just after 1600, a company of enemy infantry was spotted methodically advancing from the farthest buildings toward the airfield. Behind them, surrounded by a light cloud of dust, about 19 Japanese tanks, with infantry mounted on them were seen moving forward as well.* The enemy force maneuvered around the airfield barracks and hangar areas and advanced. Just after 1640, the entire force began a carefully orchestrated counterattack against the northeastern end of the airfield, headed for the area where 2/1 on the left had joined up with 1/5 on the right.

The naval liaison officer (NLO) attached to the 5th Marines, having seen the enemy now advancing toward them, got on his radio and was able to make contact with the USS *Honolulu*. He urgently requested a call fire mission, radioing the coordinates for grid square 134-Q, which was north of the airfield in the open area just past the abandoned barracks.

At a range of 7,800 yards (3.9 nautical miles), the light cruiser at 1643 hours opened up with its main battery and began lobbing 6-inch shells into the designated target area. In addition, a Navy dive bomber by coincidence happened to fly over. Spotting the Japanese assault developing below, the pilot swooped down and delivered a well-placed 500lb bomb onto the attackers.

Fortunately for the Marines, two more developments happened in their favor. First, when the combined enemy force had closed to about 400 yards from the Marine lines of defense, the tanks suddenly started to charge, surging ahead at some 30 miles per hour. They thus split up the attacking force, leaving the advancing infantry behind. Second, some U.S. armor had come up to back up the dug-in Marines. Three Shermans had moved forward enough to be present at the far side of the airfield and were able to augment the riflemen of 1/5, with one of the tanks dug in near the open ground. Another had been damaged by an enemy shell and could not traverse its turret, so the entire vehicle was turned to get the desired bearing. The second Sherman itself managed to take out over a half dozen of the enemy tanks.

The other Shermans that were still operational had unfortunately returned to the beach to replenish their ammo supplies. However, as close as the shoreline was to the airfield, it would only be a matter of having to move inland some 50 yards before they could engage the enemy tanks—provided they avoided

---

* Numbers vary with accounts, because after the battle, the enemy tanks were so utterly blown apart that it was hard to determine which components had been a part of which tanks (Hough p. 51 fn). The Japanese soldiers mounted on the tanks in some accounts numbered ten or so tied to the tanks with ropes. A couple accounts note that in a few cases, the soldiers rode in open-topped oil drums affixed to the tanks. (McMillan pp. 288–289)

```
              ENCLOSURE (B) TO U.S.S. HONOLULU REPORT
                 OF FIRE SUPPORT OF PELELIU
                      PALAU ISLANDS

                    RADIO LOG EXCERPTS      15 SEPT. 1944
                 3845 KCS - GUNFIRE COMMON

  0919  LOCK V SPAR    PROCEED RELIEVE IDAHO AT PT. DORIS AND
                       STAND BY FOR CALL FIRE WITH C73

  1000  SPAR V LOCK    WE ARE ON STATION AND IN CONTACT WITH
                       C73

  1256  SPAR V LOCK    C73 REPORTS HE IS IN GRID AREA 124.
                       HE STATES HE HAS NO PROBABLE TARGETS
                       FOR US

  1618  SPAR V 050     WE HAVE LOCATED WHERE FIRE IS COMING FROM.
                       IT IS COMING FROM AREA 134 QUEEN.
                       REQUEST FIRE IMMEDIATELY.

  1628  LOCK V SPAR    CAN YOU WORK C50'S PROBLEM IN 134 Q?
        SPAR V LOCK    ROGER - WAIT OUT.

  1630  LOCK V SPAR    WHAT ANSWER TO 050'S REQUEST?
        SPAR V LOCK    ROGER - WAIT OUT.
        SPAR V LOCK    AFFIRMATIVE TO YOUR LAST TRANSMISSION.

  1632  LOCK V SPAR    YOU WILL WORK WITH 050. HE WILL SPOT
                       OVER THIS CIRCUIT SINCE THE FIRING IS
                       URGENT. YOU WILL WORK IN AREA 134 Q.

  1633  LOCK V 050     COMMENCE FIRING IN 134 Q IMMEDIATELY.

  1636  LOCK V 050     PLEASE GIVE US SALVO AND SPLASH.

  1639  050 V LOCK     STANDBY ON YOUR TARGET.

  1642  050 V LOCK     SALVO 1

  1653                 (SALVO 15)

  1653  PILR V SPAR    TANKS REPORTED BY YOU HAVE BEEN REPULSED.
                       THEY ARE RETIRING. WILL YOU HAVE YOUR
                       OBSERVER WATCH THEM CLOSELY. THEY ARE
                       TRAVELING NORTHEAST.

  1655  010 V SPAR     HONOLULU IS FIRING IN 134Q. 050 SAYS
                       RESULTS ARE GOOD AND TO CONTINUE FIRE.

  1712  LOCK V 050     CEASE FIRING. YOU HAVE DONE A GOOD JOB.
                       WE HOPE THIS WILL BE THE END OF IT. WE
                       DO NOT KNOW.

                    -1-              ENCLOSURE (B)
```

Voice call log of the USS *Honolulu*, afternoon of D-Day. The log shows the NLO communicating with the light cruiser, calling in an NGS fire mission on the Japanese counterattack across the airfield. (USS *Honolulu* war diary, Peleliu Operation, p. 65.)

the Japanese tank traps at Beach White-1 and Beach Orange 3—and that is precisely what they began to do.

In Europe, the M4 Shermans were comparatively inferior and largely outgunned by the larger German Mark IVs, Panthers, and Tigers. In the Pacific though, they were superior to most of the Japanese armor, especially the 7½-ton Type 95 Ha-Go very light tanks on the island (the division's action report later mistakenly referred to them as Type 94 tanks, which were even smaller, little more than 3½-ton armored cars with machine guns). The Type

Counterattack repulsed. A couple Marines examine a destroyed Japanese Type 95 light tank at the airfield. These lightly armored vehicles were not designed for attack. Flimsy and vulnerable, they fell prey to bazookas, light antitank guns, and the more formidable Shermans (Marine Corps Photo).

95s were little more than tracked, lightly armored reconnaissance vehicles. The muzzle velocity was about the same for each opposing tank at about 1,900 feet per second, but the Japanese armament was a 37mm gun, compared to the 75mm gun on the Sherman.

If the Japanese had possessed any medium tanks on the island even remotely comparable to the Shermans, such as the Type 1 or Type 3 Chi medium tanks, their counterattack might have been far more effective. As it was though, the enemy's swiftly moving light armor was stopped cold by the advancing Shermans, some bazookas, a couple of 37mm antitank guns that a few 1/1 Marines had wisely brought ashore, and some well-placed machine-gun fire. In fact, the Sherman gunners had to switch from firing armor-piercing rounds to HE with no fuse time, so that the shells would not sail through the Japanese tank, but would instead explode on impact. Those Japanese infantrymen riding on the tanks were swiftly killed, and those on foot behind the tanks were cut down by rifle and machine-gun fire as they advanced across the open terrain. It was later suggested that had the tanks not broken away from the pedestrian infantry, they would not have made it past the middle of the airfield.

It was not long before the attacking Japanese were overwhelmed, and the few enemy survivors retreated. Some 17 enemy tanks had been destroyed, with only one or two able to get away. The counterattack did though, take

Marine tanks advancing at the airfield, D-Day. Here M4A2 Shermans of Company A, 1st Tank Battalion, advance after repulsing the Japanese counterattack. (Marine Corps photo).

the momentum out of the 5th Marines' advance, as well as keeping 1/1 and 2/1 on the left from moving up and attempting to take any higher ground. The Marines thus held their positions, while volunteers dashed back to the beaches to fetch more ammo and some rations.

In the center, the 5th Marines had been able to hold onto their half of the airfield. However, in the course of their advance, their right flank had moved past the left flank of the 7th Marines, who had been bogged down by mines, landing organizational problems, a complex series of barbed-wire barriers, periodic heavy mortar fire, and crossfire coming from a few stubborn pillboxes dug into the coral. In addition, several Shermans moving up on the left to support the 7th Marines, in maneuvering around the antitank ditch, had drifted off to the left. They thus caught up with and attached to what they mistakenly thought was the left flank of the 7th, but was actually elements of the right flank of the 5th.

Thus, a dangerous gap developed between the two regiments. To make matters worse, at around 1500, a couple shells from the sudden, accurate Japanese mortar barrage that preceded their counterattack on the airfield managed to hit the CP of the 5th Marines' 3rd Battalion. The explosions took out their communications and seriously wounded the battalion commander, Lieutenant Colonel Austin Shofner. The executive officer, Lieutenant Colonel Lewis Walt, had to take over and fill in the gap as best as he could.

The 7th Marines to the right continued to struggle to move forward. With the aid of an antitank ditch just off the beach, discovered when the first wave had come ashore, the officers were able to reposition the men within and along the sheltered ditch for another renewed assault. The going was slow.

Because the 1st Marines' communications equipment had been wiped out in the landing, making contact with the ships or with ADO Smith who was ashore was impossible for several hours. As the afternoon dragged on, Smith became increasingly worried, because not only could he not raise Puller's CP, but he did not even know where it was. It was only after a nervous runner from the 1st Marines made contact with the divisional CP in the afternoon did Smith get an idea of what was going on over on the right before being able to establish contact.

Just after sunset, with the Japanese counterattack at the airfield having been repulsed, Colonel Puller's communications wiremen finally found him near the northern edge of the airfield. They quickly ran telephone wires back to the beach, and Puller was finally able to make contact with O. P. Smith, who was back at the divisional CP in the antitank ditch. Smith, having heard all sorts of rumors about the 1st Marines' struggles and reports of heavy casualties, was thankful to hear Puller's crisp voice: "We're dug in solid, and we've got the O-1* phase line all right."

He then filled Smith in on their defensive positions. Although he had taken heavy casualties by then, he did not mention any need for assistance. He was also using 1st Battalion, which, although it had initially been designated the regiment's reserve, had been committed early, to buttress his defenses. In addition, he had managed to add to those defending the lines men from the headquarters units, and about a hundred men from the 1st Engineer Battalion.

Less than an hour later, Smith carefully made his way over to Puller's CP and again asked him how he was progressing. Despite the ordeal they had endured all day, Puller calmly replied, "All right."

Smith asked him if he needed any help, and Puller in typical Marine fashion replied that he did not. When Smith asked him about the casualties, the colonel with understatement replied, "Maybe as many as forty killed and wounded." Casualty reports would later confirm that about 500 men in the regiment were casualties, about a sixth of its fighting strength.

---

* Objective-1. O lines were graduated lines on a tactical map, used to clarify daily lines of advance expected to be achieved by the end of the day.

Meanwhile, General Rupertus, anxious and edgy, but having dutifully stayed aboard his command ship the *DuPage* all day, had tried hard to monitor the initial landing. Sitting in his folding canvas chair just below the bridge on the open starboard deck, he watched the enemy fire meet the incoming waves, and began to increasingly worry as he spotted more and more amtracs being taken out. Snippets of voice conversations between units ashore were picked up by radio sets on the deck behind him, but for the most part did not offer much information on what was going on ashore; of course, other than the fact that the entire beachhead was taking heavy fire. Obviously, the first half of his prediction that this operation would be "rough but fast" had turned out to be correct.

Communications with the 1st Marines on the left continued to be a big problem. All they had heard was that they had taken "about forty" casualties. Unknown to him, nearly all of Puller's communications equipment had been destroyed in the landing, and the colonel's regimental command post had suffered a direct hit soon after it was set up. Thus, with very little information coming in from the left, divisional staff had no clear picture of what was going on. When Rupertus finally began to receive a few messages regarding the 1st Marines that had been sent by runner to Smith and then relayed back to the *DuPage*, his concerns that the regiment was embroiled in heavy fighting were confirmed. His first concern was that Puller's men were losing their momentum in their assault. In his mind, they would simply have to push forward that much harder.

Rupertus was getting better communications regarding Hanneken's 7th Marines on the far right. Learning from Smith ashore that they were facing moderate resistance and had been slowed down by strong enemy fire coming from their front and their right, Rupertus decided to commit the division's reconnaissance company out of Lieutenant Colonel Berger's reserve group to reinforce the 7th. Later in the day, apprehensive that the 7th needed more help to roll up the island's right flank, Rupertus ordered the rest of the reserve group, 2/7, to land at Beach Orange-3, to immediately move inland, and to firm up the 7th's advance.

In giving the order, he told Selden," All right, Johnny, go ahead. But I've shot my bolt when they go in."

The order went out, but when the 2nd Battalion made ready to go ashore, they found that there were simply not enough amtracs. Still, the general remained optimistic. At one point, after having received an update about the 7th's slower than expected progress, he commented determinedly, "This won't stop us ... We'll still take the island on schedule... a week at the most." Still, his anxiety to get ashore was eating at him. Enemy resistance was much stronger than had been anticipated, and by the end of the first day, all of the reserves had already been committed on the right.

Ashore, O. P. Smith knew full well that the general was getting quite impatient to come ashore, especially since Rupertus was so keen on wanting to direct the battle himself. Finally, against Smith's better judgment, later in the afternoon, having again made contact with Rupertus by radio, he told him at that time that it was probably safe enough to bring the rest of the headquarters staff ashore. With his patience almost gone, Rupertus immediately ordered Colonel Selden, his chief of staff, go ashore with the divisional command staff. Selden though, again argued against the idea. The chance of losing the entire staff as they all moved across the coral reef transfer point and then landing along one narrow spot, all the while being under fire, was too high a risk to take. Finally they compromised. Selden would take half of the remaining staff ashore, and the general would follow them in the morning with the rest of them.

Selden did as ordered, and loaded half of the command staff onto a couple LCVPs and headed for the transfer point at the barrier reef. As the ADO had argued though, amtracs were hard to come by, partly because they had already lost so many, partly because several were ashore supporting the riflemen, and partly because those still offshore were too busy. Those that had not been knocked out that first day were hard at it ferrying ashore the reserve battalion, as well as supplies, ammo, and replacements to the 1st and 5th Marines, and then in returning, evacuating the many wounded out to the transports, all of which entailed struggling back and forth over the rugged coral of the barrier reef. The same was true of the DUKWs. Nearly half had either been taken out by enemy fire, mechanical failure, or from damage crossing the reef. The divisional command staff was just too low a priority, so even though they had safely made it to the reef, they were essentially stuck there. Angry and frustrated, Rupertus late in the afternoon finally ended up allowing them to return to the *DuPage*.

Smith, having been the first senior officer ashore on D-Day, remained ashore, and as such remained so for that entire day (with the exception of General Geiger, who had come ashore strictly as an observer). Having set up the division's command post in a Japanese antitank ditch, Smith had taken an active part in directing the battle.

That evening, Smith radioed General Rupertus aboard the *DuPage* that he had finally made radio contact with the hard-pressed 1st Marines. He then gave the general an update on the progress of all three regiments, as well as the unloading of the division's tanks and artillery. He finished by reporting that he would maintain contact with all regimental commanders, that their perimeters were in place and that they were dug in and ready for any enemy counterattack. When asked about continuing the assault, Smith replied that their own attack inland would start again at 0800 the next morning.

Fighting along the beachhead had remained intense all day long and continued as darkness fell. The Marines dug in and prepared their defenses for the enemy counterattacks they expected to come.

Because of the two openings that had formed in the landing—one between the 5th and 7th Marines, and the other between 3/1 and the rest of the 1st Marines—every fighting man who could be spared was rushed over to seal these gaps, because a determined enemy night assault coming down from the ridge there might very well take out their left flank and spill out onto the congested beachhead.

Some sort of nocturnal response would be coming though. Everybody knew it. Would the Japs sneak stealthily through the dark, or would they come down screaming and charging like they had at Guadalcanal?

Sure enough, nighttime brought the Americans no rest. All along the front, enemy activity was noted. Unlike the *banzai* charges on Guadalcanal though, the Japanese response came in the form of several localized counterattacks and a profusion of small, stealthy infiltrations. The Marines grimly held their own in the dark.

The division had by then suffered severe casualties and still had made little progress moving inland. The beachhead had been lengthened from 2,200 yards to about 3,000 yards, but the 1st Marines on the left, struggling against a determined and well-entrenched enemy, had only managed to move inland about 500 yards, and that was on their right.

As expected, the localized enemy counterattacks were especially intense on the left where 3rd Battalion was struggling. K/3/1—minus 2nd Platoon, which had been withdrawn from the tank trap—was reduced to about 30-some men, and had managed to defend The Point after hard fighting all day, but was barely managing to hold on. With failing radios and isolated some 200 yards to the left of the rest of the 3rd Battalion, this company was forced to fight alone. All that night they struggled to stay alive, desperately fighting off Japanese soldiers trying to infiltrate their lines in the dark, often resorting to hand-to-hand combat. Occasional flares and starshells fired from destroyers and sub chasers* offshore illuminated the jungle with brief flashes of eerie

---

* Designated submarine patrol craft (PC), these coastal vessels, smaller than a destroyer escort, barely qualified as oceangoing. At 175 feet long, carrying a crew of about 65, they could make about 23 knots. Armament was limited to one or two 3-inch guns, a few 20mm AA guns, a few more .50-cal machine guns, perhaps a couple small rockets, and some depth charges.

green in which the Marines spotted wraithlike figures slowly making their way toward them.

By the next morning, of an overstrength company that had landed with 235 Marines, only 18 riflemen were able to fight on (surprisingly, the reply from higher command was, "That's fine. Tell him to keep pushing.") In contrast, Hunt's unit that morning counted over 450 dead Japanese, stacked four-deep in places. One Marine later wryly remarked, "You know, the Army had 'the longest day' [in reference to the Normandy invasion of June 6, 1944 and Cornelius Ryan's celebrated book], but for us Marines in K Company, that was the longest night."

That morning, K/3/1 was somewhat reinforced with almost two dozen replacements, and after another day and night of heavy fighting, what was left of the unit was finally relieved by I Company on the morning of September 17 (D+2). By the time K Company moved off the line, it had been whittled down to just 78 men, and that number included more replacements, the wounded who were either still in the rear or had been evacuated, and those that had somehow been mixed in with other units.

Company K was not the only unit with such early losses. After three days of brutal combat, Company B, 1st Battalion, would be down from its original complement of 242 men that landed to "19 men still on their feet."

At the end of D-Day, the casualties to all three Marine rifle regiments had been terrible. In the planning, it was estimated that the first day's casualties would total about five hundred. Instead, the casualty lists for the division totaled 210 killed, died of wounds, or were missing and presumed dead, and another 901 wounded, for a total casualty list of 1,111 men. Before the dawn of D+1, that number had risen to 1,148. Nor did this total number include the many who were out of action because of heat prostration, accidents, or other causes.* The first day's casualties had already amounted to about one ninth the strength of the three rifle regiments.

In the early morning hours of September 16, General Rupertus, having closely followed his division's progress through the evening, and despite seeing some moderate casualty lists, still believed that the Japanese defenses would quickly crumble. After all, their perimeter had been broken and their counterattacks of yesterday, including the large armored one across the

---

* The actual casualty count for that first day, released by the Marine Corps in 1950, was 92 killed, 1,148 wounded, and 58 missing. The discrepancy is notable but not unusual. It is very difficult to make accurate casualty assessments in combat even by trained medical personnel (although less so today) when they are far too busy treating those that have been wounded or impaired, rather than assessing loss statistics. (Hough, p. 57 fn)

airfield, had all been successfully repulsed. His Marines had established a solid beachhead and although forward progress was stalled on the left, they were all nevertheless moving inland, especially on the right flank.

The general was still only vaguely cognizant of his high casualties, and he was mostly unaware of his enemy's change of tactics from those that he and his men had experienced at Guadalcanal in 1942. He did not seem to comprehend that the Japanese were no longer coming out into the open in massive coordinated counterattacks (the one exception being that first afternoon at the airfield). Rather, the Japanese were huddling in their well-prepared, concealed defenses, with clear fields of fire, and ready to resist to the death. Most importantly, he did not seem to understand that their defensive layout on the island was not linear, but more in-depth than intelligence had determined. So Rupertus insisted, and would continue to do so for another week, that his division was on the verge of success and thus certainly needed no backup from the Army, who could go ahead with their invasion of nearby Angaur Island.

On the left, Colonel Puller struggled to regroup his hot, weary units for the next morning's assault. The first day's casualty list had been terrible, and his men had endured enemy infiltrations that night. He had made his demands for more men and supplies up the chain of command. Now all he could do was wait and hang on. At one point, frustrated, he turned his grimy face to look over at his R-1 officer, Lieutenant Sheppard. Recalling their conversation the night before the landing, he growled, "Remember I told you that one of these days we'd get the shit shot out of us during a landing?" He took a deep breath and added, "Well, I guess all we can do now is fart in the wind and see if anybody answers." Looking up toward the front line, he added, "Meantime, let's see if we can kill a few damn Nips."

September 16

That night, while occasional bursts of starshells and flares from the light cruiser *Honolulu*, a half dozen destroyers, and some sub chasers intermittently flashed an eerie green pallor across the sky, the Navy and the Marine amphibious units worked feverishly to move ammo, supplies, and drums of the water over the reef, land them ashore, and move them up to the front. On the morning of D+1, again prefaced by a bombardment from Oldendorf's warships and several tactical air sorties from the carriers, the Marines renewed their assaults at 0800. The temperature had already begun to rise, climbing to over 100°F in just a couple hours. Navy and Marine supply units took off their leggings and shirts, and cut off their trouser cuffs as they struggled to bring supplies ashore, before loading up wounded Marines to take out to the transports.

The 7th Marines on the right resumed moving across the southeastern spur of the island, assisted by a few Shermans. In the center, the 5th Marines slowly began fighting their way out in the open across the rest of the airfield, moving eastward. Problems developed early for them. As they prepared to continue their assault at 0800, an unexpected Japanese shelling began from the high ridges to their left. One mortar round took out the field telephone switchboard and many of the wires leading to it.

Even worse, another round happened to make a direct hit on the regimental command post, which was in a captured trench next to the airfield. The explosion killed at least one staff member, and injured several others, including the regiment's chief of staff, Captain Alan Dill, the regiment's NGS liaison officer, and the operations officer, Major Walter McIlhenny, a Louisianan who carried a French accent and who in his delirium now began reverting to French. One staff member later commented, "He was parley-vooing like crazy when they carried him away."

Debris from the explosion also completely buried the 5th's commander, Bucky Harris. Although he was not wounded, he badly wrenched his knee, and would be painfully incapacitated for days. With the regiment's XO gone trying to regroup the 3rd Battalion, the regimental CP found itself missing several key senior officers. Despite this setback, and despite a number of early localized enemy counterattacks and the continued mortar and artillery fire coming from the Umurbrogols, the 5th Marines managed to advance northeast, especially the 1st Battalion, and by evening, the entire airfield had been taken.

It was the 1st Marines on the left who continued to have the most difficult time of it. Colonel Puller had singled out for his 2nd Battalion on the right one objective at the southern tip of the mountain ridges, identified on the maps as Hill 200. Talking to the battalion's commander before the attack, he was adamant. "Look, Honsowetz, I want that sonuvabitchin' ridge before sundown," he growled. "And I mean, gawddammit, I WANT it!"

Both the 2nd Battalion on the right and the 1st in the center initially made some modest gains, advancing across the rest of the northern edge of the airfield. As they turned left though and began advancing over broken ground toward the lower slopes of the Umurbrogol range, they suddenly became subject to intense, withering fire from hidden, dug-in Japanese positions on the slopes. Once again, the 1st Marines' advance came to a halt as they suffered heavy casualties. All along the front, the momentum began to slow as the heat and the intensity of combat, at times hand to hand, began to take their toll on the Marines. They became frustrated by the enemy, because as soon as they closed in on one defensive opening, the enemy would withdraw down a connecting tunnel to another and begin firing from there. Still, 2/1 on the right managed to advance the farthest, into the outskirts of the airfield's demolished barracks area before being forced to stop and dig in.

General Rupertus, impatiently determined to get ashore and to take over command, left the *DuPage* with his staff at 0805 hours. However, due to his ankle injury, it took him some time to do it. He finally limped onto the sand just before 1000 hours and again noted that the beach still looked like some sort of military junkyard.

What he saw was would later be described by *Life* magazine's Tom Lea, who wrote:

> Jagged holes in the scattered stone and dirty sand ... Splintered trees and tangled vines made a churned, burned wilderness ... We jumped over foxholes, climbed around and over smashed trees, sidestepped tapes denoting mines and booby traps, walked gingerly around those yet unmarked. Telephone lines in crazy crisscross mazes were stretched along the broken ground ...
>
> Scattered everywhere were discarded packs, helmets, rifles, boxes, rubber life belts—the debris of battle. Lying on the seared leaves and hot sands were dead bodies yet ungathered by burial parties.

Rupertus hobbled his way over to the tarpaulin-covered antitank ditch where the divisional command post was located, and which had been run so far by his ADO, O. P. Smith. After being briefed by the ADO on the current situation, Rupertus immediately took charge. He told Smith to "not hang around." Smith took the clear hint and moved his staff back to a draw between the antitank ditch and the beach. Regrouping his men, he took a break and sought out some rations and coffee.

As the fighting continued, herculean logistical efforts were made to support the rifle units on the line. All along the beaches, the Navy worked furiously to bring ashore supplies and more replacements. At the same time they evacuated the wounded and took measures to start clearing up the waterline of debris. Whenever warships could be contacted, call fire missions were directed against strong enemy defensive positions.

By nightfall, the Americans again paused and dug in. The 1st Marines had managed to get to the slopes of the Umurbrogols before they had been stopped cold. The Japanese no longer had a direct view of the beachhead and airstrip, and so their shelling now, although the areas were precisely grid-marked, would have to be indirect. The cost though, had been high.

Puller had today again suffered heavy casualties. His regiment alone had by now taken over 1,000 casualties. The rule of thumb was that a unit was to be considered for replacement in the line if their losses amounted to over 15 percent; the 1st Marines had lost twice that percentage in just two days of fighting.

A radio conversation between Puller and one of his battalion commanders reflected his frustration. In contact with the 2/1 commander on the slopes of Hill 200, he asked him, "How are things going?"

Lieutenant Colonel Honsowetz hesitated and reported, "Not very good. I lost a lot of men."

Puller pressed him. "How many did you lose?"

Honsowetz paused and replied, "I don't have a good count yet, but I think I lost a couple hundred men."

Sounding irritated, Puller asked, "How many Japs did you kill?"

"Well, we overran one position that had twenty-five in it. We got 'em all. There were a lot of Jap bodies around, but I don't know how many … Mebbe fifty."

Puller, exasperated, barked, "Jesus Christ, Hon! What the hell are the American people gonna think? Losing two hundred fine young Marines, and killing only fifty Japs!"

The 7th Marines on the right had been able to push southward to the edge of Ngarmoked Island. Most importantly though, the 5th Marines in the center had finally taken the critically important airfield, although doing so cost them not so much casualties as preciously needed equipment. By the 17th, they had lost over 70 percent of their flamethrowers and bazookas, equipment that would later be critical against the Umurbrogol positions. Again, Rupertus's orders went out: resume the attack the next morning, according to their plan. Rupertus felt justified in ordering his men forward once again; he thought he was seeing some light at the end of the tunnel. With the airfield and most of the right side of the island now in American hands, enemy resistance was probably now going to crumble, and his four-day estimate would not be too far off the mark.

He was wrong. The worst had already started and was about to continue.

September 17–18

On D+2, despite their losses so far, the 1st Marines on the left prepared to renew their assault, with the 3rd Battalion moving along the northern shoreline, Major Raymond Davis's 1st Battalion in the middle, and Lieutenant Colonel Russell Honsowetz's 2nd Battalion on the right. Despite further heavy fighting, the regiment finally managed to make some headway inland. 1st Battalion came up against a formidable enemy blockhouse clearly out in the open. Evidently, inexplicably, it had not been shelled before, even though it had been clearly spotted and identified on aerial photos before the landing. Fortunately, a fire mission that was called in to the USS *Mississippi* received an impressive response. Fifteen minutes after the call was made, her 14-inch shells blasted the structure to a shell. Still, the target should have been taken out days before.

2nd Battalion finally reached the southern tip of the Umurbrogols, and, after several brutal assaults with fire raining down on them from in front and from the ridges to their left, they managed to capture Hill 200. Their limited advance though, was made at the expense of further heavy casualties, at least half of them victims of sniper and mortar fire. Lieutenant Colonel Stephen Sabol's 3rd Battalion on the left took fire from the ridges as well, and, by later that day, could only muster 476 men, about half its original strength; half of the survivors were replacements, either from headquarters units or new arrivals.

As the regiment kept its assault going forward during the day, the toll of casualties continued to mount, and their combat effectiveness continued to shrink. That evening, after a couple limited enemy counterattacks, the 1st Marines fell back to the blockhouse to reorganize for the next day. They had taken another 240 casualties, mostly riflemen. Nevertheless, Rupertus pressed Puller and ordered him to press on the next day.

On that day, Admiral Halsey came into the area. He had been with Bogan's TG-38.2 in his flagship, the *New Jersey*. Now he sailed into the area strictly to inspect the progress of the Peleliu and Angaur landings (which he had advised against just a few days before) and for conferencing and planning. The flagship arrived in the area at around 1100, when Halsey briefly observed the operation. Then after an hour-and-a-half noontime conference with Vice Admiral Wilkinson, Rear Admiral Fort, Rear Admiral Cochrane (BuShips), Major General Julian Smith, and Major General. Geiger, Halsey departed the area, sailing away that afternoon to gather his forces for the vast upcoming Philippines invasion. In the meantime, TG-38.2 at that point took the opportunity to refuel.

It is doubtful (although certainly possible) that Halsey's flagship partook in any shore bombardment in that brief time (If it had, it would only have been for call fire missions from shore). The ship's war diary though, mentions that the crew went to general quarters at 1015 hours "and prepared for counterbattery fire." In any event, the next day, TG-38.2 was relieved of having to provide air and naval gunfire support (if any) to the operation.

Early that evening, now clearly alarmed at his casualties, Colonel Puller tried to get reinforcements. He made radio contact with Colonel Selden, the divisional chief of staff, and told him that he needed more replacements if he was to carry out his orders the next morning. Selden told him that they simply did not have any.

Puller retorted, "I told you before we came ashore that we should have at least one regiment in reserve. We're not fighting a third of the men we brought in—all these damned specialists you brought."

Selden paused and said quietly, "Anything wrong with your orders, Lewie?"

Puller knew what the question implied. "No," he growled, I'm ready to go ahead. But you know my casualties are fifty percent." (That was about 1,700 men.)

"What do you want ME to do?" Selden asked.

Puller, remembering all those auxiliary and support units working like ants on the shoreline, told him, "Give me some of those seventeen thousand men on the beach."

"I can't do that," Selden protested. "They're not trained infantry."

Puller dourly replied, "Yeah, well send them up here and by nightfall tomorrow, they'll be trained in infantry."

There was no reply from Selden, except the click from his radio.

Irritated and his leg hurting from a wound that he received back on Guadalcanal, Puller passed the word to his men: "We press the attack at 0800 tomorrow morning. No change. Full speed. Use every man."

They did just that. The next day, after a half hour preliminary softening-up by attacking aircraft and naval gunfire, the 1st Marines went into action at 0700. Their ranks were bolstered by a couple dozen "cooks, bakers, and truck drivers converted overnight into riflemen" Also shanghaied from the rear were a hundred men from a shore party battalion. Division though, was not blind to Puller's dilemma, and so, once again, hoping for a quick breakthrough, released to the 1st Marines the division's reserve: Colonel Berger's 2/7 Battalion. There were also a number of Shermans to provide some armor support.

The men pushed forward in the sweltering heat, and the Japanese responded with intense mortar and artillery fire. As the Marines came in contact with the enemy, they were met with a hail of machine-gun and rifle fire. They managed to push forward, but casualties were heavy as they struggled over the jagged crags of the southern part of Bloody Nose Ridge.

At one point in the afternoon, the 2nd Battalion commander, Lieutenant Colonel Russell E. "Russ" Honsowetz got on the field phone and contacted Puller at his command post. He told Puller that they had taken substantial casualties and that they simply could not take the hill in front of them without more men.

Puller though, under tremendous pressure from Rupertus to break through, would not give in, and repeated to Honsowetz's the orders that he had to take the hill.

Beachhead buildup. Aerial photo taken late September. Note the drums of water in the center. (U.S. Navy Photo)

Honsowetz snapped, "Christ, we can't do it! The casualties are too much, and we've been fighting all day and all night."

Puller fired back, "YOU sound all right. You're there. Gawddammit, you get those troops in there and you take the gawddamn hill!"

The 2nd Battalion renewed their assault. The entire regiment struggled on, but a late Japanese counterattack pushed a number of units back. The regiment retired at sunset and dug in for the night.

On the right, the 7th Marines on the 17th had renewed their efforts to secure the southeastern promontory, just up from Ngarmoked Island at the tip of Peleliu. After the positions were softened up by an airstrike and by Sherman tanks blasting the positions, the riflemen began to move forward, sometimes using amtracs to protect them from small-arms fire. Finally, frustrated by the stubborn enemy holdouts in caves dug out of the coral or in pillboxes, the regiment put it a call for additional flamethrowers. Using these, the Marines began to take out the Japanese strongpoints, and by evening, the entire promontory had been taken.

The next day, after a preliminary assault with artillery and tanks, the 7th Marines renewed their assault southeastward. Gormley's 1st Battalion and Hurst's 3rd Battalion moved swiftly to capture Ngarmoked Island itself. The Marines

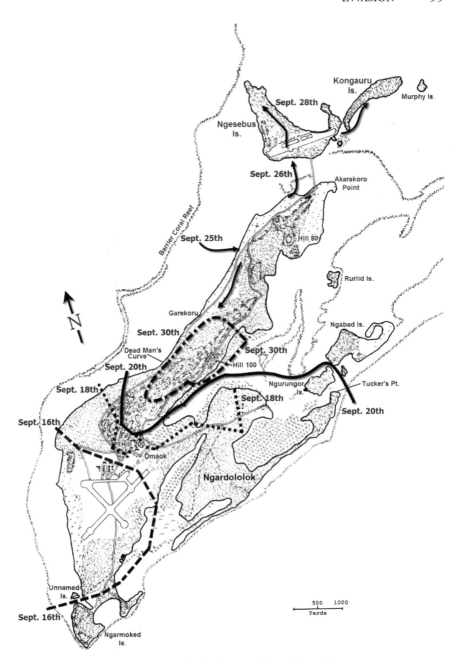

The Marines struggle inland: September 16 through 30.

made good progress, partly because the ground they moved over was relatively low, and partly because many of the Japanese defensive positions were facing the other way, i.e. toward the sea. Casualties for the 17th were quite modest in comparison to what the 1st Marines were going through on the other flank: seven dead, some 20 wounded. In contrast, the enemy had lost 441 killed. The next day though, the Marine toll was higher: 47 dead, 414 wounded, and 36 missing.

In the center, starting on the morning of September 17, the 5th Marines began sweeping across the airfield. Despite increasingly heavy fire from the lower tip of the Umurbrogol ridges around two summits identified on the maps as Hill 210 and Hill 200, they pushed forward. The next day, with 1/5 put into reserve, the regiment continued their advance. 2/5 moved forward onto the southeastern part of the Ngardololok section of the island, taking small-arms fire from the mangrove swamp off to their right. Two companies of 3/5 were able to capture the small hamlet of Omaok before enemy crossfire coming from the ridges forced them to stop around noon and dig in. In the meantime, the Seabees and advance Marine squadron ground crew personnel had almost completed repairing the airfield enough to start bringing in aircraft. With it operational, the airmen would be able to provide on-the-spot aerial tactical support for the men on the ground.

September 19–21

By September 19, D+4, Peleliu had become a congested little island. Between what was left of the Japanese defenders and the American Marine and naval personnel that had come ashore, there were about 45,000 men over some eight square miles of humid, hot coral.

Despite the fact that they had been through a good deal by now, Rupertus's orders remained unchanged from the day before, and so the division again resumed the offensive. Following an intensive preliminary bombardment from a combination of artillery on the beaches, naval warships, and both 60mm and 81mm mortars, the three rifle regiments began their assault.

The 1st Marines, battered and tired, struck on the left. The 2nd Battalion struggled to advance along the tip of Bloody Nose Ridge's right flank, between Walt's Ridge to their right, and a series of five ridges to their left, nicknamed "The Five Brothers." They managed to move forward 500 yards. To keep the momentum going, Colonel Puller threw in A Company and C Company from 1/3 to support them. However, fierce enemy resistance stopped the advance. Ordered to keep going, the units took significant casualties and finally, inevitably, had to fall back.

Of course, in the thick of the fight was Colonel Puller himself, weary, no shirt as usual, his pipe dangling from his mouth, his old Guadalcanal leg wound aching, usually standing a few dozen yards away from the front under a makeshift command post, which usually consisted of a large poncho and a rectangular piece of tin. There he coordinated the attack, as an occasional enemy shell came down nearby (Once, as his men hit the deck and a mortar round exploded a dozen yards away, he was said to have just growled and muttered, "The bastards.")

ADC O. P. Smith, when he called on Puller later that morning, found him tired but resolute in making sure the men knew that he was up there with them. Smith did not stay for long, because a sniper began taking shots at them.

In the center, the 5th continued their assault north of the airstrip, while the 7th managed to take the rest of Ngarmoked Island, as well as the rest of the mangrove swamp around Beach Purple.

General Geiger as usual again came ashore to monitor the situation; only this time, he brought with him some company: Rear Admiral Fort and Vice Admiral Wilkinson. Leaving the *Mount McKinley* at 0740, they came ashore and traveled to each of the regimental headquarters and then to Rupertus's divisional CP, assessing the Marines' progress.

The night blessedly proved to be relatively quiet, except for some sporadic mortar and machine-gun fire directed against the 1st Marines on the left. The next morning, D+5, after another heavy preliminary bombardment, Puller's three battalions assaulted the enemy again as ordered by Rupertus, this time with everything that they had, including being reinforced by Lieutenant Colonel Spencer Berger's 2/7. The Marines fought hard, pushing forward against the mountain feature known as Walt's Ridge with whatever men they could scrape together, but Japanese artillery and mortars in concealed positions above again soon stopped the advance. In response, Puller's observers called in NGS and artillery missions on specific enemy targets; in support, the regiment's light and heavy mortars were fired until "the mortars glowed red." In addition, some 18 air sorties were directed against Japanese positions. Although the enemy took casualties, they held firm in their reinforced caves and tunnels, dishing out effective counterfire. By late afternoon, the 1st Marines let up their assault and moved back to just about where they had started, hot, sore, exhausted, thirsty, and depressed. Most of the rifle units were by now depleted, mere shadows of what they once had been.

The 5th Marines on the eastern part of the island moved forward and took the island just north of Tucker's Point, designated on the maps simply as Island A (Ngurungor Island). The 7th Marines, having secured the southern part of Peleliu, moved up across the island and took a position between the 1st Marines on the left, and the 5th Marines on the right.

General Geiger once again came ashore and monitored the battle. His concerns were getting more serious. He was not happy with the way General Rupertus kept pushing his men to hurry their advance, despite the fact that it time and again seemed to incur heavy assault casualties. And with the 81st finishing up on Angaur Island, why did Rupertus still refuse to request transfer of some of their units over to Peleliu to assist?

Again, the night was relatively quiet, except for some sporadic mortar and artillery rounds fired at the 1st Marines on the left. The next morning, the 21st, again after preliminary air sorties, some naval support, and a 15-minute artillery barrage, 3/1 once more took up battle against the ridges, but with so many casualties, the men tired from several continuous days of assault, and effective enemy fire from above, they did could do very little to advance. Colonel Puller gave the 1st and 2nd battalions a break, and they moved back to the White beaches for a day's rest. The senior officers tried as best they could to flesh out the units with replacements, but all they could get their hands on were drivers, orderlies, and mess cooks.

The 7th Marines to their right tried to advance as well. The 5th Marines had the most success, crossing over to Ngabad Island and taking it with little resistance.

Logistical problems continued, as the Navy struggled to ferry supplies ashore. A pontoon causeway was built from the edge of Beach Orange-3 out to the reef and made operational by September 21 (D+6), which helped matters. So did securing Purple Beach to allow supplies to start arriving there. However, a lack of space on the beachheads made life difficult.

Rear Admiral John Reeves, who was charged with developing the base after the island was secured, came ashore soon after D-Day and was horrified by the mess. He put in a request that the artillery units be moved off the beachhead to give more logistical room, but Rupertus objected, pointing out that the artillery was providing badly needed support for the 1st and 7th Marines struggling against the Umurbrogols, and setting them up elsewhere would take precious time at the infantry's expense. Since the ground commander usually won out in such matters, Reeve's request fortunately was turned down.

Just getting supplies up to the 5th and the 7th was an ordeal in itself, because to cross the airfield in the open, zigzagging as one might, was to invite enemy fire from the Umurbrogol. For this reason, the airfield became known as "Mortar Valley," and crossing it became known as "The Purple Heart Run."

Enough for the 1st

At the end of just seven days of action, the division had sustained a great deal of casualties, but considering the conditions they were fighting in, they had accomplished a great deal. About two-thirds of the enemy on the island had been eliminated, although they were making the Marines pay dearly for every foot of ground. ADO Smith reported that the entire southern end of the island had fallen, and also, as difficult as it had been, the high ground just to the north and northeast of the airfield had been taken, as had been Island A and Ngabad Island by the 5th Marines. The White, Orange, Scarlett, Purple, and northwestern part of Amber beaches were secure and functioning, so supplies and replacements from offshore were coming in regularly, as were the evacuations out to the ships, all of this subject of course to inclement weather conditions. All the artillery had been landed and deployed, including the Corps units. Most importantly, the airfield had been repaired and was functioning, allowing several tactical air units to be deployed there to provide close, immediate air support.

Field casualty. A Marine giving water to a wounded buddy.

The next objective now was to take the top of the island in order to continue advancing across the channel to Ngesebus Island, on which the Japanese had been creating a small dirt airstrip that could be used for fighters. A wooden causeway between the two islands had been taken out, so a landing was in order. Taking the western tip of Peleliu would also isolate the many pockets of resistance on the Umurbrogol ridges so that they could systematically be eliminated.

To accomplish all this, the 1st Marines would have to move parallel to the ridges along the northeast shoreline to secure the eastern shores of the island along the rest of Amber Beach, while the 5th Marines advanced on the other side to secure the opposite shore around what had been identified as Hill 80. The 7th Marines would support the 1st Marines along their right flank and keep the enemy pinned down around hills 100 and 300 and The Five Brothers.

The entire division though, by this time was in serious condition, especially the 1st Marines. The men were drained and exhausted. They were tired, usually thirsty, hot, and disheartened. They had suffered staggering losses: the regiment had reported almost 1,800 casualties, over 54 percent of the original authorized unit strength of 3,218, with some units down over 80 percent. The 1st Battalion was down to only 74 men, out of an original 500 men in nine rifle platoons. The 7th Marines were not far behind, having lost 47 percent of their men, and the 5th Marines 43 percent.

The 1st Marines, having met the stiffest resistance, were simply depleted. They were worn down, physically, mentally, and emotionally, many of them in various stages of combat fatigue. At one point, Colonel Puller saw a small group of men shambling back from an attack and asked them what platoon they were with. One of the NCOs looked over at him with droopy eyes and said, "Platoon hell, colonel. This is Charlie Company."

It is at this point in the battle that most senior Marine officers years later would claim that the corps commander, General Geiger, showed himself again to be a true leader. In each operation, never one to sit and wait, he would often go to (or fly over) the front lines to get a current update on the situation. Peleliu was no different. Recall that soon after the landings had begun on D-Day, impatient with the conflicting information that he was getting from the shore, he had come ashore and set up his command post. Although later stunned by having nearly been decapitated by an enemy shell, the near-death experience nevertheless did not deter him, and over the following days, the corps commander usually came ashore every day to assess the situation. Although he would retire to his command ship in the evening, the next morning he would be right back on the beachhead and go up forward, sometimes to the concern (and annoyance) of the Marines around him. According to his chief of staff, Colonel Merwin Silverthorn:

> General Geiger spent nearly every day at the front lines. Almost every day he was at the front lines—and when I say front lines: he went all the way out to battalion commanders' positions, if not company commander positions …
>
> I think that … it acted as an incentive to the division and regimental commanders to be on their toes. They never knew when the corps commander was going to come around and ask some real searching questions. But that's a real compliment to General Geiger, who was in his late 50s at the time and was not a ground officer—he was an aviator, as most everybody knows, but had a complete grasp of ground operations. He was a graduate of Fort Leavenworth, and he was a graduate of the Army War College. So he could talk ground operations with anyone …

Lieutenant Colonel Jeff Fields, the First Marine Division's operations officer (G-3), recalled years later: "General Geiger was a fearless man. We always had to worry about him. He'd get out and go climbing up mountains, up the hills, right up to the front, and talk to the guys."

Colonel Frederick P. Henderson, who was on General Geiger's operational staff, saw these episodes first hand, and they often worried him. He later recalled of the general that it was not uncommon for him to suddenly show up next to some prone Marine rifleman and ask the situation. This was an effective way for him to see what kind of ground his men were up against, find out the tactical situation first hand, and assess the frame of mind of those on the line. According to author Dick Camp, in this instance, the General actually walked up to some Marines lying on a ridge, firing at some Japanese about 200 yards across the way. One of the men saw him come up to them and barked, "Get down, you old fool! D'ya wanna get us all killed?" The general realized that the young Marine was completely right. He smiled, apologized to the rifleman, and walked away.

The issue of heavy casualties had become a sore point between Geiger and Rupertus for days now, going back to September 16 (D+1). That morning, before the 81st Infantry Division had gone in at Angaur, even before Rupertus had okayed releasing Colonel Watson's 343rd RCT from Peleliu's assault force's reserve to take part in the Angaur invasion, Geiger had recommended that the 1st Marines either be reinforced or else pulled out and replaced by an Army regiment, possibly the 343rd RCT. Rupertus, confident that he could win the day, had declined the offer.

That afternoon, General Geiger showed up unexpectedly at Rupertus's division CP in the tarpaulin-covered tank trap. Each was surprised to find the other there.

Aware of Rupertus's ankle injury, Geiger said, "I didn't expect to find you here, Bill."

"Likewise, general," Rupertus replied. "I thought it was time for me to see what was going on."

The two men walked down the antitank trap a ways and talked privately. What they said exactly was unclear, but officers later recalled that the conversation became heated. Geiger again renewed his argument for Rupertus to contact the 81st Infantry and request they either reinforce Puller's regiment or replace it with one of their RCTs.

Again, Rupertus flatly refused, repeating that his men would take the heights in a day or two. The conversation finally ended, the issue still, in General Geiger's mind, unresolved.

After observing further intense combat, even though the operation was far from over—in fact, Phase 1 was not even completed—General Geiger was all but decided that he had to take some sort of action. General Mueller had radioed a message the day before to Geiger's command ship, the *Mount McKinley*:

> AS OF 1034 HOURS THIS DATE, TARGET HAS BEEN SECURED.

Angaur had been taken, although mop-up operations remained. Still, reinforcements from the Army were now available for the Marines. The 322nd RCT would remain on Angaur. The 323rd RCT, to the north with Rear Admiral Blandy's 31-ship battle force, could now land at Ulithi. That left one Army RCT to spare: the 321st. Geiger signaled to Mueller:

> MAINTAIN RCT 321 IN READINESS FOR POSSIBLE IMMEDIATE DEPLOYMENT TO PELELIU. RELEASE RCT 323 TO ULITHI ATTACK GROUP.

Geiger's worries about the casualties on Peleliu were now considerable, especially for the 1st Marines. He was resolved in what had to be done. The next morning, September 21 (D+6), as he had each day before, the general again came ashore, today with his artillery officer, Lieutenant Colonel Frederick Henderson, and Colonel William F. Coleman, his intelligence officer (C-2).

The three were accompanied by bodyguards, two sergeants armed with Thompson sub-machine guns. The general's group stepped ashore, turned left, and began walking off to the north in search of Colonel Puller's 1st Marines command post (which of course, he knew would be forward, somewhere right next to the line). The five of them finally found Puller's CP at the bottom of a small cliff, about a half mile down the coast from the small hamlet of Garekoru on Peleliu's northeastern shore. As General Geiger drew near the CP, he saw Puller on his field phone, yelling and cursing at Lieutenant Colonel Russell Honsowetz, commanding his 2nd Battalion. Puller was ordering him in no uncertain terms to keep pushing forward, even though the battalion had sustained massive losses. As the general approached the tattered canvas tarpaulin that served as Puller's CP shelter, several mortar rounds exploded about a hundred feet away. The sound of rifle and machine-gun fire, peppered with occasional grenades, could clearly be heard nearby as 2nd Battalion continued its assault on Bloody Nose Ridge.

Puller saw Geiger approaching and immediately got off the field phone. The general walked up to him and crouched down beside him.

"What can I do for you, general?" Puller asked him wearily. Clearly he had not had much sleep.

"Just thought I'd drop in and see how things were going," the general replied, looking Puller over. He hesitated then said, "Let's talk in private."

The two of them stood up and left the CP, walking off a few paces. When they were alone Geiger turned to Puller and asked him how his unit was doing, and what could corps do to help him. The colonel, bare-chested as usual and sporting his battered pipe, told him that they were managing well enough, all things considered, despite the fact that his men were exhausted. Puller himself was a sight as well. Sweating, in need of a bath, and droopy-eyed, he looked haggard and worn out. Clearly, this Marine leader was not the determined firebrand that he had been just a week before. Geiger saw that Puller seemed that morning very weary and somewhat "out of touch with reality."

Puller had yet another problem. Besides having been under fire for days and seeing so many of his men killed or wounded, he was suffering from a mortar shrapnel wound that he had received on Guadalcanal back on November 8, 1942. Perhaps aggravated by having stumbled over the coral for days and with lower resistance from cutting himself several times, the old leg wound was now infected and swollen. Whether he expressed it or not (most likely, not), Puller was now in considerable pain, which made it difficult for him to walk. In fact, on several occasions, despite his fierce objections, he had been carried around by stretcher, no doubt fortunate for the colonel. Major Ray Davis, his 1st Battalion commander, later wrote, "I was convinced if he had been able to walk around the way be was prone to do, he was going to be killed."

Geiger was convinced that Puller was spent, and, irritated with the entire situation, his voice became overly heated. He thanked Puller and left. He hitched a ride back to the beach on an amtrac that was evacuating wounded Marines. After the amtrac had dropped off the casualties at the medical tent, Geiger commandeered it to take him to Rupertus's divisional headquarters, which was now on the airstrip.

The division commander at the time was going over the situation with his chief of staff, Colonel John Selden; his operations officer (G-3), Lieutenant Colonel Lewis J. "Jeff" Fields; and his personnel officer (G-1), Lieutenant Colonel Harold Deakin. Geiger walked up to them, still accompanied by Lieutenant Colonel Henderson and Colonel Coleman. Surprising Rupertus with his sudden, unexpected presence, Geiger asked him for a situation update, while the divisional staff officers stood, respectfully silent.

After Rupertus had given him a brief synopsis of the state of affairs, Geiger—who had also for days now been concerned about Rupertus's own physical condition but had not pursued the subject—commented that the Marines really had their hands full. Geiger then asked him if he needed any reinforcements from the 81st Infantry Division, especially now that the G.I.s had taken nearby Angaur Island. Rupertus told him no, they were not needed, still insisting that his Marines could finish taking Peleliu.

Geiger then observed that the 1st Marines seemed to really be taking a beating, and demanded to see their casualty list. The not-yet-updated figures showed that the regiment had already confirmed 1,672 casualties, over half of the regiment's allotted strength. Geiger for days now had been increasingly upset over both Rupertus's performance and his stubborn, obviously unfounded and unrealistic optimism. At this point, Geiger was convinced more than ever that the 1st Marines needed to be relieved.

This issue had been a sore point between the two men for days, since D+1 in fact. But now, General Geiger had seen enough. After studying the casualty list, he remarked tersely, "The 1st Marines are finished." He then declared that he wanted them replaced by an Army RCT. Rupertus, alarmed at the idea, refused to replace his men "with any damn Army unit," especially one that was green and inexperienced. The ridges were no place for inexperienced troops to take on the Japanese. He was adamant that his Marines could still finish the job in a couple days. He continued pleading his case, going on for a couple minutes.

Geiger then turned to the staff officers present. Looking at the division's assistant chief of staff, Lewis Fields, he asked him point blank what he thought. Fields was clearly uncomfortable at being called out and understandably torn, his reluctance to get into the middle of a command feud obvious. Nevertheless, he had been asked a direct question by the corps commander and decided to give his honest opinion. Clearing his throat, he sided with Geiger, saying that he felt that the 1st Marines were spent and should be replaced by the Army if at all possible. The G.I. replacements should be landed on the island and moved up through the 1st Marines to engage the enemy in the Umurbrogols.

Hearing this, Geiger once more turned to Rupertus and said that he felt the same way. When Rupertus again started to disagree, Geiger, his eyes now blazing, cut him off. He angrily ordered Rupertus to immediately take the 1st Marines off the line. In the silence that followed, Rupertus realized that he had been given a direct order. He had no choice but to either comply or be relieved of command, something that had never happened to a general in combat in Marine Corps history. Rupertus of course, was not about to be the first; the idea of being relieved by a senior officer of the same rank would be especially humiliating.

Before he could reply, Geiger followed up. He repeated that he was convinced the 1st Marines were "totally spent," and completely unfit for combat. He directed that he wanted both Puller and what little was left of the 1st Marines evacuated off the island as soon as possible and sent back to Pavuvu to recover.

Rupertus had no choice but to obey, and Puller of course was in even less of a position to dispute the corps commander's decision, even if he could. His old Guadalcanal war wound had turned septic, and his leg had swollen up like a tree trunk. He could barely walk, even with a walking stick, and was obviously in severe pain. Eventually evacuated with his men, he would be operated on the first night aboard ship.

Geiger took stock of the circumstances: the Americans had taken the western, southern, and eastern parts of the island. However, the enemy positions on the Umurbrogols were still intact and had not been appreciably breached. One of the Marine regiments was no longer fit for combat, and the remaining two had also taken a mauling. A relatively fresh regiment was needed to shore up the situation. With this in mind, at 1625 hours on the 21st, Geiger sent a message to 81st Division commander Paul Mueller:

> MUELLER FROM GEIGER XXX URGENTLY REQUEST RCT 321 IMMEDIATE TRANSFER FROM ANGAUR AND ASSIGNMENT TO COMMANDING GENERAL 1ST MAR DIV PELELIU HQ XXX REPLY SOONEST XXX HQ III AMPHIB CORPS XXX.

That evening around 1800, Geiger arrived at Mueller's divisional headquarters and confirmed his earlier request that an RCT be sent over to relieve the 1st Marines. Mueller immediately acknowledged, and the 321st RCT, having already been ordered to immediately begin preparing to leave Angaur Island to replace them, continued with the arrangements.

Soon, the 1st Marines were immensely relieved to hear that they were to be taken off the line and evacuated from the island. The next day, elements of Colonel Robert Dark's 321st RCT started arriving, as the Marines wearily began to move back, southwestward toward the airfield. The 321st was fully on the line by the 23rd, while the 1st Marines were slowly making their way over to the now secure Purple Beach at the southeastern part of the island. There they set up a defensive perimeter to defend the beach area before resting and trying to recover from the staggering battle that they had gone through the last week and a half. Although Puller told them they would be going back to the line in a few days (which did not go down well at all), they did not. A few patrols were sent out, but that was it. The 1st Marines were no longer an effective fighting unit.

They were finally evacuated a week later to the hospital transports USS *Pinkney** and USS *Tryon*, and on October 2, in bad weather, the regiment was finally evacuated off the island. One soaked, worn-out group was approached by an eager, clean-shaven young naval officer who asked them with a smile, "Got any souvenirs to trade?"

One sunken-eyed Marine looked at him wearily, and, reaching behind, patted his rear. "I brought my ass out of there, swabbie," he grumbled. "That's MY souvenir of Peleliu."

The division so far had paid a heavy price for their partial success. In just seven days of fighting, the entire division had incurred almost 4,000 casualties, nearly half of them from the 1st Marines. And the fighting on the island was far from over. Another two months of combat would occur.

Along with the 1st Marines, at General Rupertus's direction, those Shermans and their crews of the division's 1st Tank Battalion that were still operational were (to the amazement of the infantry) evacuated off the island as well. Even O. P. Smith saw that this was a mistake. The only armor support the riflemen would have now was the recently arrived Company A of the Army's 710 Tank Battalion, a unit that had only seen two days of combat in the war, on Angaur. Rupertus had concluded that the tanks were in dire need of maintenance and their crews tired. At any rate, they would not be useful against the enemy positions higher up on the ridges.

He could not be more wrong.

---

* USS *Pinkney*, APH-2 was a Tryon-class transport that served in the Pacific to medically treat and evacuate casualties, and shuttle replacements back out to forward areas. She could make 18 knots, and carried a crew of 475, with capacity for some 1,200 men in her compartments and wards. Like most transports, she was armed with a 5-inch/38-cal. gun at her stern and several 40mm antiaircraft guns. The *Pinkney* eventually was used to repatriate soldiers and Marines back to the States. Decommissioned in September, 1946, she was turned over to the Army, and renamed the USAT *Private Elden H. Johnson* (T-AP-184). She was eventually sold for scrap in September 1970.

The 5th and the 7th Carry on

In the meantime, operations on Peleliu continued. Harris's 5th Marines had made the most headway by now, driving across the center of the island. The going for them was easier, and by September 21, they had cleared the eastern part of the island (the bottom lobster claw) called Ngardololok. This included all of Purple Beach, which would now provide another logistical transfer point. The 5th Marines pivoted to their right and, moving back down, continued their advance clear up to the eastern tip of the peninsula, identified as Tucker Point. They could now ferry across to what was simply labeled Island A, and further advance onto Ngabad Island, just northeast of it.

With the airfield now secure, Seabees and Marine engineers had begun to repair the airstrip, and very soon, a couple of Navy fighters were flown in to start providing close air support and to spot for both the artillery and for the infantry.

Hanneken's 7th Marines, having secured the promontories at the far southern tip of Peleliu, were withdrawn and repositioned up the center of the island between the 1st Marines on the left, still struggling and about to be relieved, and the 5th Marines advancing on the right.

As the Army's 321st RCT began taking over the shattered 1st Marines, the 7th Marines began moving across the island to fill in the gap between the 321st moving up the West Road and the 5th Marines advancing along the eastern shoreline.

Because of the rough terrain, fighting was now mostly localized in the Umurbrogols. Frontal assaults on the ridges were impractical, not to mention deadly. Large-unit tactics did not work here, and the Marines often found themselves having to improvise in taking a position. Often while regrouping, so close were they to the enemy, the Marines could often smell the Japanese cooking in the myriad caves and tunnels. Explosives, napalm, and antitank shells were used to either blast the enemy out, or to kill them in their enclaves. The ridges, stripped of their foliage, began to look craggier and sharper. One Marine described the area like "the face of the moon, defended by Jap troglodytes."

As the Army advanced along the coast up the western road toward the hamlet of Garekoru, the 5th Marines closed in from the northeast. The Japanese, now firmly trapped in their holes in the Umurbrogol, were unable to go on to the offensive: they could only bitterly defend their underground positions. So the 5th Marines began outflanking them, concentrating on simply securing the eastern part of the main peninsula, where the last of enemy remained holed up.

Or so the Americans thought. In the predawn hours of September 23, (D+8), the Navy discovered a Japanese effort to reinforce the island. A battalion-sized group of troops tried to infiltrate the island by sea. The 2nd Battalion, 15th Infantry Regiment, having originated on nearby Koror and Babelthuap islands to the north, had worked its way down, past Eil Malk and Garakayo islands. A total of 13 landing barges and a motor sampan were spotted off Akarakoro Point at the northeastern tip of Peleliu, heading south through the mined area.

By 0525 hours, they had all been destroyed or sunk by LCI(G)s and destroyers from TF-32 picketing the area, including the USS *Heywood L. Edwards* (DD-663), as well as by a Marine artillery unit, which later claimed sinking several barges. However, scores of enemy troops managed to struggle ashore (of course, without their heavy equipment), whereupon they were fired upon by the artillery and later strafed by tactical aircraft as the sun came up. The survivors immediately melted into the jungle, moving southwestward to join up with their comrades still hiding out in the caves and tunnels. According to Japanese reports, their casualties were not nearly as severe, and nine of the barges managed to land safely.

Two nights later, another couple barges tried to infiltrate to the northeast, but they too were spotted and destroyed.

Later that day, the 2/5 was ferried over from Ngabad Island north onto Carlson Island, which they took by the evening.

In the early morning hours of September 25 (D+10), another enemy barge moving down was spotted and destroyed. That morning, while several vessels pounded Ngesebus Island, the entire 5th Marines regiment was ferried over to the other side of the island and landed near the northeast tip of Amber Beach. The 1st Battalion on the left flank pivoted north to advance toward the phosphate refinery at the tip of the island. The 2nd Battalion on the right turned southwest and moved down along the coast so that they could hook up at the small hamlet of Garekoro with the 321st RCT, which that morning had begun advancing up along the shoreline, past the Umurbrogol ridges to their right. They managed to hook up with 2/5 by nightfall. To their right, the 7th Marines had advanced along the eastern road of the peninsula.

After a night of heavy mortar fire from Ngesebus Island on the left and the higher Umurbrogol ridges on their right, the 5th Marines the next morning continued up onto the northern tip, with fire from Ngesebus getting heavier as they advanced. Their drive stalled as they came upon what had once been a functioning phosphate mine and factory. There, the Japanese had turned the main building into a blockhouse, and it took a considerable effort to take the factory.

That same day, the Marines all over the island cheered as they saw sleek, gull-winged Marine F4U Corsairs of Major Robert F. "Cowboy" Stout's fighter squadron VMF-114 fly over, make a few strafing runs against the enemy, before landing on the airfield. The riflemen would now have continuous, close tactical air support—and not from Navy carrier pilots, but from daunting Marine pilots, specially trained for tactical coordination in amphibious operations. They would be followed in a matter of days by the rest of Colonel Caleb T. Bailey's Marine Air Group, MAG-11.

At dawn on September 28 (D+13), Ngesebus was hammered by an intense naval bombardment, a heavy artillery barrage, and several air attacks in which VMF-114, now firmly based on the island, delivered several strafing runs from treetop level. Then 3/5 crossed the small channel from Peleliu to Ngebebus Island to the northeast and captured the small partially complete airstrip there. They then moved onto Kongauru Island, supported by amtracs and Marine air cover. The 3rd Battalion met little resistance, and the islands were swiftly taken. The Seabees landed to repair the small Ngesebus airstrip, and the 5th Marines returned to Peleliu to advance once again on the ridges from the east.

While the 5th Marines were clearing the eastern part of the island, the 321st RCT and the 7th were slowly advancing across the Umurbrogol from the west. As the Army units fought their way along the northern side of the cliffs, the 7th Marines took on the role of battling eastward over the cliff themselves. Positions known as Baldy Ridge, hills 120 and 140, and Wattie Ridge were bitterly contested, overrun, and finally taken.

On September 27, as the 5th Marines continued fighting up to the eastern tip of the island, a peculiar ceremony took place. At General Rupertus's new divisional command post next to the airfield, not even 300 yards from the enemy on the high ground, a flag-raising ceremony took place to commemorate taking the island. The general, "a scattering of brass," and some administrative enlisted took part to celebrate the island being reduced to mere "pockets of resistance." Ominously, as the flag went up, mortars and machine-gun fire could be heard off in the distance, while near the waterline, wounded were being evacuated onto DUKWs.

By the end of September, the Americans had completely surrounded the Umurbrogol. The Japanese dug in in the caves and tunnels were now totally surrounded and isolated. Still, they resisted. The Marines continued relentlessly, resorting to tank fire, flamethrowers, and 100lb demolition charges. Still the Japanese returned fire, even when the Shermans fired into the caves at point-blank range.

The end of September brought rain, and attacks slackened as the area became a sea of mud.

*

Bucky Harris, still recovering from the wrenched knee that he had sustained on D+1, was constantly with his 5th Marines to close up on the right what remained of the Umurbrogol pocket, now about 900 yards long by 400 wide. In doing so though, he now faced the prospect of having to advance up Bloody Nose Ridge from the back. Most of his men, while having taken out their share of heavy enemy positions, had mostly done so on relatively flat ground. Now they faced the high, steep ridges of the fortified enemy stronghold.

Knowing what Puller's men had gone through, he wanted to make sure that his attacks on the dug-in, diehard defenders would entail for him a minimum of casualties. That meant implementing coordinated assaults of riflemen, working with Shermans, LVTs, air assaults, artillery, and flamethrowers. Comprehensive synchronization would be the key. So commandeering a pilot and one of the airfield's "Piperschmitts"* one morning, he took off for a short recon flight over the area his men would be assaulting. The terrain, having for over two weeks been subject intermittently to heavy naval bombardment, artillery barrages, airstrikes, and occasional ground assaults, had been stripped of nearly all of its foliage. Now, amid the burnt, broken and shattered tree trunks, branches, vines, and craters, the coral and limestone surfaces lay bare, and what Harris saw below in the morning light worried him. A few years after the war, he described the scene:

> I was appalled at the sight of those ridges from the air. Sheer coral walls, with caves everywhere; box canyons, crevices, rock-strewn cliffs, and all defended by well-hidden Japs. I knew then that would be no breakthrough.

Harris's men, after careful planning, continued to carefully assault the enemy positions, but, as he had feared, the going was slow. General Rupertus continually urged him to hasten his advance to speed up the operation. One morning though, when he visited Harris's CP, his exhortations were observed. Looking over the map that Harris had been studying, Rupertus said, "I've just been over talking to Colonel Harrison [commanding the 11th Marines], and he told me that he had fired 75 percent of his ammunition in support of the 5th Marines."

After a few moments, Harris broke out in a grin. "Walt† and I figured that so far, the 5th has taken about 70 percent of the division's objectives, so it looks like Colonel Harrison still owes us five percent more."

However, unseen by anyone, General Geiger himself had entered the rear of the tent and had overheard the conversation. He now cleared his throat and

---

* A nickname—a sardonic cross between "Piper Cub" and "Messerschmitt"—given to the Piper L-4 and L-5 Grasshopper two-seater observation planes used for artillery spotting, reconnaissance, and observation patrols. Other nicknames included "Cub,' 'Puddle Jumper,' and "Messercub."

† Lieutenant Colonel Lewis W. Walt, the regiment's executive officer, later becoming commanding officer of the 3rd Battalion, 5th Marines.

told them that when he had gone to school, he had learned that in war there was always a lot of shooting going on, and the ones who shot the most and the best usually ended up being the winners. He paused and then added that he always liked to come to Harris's CP, because his men were always shooting and he seemed to be the only one who was getting anywhere doing it.

Chastened, Rupertus primly said, "Bucky can have all the artillery support he wants." He then turned on his heels and left the tent.

As the main fighting shifted to the Umurbrogols and while the rifle units up there slowly took out one cave or tunnel after another, day after day, the soldiers, sailors, and airmen who served in the administrative and logistical units back at the airfield were shielded from the savagery and close intensity of the fighting nearby.

Incredibly, perhaps inevitably, a number of these men sometimes wondered if conditions up at the front were as bad as the rumors made them out to be. With the black market continuing to thrive on captured enemy items, the thought of obtaining souvenirs enticed a few to go looking for a few or perhaps trade for some with the front-line units. Those who did venture up near the lines were just a nuisance, and so were unceremoniously shanghaied into the nearest front-line unit by direct order of the regimental commanders.

One captain, Joseph E. Buckley was so good at obtaining these "recruits" that he was actually promoted to major. His technique was surprisingly simple. As historian Major Frank Hough later wrote:

> Any men found in Buckley's area without good reason for being there were promptly seized, handed weapons, and placed in the line, where they were held by force if necessary. If they behaved themselves, he notified their unit commanders of their whereabouts and employment; otherwise, he did not bother, and they were carried as AWOL for as long as Buckley chose to hold them.

Other explorers met more tragic fates. Colonel Joseph Hankins, commanding the division's headquarters battalion and the division's provost marshal, decided in the afternoon of Tuesday, October 3 to take a patrol up the West Road to a point near what was known as Dead Man's Curve. It was so dubbed because the road was only 50 yards from the Umurbrogol cliffs, and Japanese sharpshooters hiding in caves up there had regularly been taking pot shots at traffic below. Having heard reports for days of snipers there, Hankins was to ostensibly check out a report of snipers and see what he could do about the situation. Going up the West Road, his jeep stopped alongside the dirt roadway. An LVT and a few trucks behind been abandoned when the drivers had been shot at from above, and some of his MPs were now trying to direct traffic. Hankins stepped out with his M1 and a set of binoculars to take charge.

"I'm gonna do a little countersniping' myself, he said with a grin to the driver, who immediately took off.

Hankins walked over to the traffic jam and began shouting instructions to the drivers hiding in the nearby ditch.

He was promptly shot through the heart by a sniper, killed instantly.

Joseph Hankins, who was posthumously awarded the Navy Cross for command of 3/1 at Cape Gloucester, would be the highest-ranking Marine in the division to die on Peleliu. Dead Man's Curve remained a threat to traffic on the West Road for a while, even though a company of Marines was sent to the area to take out the snipers. The snipers though, soon returned, and finally three Shermans were eventually dispatched to the area to act as a permanent deterrent. If any shots were fired from the ridges on traffic below, the Shermans were ordered to open fire on that spot.

It had not taken long for Peleliu's airfield to become operational. About a week after D-Day, a Seabees unit, showed up at the airfield, announcing to the advance ground support crews, "We got some "f*cking big crates for

Dead Man's Curve, as seen from the Japanese positions on the cliffs. It was along this road that Colonel Hankins was killed.

you ... I think they're airplanes. Unload 'em quick so we can get the hell outta here."

They were indeed airplanes: seven large crates that had made the trip over in an LST. Each comprised a Marine artillery Piper L-5 spotter airplane ("Piperschmitt") that had to be unloaded and assembled, the wings and landing gear having been removed for the trip and packed in separate crates.

On the first day of October, with several Navy fighters already operating off the airfield, flight operations were expanded. The 24 Corsairs of Marine fighter squadron VMF-114 were joined by another 24 from VMF-121, 25 more from Major Joseph Reinburg's VMF-122, and the 15 F6F Hellcats of VMF(N) 541 that somehow made it to the island on October 3.

Then a typhoon hit the island on October 2 for three days, preventing any air support for the next few days. Worse, heavy seas and pounding surf prevented any supplies from being unloaded. The pontoon causeway off Beach Orange-3 was damaged. Two LSTs unloading supplies were swept ashore with serious damage. Other smaller craft bucked wildly in the frothy waves, several of them driven violently onto the shore. Purple Beach, now the main drop-off point for supplies, was hit the hardest.

When the storm let up on October 5, the 5th and 7th Marines were ordered to resume their assault on the Umurbrogol pocket; the Marine aviators took off to give them close air support in what would later be concluded as the shortest tactical bombing and strafing runs of the war. Using the shorter of the two runways, which ran southeast to northwest, the pilots could take off, circle around and attack the enemy positions in less than half a minute, before landing to rearm. The pilots did not even had to even retract their landing wheels, which made the missions even easier. Because the target openings were small, aircraft making bomb runs had to be precise, which meant the aircraft had to come in low. To allow the pilot time to distance himself from the explosion, the bombs were armed with delayed-action fuses. Making runs with napalm was particularly hazardous, and so the pilots began dropping the tanks without fuses. The tanks would burst, but not ignite. After the aircraft had cleared the area, Marines nearby would ignite the napalm with white phosphorus grenades.

Even with the additional air support, attacking the enemy on the ground was still a slow-going affair. The terrain was broken, with crags, sinkholes, moles, and ridges. Trying to advance across this amorphous, jagged ground was difficult at best. The bodies of those killed had to (at least temporarily) lie wherever they fell, and evacuating the wounded by stretcher was guaranteed to be a bumpy and painful ride indeed.

Exacerbating the situation was the Navy's partial inability to continue to provide adequate supplies of rations, especially when the typhoon hit. The

Seabees had come ashore in force, but were stymied by the fact that their equipment aboard the LSTs had to stay offshore for almost a week because of the shortage of craft to bring them in. Thereafter, the Seabees had worked feverishly to repair the airfield and turn the beachhead into a viable supply point. They had cleared nearly all of the broken hulks of amtracs, DUKWs, and equipment that had been destroyed. By now there were neatly identifiable piles of supplies, brought in by DUKWs, and loaded out by trucks, small jeeps, or individuals. The craters had been filled in, and the area was constantly being worked on by earthmovers, and large support units with generators, communications trailers, and all levels of medical aid and evacuation stations. Still, the area, which occasionally took a stray enemy mortar or artillery round, was far from an ideal logistical transfer point, and ammo shortages were regular.

The Seabees, by September 21, had finished constructing a pontoon causeway from Beach Orange-3 out past the coral reef. UDTs had blasted huge gouges in the barrier reef off Beach Purple, so that LSTs could now meander right up to the water's edge and unload vehicles, equipment, and supplies through their bow ramps. Still, supplies were not getting landed and moved up to the front fast enough. So at the beginning of October, after the Seabees had upgraded the runways and constructed additional roadways, and after the storm had roared across the island, ration supplies began coming in by air from Guam, using the tactical bombers and scout planes of Colonel Bailey's MAG-11.

One grisly construction development was troubling to all those who passed it. In a palm grove some 50 yards in from Beach Orange-2, right next to the southwestern edge of the airfield, the graves registration units took on their adverse task. As the battle progressed and the numbers of casualties increased, burial details were busier and busier burying the dead, naturally though, with Marine Corps precision: the bodies exactly three feet apart from centerline to centerline, with 50 corpses per row, and three feet from one row to the next.

*

The weary Marines were ordered to press forward. The cliffs facing them now at the eastern end of the Pocket were as stiffly defended as the others had been. Two steep ridgelines, the Five Sisters facing the Army, and the Five Brothers facing the 5th Marines, were impressive groups of stalagmite-like tall ridges. To the west of the Five Brothers was a parallel ridgeline dubbed the China Wall. To the east of the Five Brothers was another ridgeline identified as Hill X (later named Walt Ridge by the mapping units, after 3/5's commanding officer Lieutenant Colonel Lew Walt, and known to the Japanese as *Kansokuyama*).

Between them was a deadly valley known as The Horseshoe (Army reports registered this area as "Mortimer Valley.") At the eastern end of the pocket were four smaller ridgelines, named Watty Ridge, Baldy Ridge, Ridge 3, and Boyd Ridge (so named by the mapping parties, after the 1/5's commanding officer Lieutenant Colonel Bob Boyd, who had seized it; to the Japanese, it was referred to as *Suifuyama*.)

The Marines in the valleys and draws, even during periods of relative quiet, could swear that they could feel the hostile eyes looking down at them, ready to open up on any American advance.

Nor was it any better from above. The enemy grimly defended every position, and the Americans found to their dismay that even taking a ridge offered little relief or satisfaction. For one thing, it seemed that capturing a summit only made you the subject of fire from enemy positions on nearby ridges, and the type of fire varied. Sometimes it would be a distant machine gun, or small arms, or perhaps just a deadly sniper. On top of that, there invariably would still be enemy caves or holes below you that continued to hold out, sometimes taunting the Marines above with the aromas of fish and rice cooking wafting up to them. There was frustratingly little that you could do to remove the enemy positions below, except to take them out individually, or if lucky, to find air vents and destroy them with flammables.

One corporal described it: "Once you got on top of a hill … it was like getting on top of an ant nest. You thought you had it made once you were on the hill, but then at night they'd crawl out and try to crawl in the hole with you."

The 7th and the 5th Marines continued the chore, and on October 4, as ordered by General Rupertus, they continued their assaults, moving against those series of formidable ridges that sat perpendicular to their lines, and through the draws between them. An Army tank was there to support them, but it immediately got stuck in the coral crags, and could not advance. Call missions to naval warships or artillery was often ineffective, because even larger-caliber shells, even when accurately laid down, did little to eliminate an enemy deep inside a tunnel or cave. An officer later recorded that in one instance, thousands of rounds of 75mm shellfire were thrown at one cave with little effect, except to take out the nearby undergrowth and topsoil. One rifleman grumbled: "It was just like throwing a handful of bee-bees against the wall, for all the good it was doin'."

The list of killed and wounded continued to grow each day as the men slowly took out the enemy. Evacuating the wounded under fire was a deadly task as the enemy showed no mercy. The Japanese, stubborn in their defense, bitterly fought back, hitting the advancing Marines with crossfire from their many bunkers, tunnels and caves (An Army survey taken early in 1945 discovered that a third of all the fortified underground enemy positions were there in

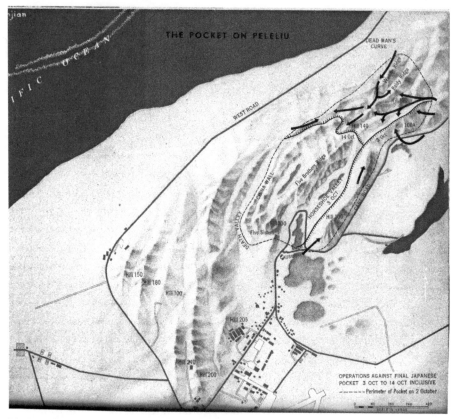

The Umurbrogol pocket. Each ridgeline was honeycombed with dozens of enemy caves and tunnels. (Map courtesy of George McMillin, *The Old Breed*, p. 324)

the Pocket). Slowly, the Japanese were killed off in their caves and tunnels. Rarely did one ever surrender.

One attack of some 50 men against Baldy Ridge by L Company, 3/7, while initially successful, ended in a slow, murderous retreat: when the men eventually returned to their jump-off position, there were only 11 of them left. The dead included the company commander, Captain James "Jamo" Shanley (who had won the Navy Cross at Cape Gloucester), the company's executive officer, First Lieutenant Harold Collins, and one of the platoon commanders, Second Lieutenant James Dunn.

Surprisingly, many of the surviving Japanese, who knew that their time was running out, decided at this time to make a last-ditch effort. That night, about a hundred of them, after stealthily moving out of their caves, suddenly charged the Marines holding the slopes. American reinforcements quickly arrived, and the Japanese finally retreated to their underground positions, leaving over half their number dead on the field.

The Marines, worn out and mentally low, continued day after interminable day. After resting in the evening from a hard day of fighting, they would try to get some rest in what were appalling conditions. Field sanitation was next to impossible, and dysentery became a common ailment. The occasional rains did not help much either. Just moving about, because of both the enemy and the sharp, craggy terrain was difficult. Relieving one's self was usually done next to your foxhole, and often, because of the coral surface, the feces was left uncovered. Retrieving a dead buddy might mean taking a bullet, so the dead often remained where they fell for a couple days, which, because of the heat, made them bloat quickly.

Even one's rations on the line offered little relaxation, because the "gawddamn bugs" got into everything. The men soon learned to shovel their chow with their right hand while at the same time picking the bloated flies or mosquitoes out with their left. What little sleep they could get (when the swarms of insects let them) was often punctuated by nearby explosions or occasional infiltrations by stealthy Japanese.

On October 6, after having fought in the Umurbrogols for some 16 days, Colonel Hanneken's 7th Marines finally began to be relieved by elements of the 81st Infantry Division. Again, this was at the bidding of General Geiger, who, as with the 1st Marines, had been concerned for days about the mounting casualties. They had by this time suffered over 46 percent casualties. Again, Rupertus had argued against this, his answer being the same. "Give 'em a little more time, and they'll take the Pocket, and the battle will be over." Now though, he reluctantly realized that Geiger was right (and he did not want to again be ordered to relieve the men). He could see that the 7th was done as an effective fighting unit. At this point, of the original 3,217 men, casualties amounted to 1,486, nearly what their predecessors, the 1st Marines, had suffered. Hanneken welcomed the relief order, and his men began moving back toward the hamlet of Garekoru on the coast, where Colonel Dark had his 321st RCT headquarters. From there, Army trucks and jeeps ferried the Marines three miles south, down to Ngarmoked Island, and a few days later, two transports evacuated the men and began sailing down to Pavuvu. For the 7th Marines the fight to take Peleliu was over.

Colonel Harris's 5th Marines, now with a total of some 1,378 casualties, would remain, although supposedly they were to start getting relieved two weeks later.

Now the last Marine unit on the island, they wearily continued the task. Shermans with attached bulldozer blades cleared the approaches to the enemy ridges, the riflemen, now supported by a number of Shermans, nearby heavy artillery, and flamethrowing amtracs, once again made the assault. Baldy Ridge was taken in three days, as intensive fire was put onto Walt Ridge and Boyd Ridge. As he had in the previous weeks, General Rupertus tried to keep up the pressure. Often times he would phone a battalion CP and exhort him to continue. "Hurry it up! Gawddamit, don't lose your momentum!"

By October 10, most of the ridges had been reduced, and the enemy was at last unable to mount any organized resistance. It was now a matter of guerrilla warfare, with dozens of small groups in isolated caves and tunnels simply trying to survive.

Exit the Marines

On October 7, D+22, Admiral Nimitz, having monitored the message traffic coming out of Peleliu, concluded that Peleliu had been taken. An announcement to that effect went out to the media, who promptly reported the information, along with Navy-release statistics on the battle.

That day, the 5th Marines continued their assaults on the Pocket, taking out enemy positions on the Five Brothers, Baldy Ridge, and the China Wall. General Geiger in these final days usually stayed aboard his command ship, the *Mount McKinley*, since there was little more that he could do. He did though, from time to time, urge Rupertus to let the 5th Marines stand down, and allow the relatively fresh Army units to take over. As he had for weeks, Rupertus refused, saying in essence that he commanded the 5th and that it was his decision as to when they would be relieved.

Geiger found himself in the same predicament he had been in back on September 21 when he had decided to order the relief of the 1st Marines. If he relieved Rupertus now, it would be the first time in Marine Corps history that a general was relieved in combat. Or, he could order Rupertus to relieve the 5th, as he had with the 1st. This time though, coming near the end of the campaign, the repercussions would be considerable. The man's career would be over, and Geiger's move would come off looking like a vain boost to his command ego. His own downfall in the Corps would be close behind Rupertus's, not to mention the havoc all of this would wreak back in Washington.

It was here that luck (and the Navy) kept Geiger from having to relieve Rupertus. On October 12, D+27, orders were received from CinCPac. Admiral Wilkinson was to report back to Hawaii for a new assignment. He therefore chose Admiral Fort to replace him, and Fort immediately declared that Phase 1 of the campaign—the assault phase—had been completed. At this point, the 81st Infantry Division would begin to complete its takeover of the entire operation.

General Geiger received the news with considerable relief. "I'm glad it's finally over, and the Marines can leave," he said. Rupertus added simply, "I am too."

Colonel Dark's 321st RCT took over from here, and by the third week in October, the Umurbrogol pocket had been whittled down to about a fifth of a square mile. The Japanese feebly continued to resist, but by now they were physically and mentally exhausted, low on ammunition, and living off emergency rations. The island was considered all but taken.

Two days later, Army units began relieving the 5th Marines who were to spend a week or so as occupational reserve on the islands of Ngesebus, Kongauru, and Garekayo. On Ngesebus, they found tents, showers, and even a cookhouse, originally set up by the Army before transfer to Peleliu. The Marines could but shake their heads.

*

The Japanese positions were slowly taken out by the 321st RCT in the eastern part of the pocket, and eventually the 323rd RCT, which had finished with the Ulithi operation, in the western part.

On early Friday morning, October 20,* Geiger unceremoniously turned over all operational command to General Mueller of the Army, who assumed the title of Commanding General, Ground Defenses, Southern Palau Islands. General O. P. Smith temporarily remained behind on Peleliu to oversee turnover of the campaign to the Army; after the war, he wrote that Rupertus was very, very anxious to be relieved. Even so, Rupertus to the last showed disdain toward his ADO, by wanting to leave him just one divisional officer to assist him. It was only after Smith confronted him and vehemently insisted on more that Rupertus sullenly relented.

After handing command over to Mueller, Geiger and what was left of his staff, at 0830 took off from left Peleliu in a comfortable, converted B-24 Liberator, which had been provided compliments of Admiral Halsey. Rupertus flew out of Peleliu that evening with some of his staff at 2330. Geiger's plane arrived on Guadalcanal at 0730 hours the next day, where Geiger and his staff remained. Rupertus on arriving was given orders to

---

* Ross in his book (p. 336) mistakenly wrote that this took place on October 30.

General Paul Mueller, Commanding Officer, 81st Infantry Division.

report to Washington and immediately left for the States. The two generals never saw each other again.

In the meantime, the 5th Marines began their evacuation process. They had come to Peleliu with 3,117 men. They had taken a total of 1,309 casualties, or about 42 percent of their unit. The last of them sailed from the island on October 30, and General Smith flew out on November 1. The Marines were finally off what one had once bitterly called the "Nothing Atoll."

Although nearby Angaur Island had been overrun in four days and declared taken on September 21, small pockets of holdouts would last well into October. The 81st Infantry (minus the 323rd RCT, which was assaulting Ulithi, some 420 miles to the northeast, and minus the 321st on Peleliu) eventually finished Phase 2 and took the island after several weeks of additional combat.

By then, the invasion of the Philippines had begun, with MacArthur's Sixth Army storming ashore at Leyte Gulf on October 20. Five days later, Admiral Oldendorf, who had commanded Western Gunfire Support Group TG-32.5 for the shelling of Peleliu, now commanding his six old battleships (the USS *California* had been repaired by then and had rejoined the force), eight cruisers, over a dozen destroyers, and some three dozen PT boats, in a classic crossing the T of an approaching enemy force, decisively defeated the Japanese in the battle of the Surigao Strait. In this momentous battleship-to-battleship action, the last to ever take place in history, his concentrated, intensive fire all but destroyed the two attacking enemy forces, and both enemy battleships, a heavy cruiser, and a half dozen destroyers went to the bottom.

Back on Peleliu, the battle continued as the Army took over the operation in Phase 2. The Umurbrogol pocket was slowly reduced as one after another

Japanese underground defensive position was slowly taken. Peleliu though, had become just a backwater struggle, now of little importance.

On November 24, on Kondor Island, the Japanese commander or the Palaus received a message from Peleliu: *Sakura, sakura* ("Cherry blossom, cherry blossom").* This was the codephrase for "Resistance has collapsed." The next day, the 25th, the Japanese commander on the island, Colonel Nakagawa, sent a final message to his superior, General Inoue on Babelthuap:

> ALL IS OVER ON PELELIU.

He subsequently reverently burned the ceremonial ribbons and colors of his command, the 2nd Infantry regiment of the Kwantung Army. Then along with his assistant, as true Samurai warriors, he performed the traditional ritual of *Seppuku.* Their bodies would not be found for several weeks.

Although the U.S. high command had considered the operation to be a victory by mid-October, the island was not actually declared secure until November 27, when the commander of the 323rd RCT officially made a report to that effect to the division (and island) commander, General Mueller. Even after that day though, there still remained several Japanese holed up in caves, and enemy resistance continued to be a nuisance for months.

In the scheme of things, Peleliu's strategic value by now had vanished. No other islands in the Palau were assaulted, and the Japanese holed up on them were simply ignored. While on paper the island theoretically remained a threat to MacArthur's flank, in reality it was nothing of the sort. The Japanese were isolated, without any vessels or aircraft to assist. And the U.S. Navy made sure that none ever made it to the islands to change that. That once considered all-important, strategically vital airfield for the area became just a stop for aircraft transiting to the battle area. A strip was developed on Angaur Island for short-range bombers, but they did not play any significant role in the

---

* The beautiful cherry blossom, which abounds all over the Japanese islands in the springtime, has a deeply symbolic, spiritual meaning for the Japanese. Lovely to see but fragile and short-lived, it was often used by Imperial leaders as a propaganda gimmick, reflecting man's mortality and the Buddhist-styled philosophy of the transitory nature of life. The leaders would compare their "mighty warriors" to cherry blossoms as a motivation to target their young soldiers to give their lives in glorious battle for their country and the Emperor. Along those lines, Japanese kamikaze pilots would sometimes paint a cherry blossom on their aircraft, or take a small sprig with them on their fatal mission. Family members would sometimes plant a cherry tree in remembrance of a fallen son or husband.

taking of the Philippines. Even Ulithi, which the 323rd RCT took with very little resistance, played a more important role in the war. Developed into a major naval anchorage, it became an important staging area for the invasion of Okinawa in April of 1945.

For the Marines, weary and combat-fatigued, leaving the island had been a blessing, and even though they were returning to miserable Pavuvu to recover, it was a comparative godsend.

Coming ashore in small boats, the men noticed two improvements: the area had been further developed as a base, and facilities had been built. Second, unbelievably, there were a few Red Cross nurses there to offer them grapefruit juice. The healing would now begin.

*

Because of the resistance the Japanese had mounted, it had taken the Americans an enormous amount of firepower to finally reduce the island. Statisticians later determined that the Americans had fired some 15.7 million rounds of ammunition of all calibers, averaging an amazing 1,590 rounds per Japanese. Nor did that number include all sizes of naval shells, naval small arms fire, and rockets. The average did though, include the following totals expended for each enemy soldier killed:

- 1,331 rounds of .30-cal. bullets (carbine, rifle, BAR)
- 152 rounds of .45-cal. bullets (pistol and sub-machine gun)
- 60 rounds of .50-cal bullets (machine gun)
- 9 rounds of 60mm mortars
- 5 rounds of 81mm mortars
- 1 rifle grenade
- 10 grenades
- 6 rounds of 75mm Pak howitzer
- 5 rounds 105mm howitzer
- 1 round 105mm howitzer
- 1½ round 155mm field gun

The First Marine Division expended the following:

- 13,319,488 rounds of .30-cal. bullets (carbine, rifle, BAR)
- 1,524,300 rounds of .45-cal. bullets (pistol and sub-machine gun)
- 693,657 rounds of .50-cal bullets (machine gun)
- 97,596 rounds of 60mm mortars

- 55,264 rounds of 81mm mortars
- 13,500 rifle grenades

The Marine artillery expending the following:

- 65,000 rounds of 75mm Pak howitzer
- 55,000 rounds 105mm howitzer
- 8,000 rounds of 155mm howitzer
- 5,000 rounds of 155mm field gun

While a final report on the total aerial ordnance used on Peleliu was never made, the following tonnage was reported for September:

	D-3 to D-1	D-Day to D+14
Number of Sorties	916	2,142*
Rockets	147.4	168.5
1,000 lb bombs	132	78.5
500 lb bombs	0	238.9
250 lb bombs	66	38.5
100 lb bombs	119	108.6
325 lb DC	18.2	46.2
1,000 lb napalm	25	46.2
400 lb napalm	0	5
TOTAL	507.6	715.3

*These numbers include those of TU. 32.7.3 (three CVEs and four destroyers), a total of 616 Navy sorties (403 VF, 213 VT) from D-Day to D+8.

Although the battle would go on for another month, for the battered First Marine Division the nightmare of Peleliu was finally over. The division had lost 6,526 men. Of this number (released by the Marine Corps Personnel Accounting System on June 1, 1950), 1,252 were listed as dead or missing and presumed dead. This includes casualties in the other battalions beside the infantry—tank, hospital, amphibious, etc. In comparison, the Army lost 1,393 men on Peleliu, and another 1,676 on Angaur.

Of the three rifle regiments, the 1st Marines had the most losses at 56 percent, the highest percentage of any Marine regiment in American history. All the platoon leaders in 1st Battalion's nine platoons were gone, and the battalion could only muster 74 of the original 954 men.

Numbers of course vary with sources, and questions of reliability arise. Halsey in his report of December 28, 1944, unrealistically put the number of dead at only 842. Another source puts Marine casualties at 6,336, with 1,252 dead, 5,142 wounded, and some 73 missing. The missing were all later ruled as dead: mostly because of the sustained heavy enemy fire, there was often no chance to identify those who had fallen, especially since many bodies had been dismembered by explosions. Another consideration is that there was often not enough time, especially in the first couple days, to remove all of the dead along the shore before many of them drifted out into the surf and floated away, never to be seen again.

The First Marine Division would stay out of the war for five months before it again went into action: that would be at Okinawa.

CHAPTER FOUR

Analysis

Was the Invasion Necessary? The Halsey Factor

Strategic necessity was one of the biggest and perhaps saddest lessons that emerged from this operation, and it is often argued, even today. For decades, historians have studied the elements surrounding the simple question of whether the Peleliu invasion was even needed. Most, with hindsight, have concluded that it was not.

Recall that at the summit conference on July 27, Admiral Nimitz himself had suggested to the president that Peleliu be bypassed in favor of a more direct approach to the Japanese Home Islands. One point that so many have pointed out was a famous last-minute message sent by Admiral Halsey to Nimitz exactly 52½ hours before H-Hour.

As background, Halsey had for weeks wanted to ensure that the Palaus operations would not be interfered with by the Japanese Navy. Indeed, one of the directives given him was to "seek out and destroy hostile air and naval forces which threaten interference with the Stalemate II operations, in order to inflict maximum damage on the enemy and to protect our own forces."

Halsey, in a fashion typical of his leadership style, pursued this goal with vigor. Near the end of August, Vice Admiral Marc Mitscher's fast carriers of Task Force 38 left Eniwetok in the Marshalls. Sailing westward, they carried out extensive air raids throughout the Philippine Sea area, from the Bonin Islands south of Japan, to Iwo Jima, down to the Palaus, from Yap west to Mindanao.

Hunting down enemy air assets, the carriers of Halsey's Task Force 38 on September 12 conducted a number of effective raids on Japanese forces in the Philippines. The raids were surprisingly effective: Halsey's planes destroyed some 200 aircraft. In addition, they destroyed or damaged a number of key facilities and sunk a dozen support vessels. American losses were only eight aircraft, with one of the pilots rescued by Philippine guerrillas. When he returned to the fleet, he had vital intelligence information. His rescuers told him that there were hardly any Japanese left in the area, and that Leyte was virtually undefended.

Halsey had never really been in favor of a landing in the Palaus. In fact, he had expressed apprehension over the operation a couple times before. He had voiced some trepidation about the necessity of taking Peleliu way back in May, and when queried in mid-June, he later formally made his concern known. At that time, he had stated that taking the Palaus just to use their airfields might bring "a prohibitive price in casualties." His concerns at that time were noted and then dismissed.

Now, on September 12, with the invasions Peleliu and Morotai to the southwest just three days away, Halsey had seen how very effective his airstrikes had been on the Philippine Islands. He was now convinced that Japanese power in that area was very weak. In fact, air recon photos from the Mindanao operation on September 9 had showed that a landing there was not even needed.

He pondered the Peleliu operation for a while in a last-minute analysis, taking into account the savings in time, manpower, and resources against the possible command repercussions of again recommending the changes he had in mind. He again discussed the issue thoroughly with his staff for hours before at last making his decision to politically risk going forward with some recommendations. Convinced that the Japanese there could be taken easily, Halsey decided to wire Nimitz with that information, along with the possible changes in strategy that he and his staff had discussed. Halsey wrote a summary stating that due to this recent discovery of unexpected light resistance in the entire area, he was making three recommendations:

1. That the invasion of Peleliu and Morotai should be scratched and that both the Palau and the Talaud islands be bypassed altogether;
2. MacArthur's invasion of the Philippines should be moved up to take advantage of this glaring enemy weakness that he had recently discovered in his operations, and that the preliminary landing at Mindanao before Leyte be cancelled;
3. The 1st Marine Division, which had been slated for the Peleliu invasion, should instead be put at MacArthur's disposal for the landings in the Philippines, along with the Army XXIV Corps, which had been slated for landings at Yap and Ulithi.

Together with his chief of staff, Admiral R. B. Carney, Halsey drafted his set of changes for Nimitz back at Pearl Harbor, radioing the information to Nimitz in two classified messages. The first was transmitted at 0230 hours. It read:

> DOWNED CARRIER PILOT RESCUED FROM LEYTE INFORMED BY NATIVES NO NIPS ON LEYTE. PLANES REPORT NO MILITARY INSTALLATIONS EXCEPT BARE STRIPS ON LEYTE.

The essence of Halsey's thoughts though, came in the longer subsequent message. Classified as top secret and given a precedence of Flash priority, it was finally transmitted at 0300 hours on September 13. Because of the time-zone differences and the fact that his message was sent eastward across the International Dateline, Nimitz only received it at 0800 hours on September 12. His daily summary reviewed the points of both Halsey last-minute messages:

> COM3RDFLT 130230SEP44 (PINK) REPORTS RESULTS OF CARRIER STRIKES AGAINST CENTRAL PHILIPPINES BY TG'S 38.1, 38.2, 38.3 ON 12 SEPTEMBER (E.L.T.) ... DOWNED CARRIER PILOT RESCUED FROM LEYTE INFORMED BY NATIVES THAT THERE ARE NO ENEMY ON LEYTE, BOHOL, APIT, OR SMALL ISLANDS IN THE VICINITY.
>   COM3RDFLT 130300 (PINK) BELIEVES THAT PALAUS NOT NOW NEEDED TO SUPPORT OCCUPATION OF PHILIPPINES, AND THAT WESTERN CAROLINES, EXCEPT ULITHI, NOT ESSENTIAL TO OUR OPERATIONS; BELIEVES LEYTE FLEET BASE CAN BE SEIZED IMMEDIATELY.

Nimitz read Halsey's second message and analyzed the content for about an hour before making his decision. For various reasons, he rejected Halsey's Peleliu recommendation. One considerable one was the fact that the operation had already commenced. The naval bombardment of the beachhead was already underway. The attack transports with their Marine units were nearing the area, and it would be quite difficult (as well as puzzling to the units) to recall them. Moreover, Halsey's idea of using carrier and surface forces to isolate the Palaus seemed to Nimitz a waste of resources.

Nimitz's also probably thought, like so many others, that Peleliu would be an easy operation anyway, and that the island would be taken without much effort. This impression was no doubt reinforced by General Rupertus, whose opinion must have carried some weight with Nimitz, seeing as he a) commanded the Marine division going in, and b) was an experienced leader in the Pacific, having been the division's ADO on Guadalcanal.

There was also the potential for the enemy to put a positive spin on a cancellation. Nimitz perhaps feared that by calling off the invasion, the Japanese might declare in the media that the Americans were afraid of trying to take the formidable island, and thus turn Peleliu into a political victory, or even that the Americans had attempted a landing and the Imperial Japanese forces had successfully driven them off.

Some historians also claim that Nimitz probably considered the source of the suggestions. While Nimitz and his staff considered Halsey an excellent tactician, as a strategist, they found him to be mediocre at best, and decidedly too impulsive and too aggressive. Some scholars feel that Nimitz probably also thought that Halsey was too inexperienced at overseeing large amphibious operations. Halsey's points might possibly have been taken in that vein. Nimitz thus perhaps concluded that although he was a fine commander for aerial strategy, he was only fair when it came to island strategy.

Nimitz's staff had carefully planned the Philippines operation, and it has to be remembered that the original objective of securing Peleliu was to provide a suitable airfield to support the Leyte operation. Since the latter was going to happen, Nimitz now felt that the former was a solid point.

This in itself is an interesting turnaround, because recall that Nimitz had actually argued against taking Peleliu back at the July summit conference. The president though had eventually sided with MacArthur on the Philippines operation, so the implications of canceling the operation would not just be strategic, but regarding the admiral, political as well. For Nimitz to call off the Peleliu invasion now, he would in essence be reneging on his promise to support MacArthur, a pledge he had made on behalf of the Navy in front of the president himself. Moreover, to back out here would in a sense indirectly give MacArthur complete command of all operations in the Central Pacific; the idea of the Pacific theater being under one commander and one service was still being bandied about in Washington, often bitterly. This was especially true in the overall planning of the final defeat of Japan. Both the Army and the Navy wanted to be the controlling command force in the ultimate victory.

In later years, historians have theorized that perhaps some other political issues were discussed and agreed upon back at the July conference, a sort of quid pro quo. Again, with the consideration of the services fighting for control, perhaps Nimitz might have been persuaded to support MacArthur's proposal to invade the Philippines if MacArthur in return agreed that doing so would cut off Japan's vital supply lines and that the Japan would have to sue for peace. Thus, the Home Islands would not need to be invaded and all operations in that area would be carried out exclusively by the Navy.

Along these lines, a couple writers have suggested that the president himself had weighed in on such an agreement. Perhaps Roosevelt had decided to support MacArthur's plan if the general in turn used the media to show that his victories reflected the president's leadership, and thus help in the upcoming November election. As an extension, Roosevelt might also have agreed to then let MacArthur be appointed overall theater commander if it ever became necessary to invade Japan. Again, if such a secret agreement existed, it would be in the Navy's best interest to agree.

So for whatever reasons, Nimitz, after an hour of deliberation, decided to reject Halsey's recommendation of canceling Peleliu. At any rate, he certainly could not do so at this late stage without approval from the joint chiefs, currently attending a conference in Canada. He did though go along with Halsey's other suggestions. To that effect, he did endorse canceling the invasion of the two northern Palau islands and the Yap operation (although, as with Peleliu and Angaur, the invasion forces were already at sea). He endorsed the recommendation of stepping up the Philippines invasion. That would be moved up to October 20.

Nimitz immediately forwarded all of Halsey's recommendations as well as his endorsements of Halsey's recommendations (except of course the Peleliu cancellation) on to the Joint Chiefs of Staff, currently in Quebec with President Roosevelt and Prime Minister Churchill attending a summit, codenamed "Octagon." Curiously, Nimitz never directly documented the reasons for his decisions, even after the war.

The joint chiefs in Quebec, which included CNO Admiral King, analyzed Halsey's original message and Nimitz's additions for an hour and a half. They readily approved Nimitz' endorsements, including bypassing Mindanao, and finally sent their findings back to him. Reinforced by this response, Nimitz went forward with the now-modified plans. And, of course, the Peleliu landing would still be made.

His response went out to Halsey, with MacArthur and King copied:

CINCPAC 130747SEP44: CARRY OUT FIRST PHASE OF STALEMATE AS PLANNED. AM CONSIDERING ELIMINATING OCCUPATION OF YAP ... IN ANY EVENT WILL OCCUPY ULITHI AS PLANNED.

A few minutes later Nimitz sent a message to MacArthur, advising that:

IF OCCUPATION OF YAP IS ELIMINATED, 24TH CORPS, INCLUDING 7TH, 77TH, AND 96TH DIVISIONS... WOULD BE POTENTIALLY AVAILABLE TO EXPLOIT FAVORABLE DEVELOPMENTS IN THE PHILIPPINES. YOUR VIEW ON THIS AND COM3RDFLT'S 130300 REQUESTED.

MacArthur agreed and responded the next day:

> IN VIEW OF COM3RDFLT'S LATEST REPORT ON CARRIER OPERATIONS IN
> THE PHILIPPINES ISLANDS AREA, I AM PREPARED TO MOVE IMMEDIATELY
> TO EXECUTION OF K2 WITH TARGET DATE OCTOBER 20TH.`

Most historians have argued that Peleliu in the end was a wasted effort. Even Admiral Oldendorf commanding the Western Gunfire Support Group wrote after the war that he personally had made some fundamental mistakes in the operation, and that if the planners had had the same amount of foresight as hindsight on the operation, the Peleliu operation would never have occurred. Even while Peleliu was still being secured, MacArthur's epic invasion of the Philippines began, dwarfing the Peleliu campaign in importance and essentially turning it into a needless backwater operation. Certainly it was not worth the heavy cost in lives. After the war, Bull Halsey echoed his earlier concerns:

> I had been weighing this operation ever since it had been broached to me, early in May, at a conference with King and Nimitz in San Francisco, and the more I weighed it, the less I liked it. Ulithi had a useful anchorage, but I saw no need for any of the other islands. Yap's only value was as a minor staging point for aircraft. The Palaus threatened the route between New Guinea and the Philippines, but although they also offered an anchorage—Kossol Roads—and several sites for airfields, I felt that they would have to be bought at a prohibitive price in casualties. In short, I feared another Tarawa—and I was right.

Nimitz himself never went to Peleliu. This is interesting because, as it turns out, it was one of the few major island invasion sites that he did not visit. Halsey though once did. On September 17, aboard his flagship the *New Jersey*, he sailed into the area, but only to observe the ongoing operation and to have a conference with his admirals, before departing that same day.

A week and a half later, Halsey came back to Peleliu a second time, and this time, stepped foot on the island. On Saturday, September 30, arriving in Kossol Passage, at 1150, he hitched a ride southward on the destroyer USS *Hunt* (Halsey a couple of times used the *Hunt* as a sort of taxicab to travel from one vessel or site to another).` The destroyer took him south to Peleliu, where he arrived at 1551 off Purple Beach. An hour later, he went ashore to inspect the progress.

` USS *Hunt* (DD-674, Commander Halford. A. Knoertzer commanding), was a Fletcher-class destroyer named after President James Garfield's Secretary of the Navy, William H. Hunt. Commissioned September 22, 1943, it displaced 2,930 tons and carried a crew of 275. She had a top speed of 38 knots (quite a remarkable speed for a warship in those days). She was armed with five 5"/38 single turret guns, four 40mm AA, four 20mm AA, ten torpedo tubes and eight depth-charge racks. Attached to TG-30.1, the *Hunt* was part of the escort screen for Halsey's carriers. She was decommissioned December 30, 1963 and scrapped in late 1975.

Riding along the beachhead in a jeep, the admiral was sickened by the images that he saw and the stench that was everywhere. It was on this once-only visit to the island that he was directly made aware of how dangerous the operation had been and continued to be. Despite the fact that the beachhead area had long been declared secure, the admiral was nearly killed when a Japanese mortar shell landed near his jeep. Somewhat rattled, he left the island less than an hour later and was taken to the *Mount McKinley*, where Admiral Fort's staff gave him a full briefing.

Halsey departed on the *Hunt* the next morning at 1000 hours to return to his flagship. He left more than ever convinced that this invasion which he had been against was as costly as he had earlier predicted. A week later, Halsey surprisingly advocating use of chemical weapons, wrote to Nimitz: "Peleliu and Angaur were the usual thing on recent visit. The interconnecting caves in the hills, utilizing many entrances and exits and various connecting tiers was a new phase. It is a slow progress in digging the rats out. Poison gas is indicated as an economical weapon."

Starting several months later (and continuing thereafter for many years), when Peleliu's insignificance in the war effort was concluded, many Marines came to bitterly resent the idea that so many of their comrades had died or been crippled or had just suffered needlessly on that lousy island, the "Nothing Atoll." Eugene Sledge, 3rd Battalion, 5th Marines, wrote exactly 50 years later: "I shall always harbor a deep sense of bitterness and grief over the suffering and loss of so many fine Marines on Peleliu for no good reason."

Preparation

One factor that negatively impacted the campaign was that planning for this operation had been inadequate and hurried. This was mostly because of three critical points.

First, so many other operations were ongoing or about to be undertaken at that time, both naval and amphibious:

- The Marianas campaign. Started in June with the invasion of Saipan, this would continue into July with the invasions of Guam and Tinian.
- The sudden naval engagement with the main body Japanese Navy, which had sortied in response to the Saipan invasion. Admiral Raymond Spruance's Fifth Fleet found itself engaged in mid-June with a large enemy force that included nine aircraft carriers, five battleships, 14 cruisers, 32 destroyers, and two dozen submarines.
- In the south, MacArthur's continuing offensive, including the ongoing Bougainville campaign in the Solomons, begun in November, 1943, and

projected to continue through 1944. Also ongoing was the battle of Biak, part of his New Guinea campaign.

- Planning for the massive invasion of the Philippines. Ever since early 1942, MacArthur had vowed he would lead this campaign of liberation, and, finally in late July, President Roosevelt had agreed to undertake it.
- Coordination with and support of American Army Air Corps assets in southeast China working with the Chinese to counter the large, unexpected Japanese offensive there (code name Ichi-Go) started in mid-April.
- The ongoing submarine war against Japanese shipping.

A second and far worse factor that hampered proper planning was misinformation. Although the Americans acquired through the capture of vital maps and reports in the Marianas operations vital, accurate intelligence on the strengths and composition of enemy forces in the Palaus, they critically underestimated the extent and determination of the Japanese on the island. The invasion planners held the firm belief that enemy resistance was not expected to be heavy. This was based upon the optimistic conviction expressed by several senior officers (most importantly the division commander himself, Rupertus) that the operation would only take a few days. The element of surprise was considered a key factor, with the enemy assumed to have minimal defenses on the island. Moreover, the naval planners felt that the firepower of several battleships and cruisers in a brief but savage softening-up of the island would all but take care of whatever enemy positions there were.

Thus because of these two important suppositions, those planning the operation drew up critically inadequate lists of supplies that would be needed, including sizes and lists of replacements, ammunition, and, most importantly, medical supplies and medical personnel. This paucity of medical attention and the resulting problems that arose undertaking a much larger evacuation effort, negatively affected by this shortsightedness, would be made even more serious by the number of ferrying LVTs and other amphibious craft destroyed by unexpectedly strong enemy artillery and mortars. It was only at the last minute that the Marines were given LVT-4 amtracs and a number of flamethrowers, both of which would prove to be invaluable in the operation.

Engaging just two divisions as it turned out was not adequate for this operation, especially given that there were few reserves that could readily be committed. Granted, the 77th Infantry Division had early on been designated as a floating reserve for this operation, and, if truly needed, the Fifth Marine Division could be brought in as well. However, the 77th was recovering on Guam from its recent operation there in late July, and the Fifth Marine Division was way back in Hawaii. The 77th, some 860 miles away, would have needed at least a week to get to Peleliu, and the Marine division, some 4,600 miles away, might as well have been on the moon for all the help it could provide.

As mentioned, General Rupertus amazingly thought that only his division was needed, despite several reliable intelligence reports that all but confirmed that there were now some 8,000 to 10,000 entrenched Japanese on the island. Unfortunately for the Americans, most of these defenders were recent additions to Peleliu. Back at the beginning of March, when Admiral Marc Mitscher's fast carrier task force, Task Force 58,* had hounded the Japanese out of Truk, followed them almost 1,200 miles west to the Palaus and then bludgeoned the islands with massive air attacks (especially Peleliu), there were at that time only about 3,000 Japanese on the island, mostly naval personnel. It was only in the following months that the enemy had extensively increased the island's defenses and significantly increased the defending force, including the addition of the veteran 14th Infantry Division. Some Marine planners had voiced concern over this in early July. The just-taken island of Saipan had been smaller and less rugged, and yet it had taken three divisions nearly a month to capture it.

Also as mentioned, a critical point that factored into the inadequate planning was the unexpected, extended struggle in the Marianas. It was anticipated that these operations would be over by the beginning of August. The battles first for Saipan, then Tinian, and finally Guam, the last of which started in the third week of July, carried on longer than expected. As a result, Oldendorf's NGS commanders, the Navy later argued, were not given enough time to coordinate with the Marine commanders. Admiral T. S. Wilkerson, in his

---

* In late August, 1944, TF-58, like most of the other forces in Spruance's Fifth Fleet, was transferred to Halsey's newly created Third Fleet, and redesignated TF-38 to reflect this reassignment. While Halsey commanded his fleet in specific Central Pacific operations, Spruance and his Fifth Fleet staff stayed ashore, planning for their next major offensive. Then in the spring of 1945, Spruance took over from Halsey, and their roles (as well as their designations) reversed. Thus, TF-38 became again TF-58. This technique not only allowed each staff a respite from battle and time to plan, but also confused the hell out of the Japanese, who were convinced that two separate major fleets were operating against them.

December 22, 1944 endorsement of Admiral Ainsworth's October 5 report on the operation, wrote:

> due to the prolonged presence of the Fire Support Group in the Marianas operation, the ships barely had time to reservice and reach the objective area by the scheduled date. There was accordingly little or no opportunity for the principal commanders of the Fire Support Group to meet with the amphibious force commanders and, as customary, jointly confer in the preparation of plans.

Logistical Shortcomings

A direct result of the lack of time between the end of the Guam operation and the beginning of *Stalemate II*, as well as other operations going on at the same time, was a series of shortages of supplies that occurred, first in the planning, and later in the preparation.

Fresh food was in limited quantity, frozen food supplies much less so. Making matters worse, as so often unfortunately happens in war, a good many of those supplies were given out to the crews on the warships and to rear areas, and less were delegated to the Marine units preparing to take part in an invasion. The First Marine Division had seen strong evidence of that during their stay on Pavuvu. Luxuries like ice-cream and cake were unheard of, and even normal treats like chocolate and spam were somehow held up in logistical centers.

Another problem was going to be water supply. The military had concluded that in steamy climates such as this, at least two gallons of fresh water was needed per man per day. Coupled to the tropical climate was the fact that there were no natural lakes, rivers, or springs on the island. Indeed, the only water the natives received was from rainfall that they collected and stored. Intelligence had determined that the Japanese on the island did so as well, normally stocking rainwater in large cisterns near the airfield, supplemented by supplies occasionally brought to the island.

Each Marine would only be carrying ashore a pair of one-pint water canteens. Thus in the intense sun and the pounding heat, the perspiring men quickly became dehydrated and thirsty from combat. Since fresh water access would be almost non-existent, it would have to be transported ashore. Allotting two gallons a day per man, the Navy was preparing a few thousand 50-gallon drums of water to alleviate this situation Additional supplies of salt tablets were planned as well.

Bearing in mind that the men landing and assaulting the beaches would only have a limited amount of supplies on them, it was going to be quite an operation to keep the men who landed supplied with what they needed to carry out their mission, be it food, water, ammo, or medical supplies, especially since it all would have to be hauled over that barrier reef. Compounding this problem was a shortage of landing vehicles. The numbers of amphibian tractors, amtracs, and DUKWs available were not enough to provide any kind of a safety margins. These were the critical units that were going to get the men, ordnance, and supplies over the reef and onto shore. Further complicating the matter was a sudden decision by command to reorganize these amphibian units, thus necessitating extensive retraining all round.

To partially remedy these amphibian problems, a number of barges with mounted cranes and a floating dry dock were to be used to help get supplies over the reef. Any way they looked at it though, that first day would be logistically hectic, and if unexpected stiff enemy resistance was encountered, things could get desperate.

Added to these logistical difficulties that arose in the planning was the fact that loading operations would be conducted at five different areas, each some distance from the others. Coordination would have to be exact, and as it happens so often in war with such complex elements, Murphy's Law frequently comes into play when complex movements are required.

Also, because of the aggressive advancement planning by the high command, transport problems inevitably arose (a serious problem for the Allies across the globe). Transports were in short supply strategically because of the logistical demands required to continue the offensive in the European theater. In the Pacific, the problem was compounded because several other operations in the area were ongoing, with others in the planning, including the upcoming massive Philippines campaign, starting with the invasion of Leyte.

Shortages of vessels for Peleliu were further compounded by a series of mishaps at sea, many occurring during practice exercises when a number of landing craft collided and were swamped. The worst incident involved two of the major warships slated as part of the operation's fire support team. The battleship USS *California*, veteran of Pearl Harbor, collided with the *Tennessee* on August 23, and was knocked out of the operation. (Repairs expedited, and, as a result, the *California* left port three days after the Peleliu invasion had begun. She did not though, participate in that operation. Instead, she sailed to Manus Island off New Guinea to prepare for the Leyte operation.)

There were other important problems as well that directly resulted from the vessel shortages. Because there were not enough transports available, sacrifices had to be made. A significant one involved the division's only armor, the Marine 1st Tank Battalion. Only four LSDs to ferry tanks were available for the operation, and two of them had to be given to the Army component for their operations. This meant that the number of LCTs was limited, and because of this, so were the number of tanks that could be loaded. Thus, the Marines could only bring 30 of the battalion's 46 Sherman tanks with them, along with only two-thirds of the battalion's 900 men. They were forced to leave 16 Shermans behind, along with 300 men. Because the operation would take much longer than estimated, this became a critical factor that, by the time the operation was over, had cost the Marines many more casualties.

General Geiger confirmed this in his action report after the battle:

> The First Division requested shipping to land all its tanks in the seizure of PELELIU. Shipping made available permitted only thirty tanks to be employed. Sixteen were left with the Rear Echelon. These tanks were sorely needed and the Division was handicapped by their loss on an operation of a type which particularly required them.
>
> PELELIU Island was known to be generally flat, hard terrain, with an airdrome area composing the bulk of its surface. It was known to be defended by a strongly entrenched garrison of 10,000. The economical assault of it required maximum tanks strength.
>
> The insufficient number of tanks which could be taken delayed the complete seizure of the airdrome area, and further rendered its seizure very costly in casualties. Throughout the first five days of action, all three infantry regiments repeatedly requested and needed, additional tanks support.

Perhaps adding to this drawback was the fact that the Angaur operation was also allocated a tank battalion, but no more than one Army company from it was ever deployed at any time. In a similarly short-sighted vein, the Motor Transport Battalion was broken up into individual companies, only one of which could bring its organic equipment and be effectively used for supply replenishment.

Yet another problem with the armor was supply and maintenance of the tanks. Few replacement parts had come over, and nearly all were loaded next to the tanks themselves in the LCTs. Thus, between combat conditions, the lack of adequate parts, and mechanics killed or wounded, repair was often difficult or impossible. These problems, coupled with a stout enemy defense, resulted in an average of only two-thirds of the Shermans being operational at any one time. Of course, for any given day, any Sherman that could move and shoot was used in combat. Even then, ammo was often found to be lacking, and in the first couple days, spare shells and ammo belts had to be salvaged from disabled tanks.

Equipment failure was a problem too. Walkie-talkies were unreliable in the jungle environment. Some ammo for a few types of weapons was found to be faulty because of the environment. Most of the grenade launchers, for instance, which would have been effective weapons against dug-in positions, were discarded soon after landing, because the cartridges had deteriorated from the humidity.

There were other shortage difficulties as well, including mobile flame-throwers, explosives, machine guns, and bazookas. Engineering equipment that had been used extensively in the Marianas was now in short supply. And with the frequent showers the islands experienced, quantities of waterproof material that so often made life in the rains slightly more tolerable were also lacking.

Even the ammo that the men were to use was often not up to par. Machine-gun belts were often found rotted from the tropical environment. Explosive material was sometimes found to be faulty, included crumbling mortar powder rings, shotgun shells, and some artillery shells. Brass shells corroded, and metal containers rusted. All of these things would need replaced before the division went into battle.

Logistical problems both during and after the landing were serious as well. A considerable problem that hindered logistics was the very nature of getting men and supplies ashore. The reef was far wider than those at Guam and Tarawa, and in addition, it was infused with various enemy offshore obstacles, such as barbed wire and girders laid into the coral. Complicating matters was the fact that this division had never negotiated a landing across a reef before. Worse was the fact that in the rehearsals of August 27 and 29, no reef simulation was factored into the landing exercise. Getting supplies over the barrier reef was the first critical concern, and it proved to be quite the headache until a pontoon causeway and later, the use of Purple Beach eased the shortages. To be sure, the unexpected enemy resistance that had been so passive during the pre-landing bombardment was a major factor contributing to this: enemy fire taking out a considerable number of LVTs and DUKWs significantly slowed down the landing process.

Getting supplies and replacements over the reef, proved to be considerably more difficult that had been anticipated. Because the casualties were far worse than had been expected, medical supplies and processing were overwhelmed, and considerable time and fuel were expended evacuating the wounded.

While the reef next to landing beaches was not as wide as the 1,000-yard-wide reef opposite the Amber Beaches, it still was a good 500–700-yard stretch that the landing vehicles would have to struggle over time and again. The rough coral tore at the DUKW bottoms, and the amtracs found traversing it difficult as well. Plus there was the fact that while they were relatively stationary in crossing the barrier, they were far easier prey for enemy mortar and artillery fire. Supplies to a limited degree could also be carried in by hand, but that was a slow and dangerous process. The causeway built from the edge of Beach Orange-3 by D+6 improved supply flow, as did securing Purple Beach to allow supplies to start coming in there. Still, logistical units struggled to land ammo and supplies to allow the Marines to keep up the pressure. Because of this limitation, moving vehicles across the barrier was even more of a challenge, and, as a result, there was very little transport brought ashore in the first week.

One significant result of this slowdown was getting the supporting artillery ashore. The 75mm Pak howitzers had to be brought ashore individually, and not all together as had been planned.

It was even worse for Colonel William Harrison's 3rd and 4th battalions with their 105mm howitzers. Most of the batteries actually had made it ashore on D-Day and were unloaded. One was even able to provide support fire for the 7th Marines. Two of the batteries though, landed later in the day, but the embattled Marines were unable to unload the guns and equipment. As darkness fell, rather than let the transporting DUKWs sit in the dark exposed to enemy fire, they were ordered to return across the reef and re-embark back to their respective LSTs. These DUKWs had already sustained some damage crossing the reef, and returning now in the dark was to prove a dangerous undertaking. Before they could make it to the LSTs, three DUKWs took on more water and sank, each one taking its 105mm howitzer and equipment down with it.

Pre-Invasion Reconnaissance

Poor target investigation of the island resulted in severe misjudgment, most notably in the nature of the target terrain. Planning had been based upon photographs taken by two sets of sources: by two submarines that at different times took images from far offshore, and aircraft, usually flying high above the island.

The Marines concurred. W. F. Coleman, the assistant intelligence officer for the First Marine Division, even as the 1st Marines were starting to evacuate on October 1, wrote on behalf of General Geiger:

> Unfortunately, the maps of PELELIU and ANGAUR were found to be extremely inaccurate in their representation of the configuration of the terrain. The representation of the coastline and major road and trail net was quite accurate, but the hill masses were not portrayed anything like the actual terrain. It is believed that this was caused by the fact that maps were made from unsatisfactory aerial photographs.

The two submarines tasked with photographing the island were the USS *Seawolf* and USS *Burrfish.*[*] The *Seawolf*, on her 13th war patrol, took photos of the island from June 4 to July 7, avoiding enemy air patrols. The *Burrfish*, on her third war patrol, reached the Peleliu area at the end of July. Patrolling south of the island, she stayed in the area for a few weeks, taking photos by periscope, charting ocean currents, and collecting data on the reef, before finally leaving the area on August 13.

Each sub had to be discrete in its mission, particularly since the island had extensive radar and a viable airfield, from which Japanese aerial reconnaissance and anti-submarine flights were commonplace. Only once was a frogman team landed onto the intended landing area. This was conducted by the *Burrfish* on August 11, and while anti-invasion devices were noted, the larger point emphasized by the report was that the beaches were well suited for landing craft. And, of course, there was no investigation of the enemy defenses in the area. Further UDT missions were not possible over the following nights, because the moonlight was too bright, and Japanese radar was too intense.

Details of any features inland could understandably only be photographed from the air. The aerial photos that were used included a wide variety of images. Some had been taken before the war, and proved of little value. The first useful aerial reconnaissance photos were taken back in early March 1944 when the Palaus had been hit by several airstrikes from Halsey's fast carriers. A series of missions, spurred on from requests by the Marine planners, were later conducted in July and August to obtain updated photos.

Just about all of the aerial reconnaissance images had been taken from considerable altitudes. As a result, they thus appeared low and misleadingly flat, even though some early reports showed spots as high as 250 feet. Except of course for the open airfield and the thick mangrove swamp to the east of the airfield, the photos repeatedly showed stretches of thick jungle, naturally appearing deceptively flat to the analysts, who also severely misjudged the extent and size of the thousands of coral ridges, valleys,

---

[*] USS *Seawolf* (SS-197) was a Sargo-class submarine, launched in mid-August, 1939. On her 15th war patrol she disappeared with all hands in early October, 1944. USS *Burrfish* (SS-312) was a Baleo-class submarine, launched in mid-June, 1943. She survived the war and, in 1960, was loaned to the Canadian Navy, recommissioned as HMCS *Grilse* (SS-71). Returned to the U.S. Navy nine years later, she was sunk during target practice off San Clemente Island by a torpedo dropped by an SH-3 helicopter.

crevices, cliffs, and crags that the thick mantle of jungle masked, especially in the Umurbrogols.

The photos, even the very few taken at lower altitude, did no justice to the highly irregular hidden surface terrain that resulted in the Marines going into action with inaccurate, poor-quality maps. This was especially true for the Umurbrogols: the maps showed the area to be a single, for the most part continuous, ridge that ran up the peninsula, and that there was a decent road running along it on each side.

Even more critical were the hundreds of hidden, fortified caves and bunkers that went unidentified. Very few revealed any type of significant Japanese position, especially on or around the Umurbrogol range. What the jungle did not hide the Japanese made substantial efforts to camouflage. Some positions, such as prominent airfield points, a radio direction finder, the power plant, and some minor utilities were identified. More were spotted but could not be identified. However, many were not even seen. The photos did not reveal the dozens of hidden resistance points that the enemy had built, nor any aspect of the complex honeycomb of solid, underground fortifications and bunkers they had created along the slopes, most of them connected by a series of tunnels and passageways.

Thus the aerial images showed very few signs of the enemy defense anywhere north or east of the airfield. No caves or tunnels could be seen (and were thus not mentioned in the reports). These image limitations were further pronounced by the fact that several areas were only detailed by enlarging areas that had been taken at high altitude, which of course did little to enhance what was being viewed.

Added to this was another dangerous habit that the analysts had exhibited in the past and that to an extent was in play here. Whenever ground features taken in aerial images were covered by haze or by clouds, those areas understandably had no enemy positions identified and were simply left blank. The analysts had done that a few times before the Guadalcanal and Cape Gloucester invasions.

Coupled to this was the fact that even in areas not covered by cloud or haze, the enemy had taken extraordinary efforts to hide their positions. Despite the fact that the Americans had a remarkably accurate estimate of the enemy forces on the island—detailed lists of units had been discovered in comprehensive enemy documentation that was discovered on Saipan when the island was taken in July; force dispositions on Peleliu were later verified by Ultra intercepts of Japanese radio transmissions—they fell far short of understanding how these units were deployed, in what sort of positions they were, and thus where the

Aerial recon photo of Peleliu. At the bottom of the photo, just below the airfield, are the White and Orange beaches. Clearly notable to the left of White Beach is The Point, as well as the small promontory to the right of Beach White-2. From these two positions, the Japanese were able to rain down murderous fire onto the Marines coming ashore.

enemy's strengths and weaknesses were. Complicating the matter was the fact that human intelligence for the island was non-existent. There had been no coastwatchers, no cover operations had been undertaken, and almost no one could be found who had lived on the island before the war. Certainly there was no one available who could attest to the fact that the Japanese had gone to great lengths to fortify the island and to conceal their positions.

Critical to the American lack of knowledge regarded the locations and dispositions of hidden enemy positions near the beachhead and the airfield. This was crucial, as-yet-undiscovered information for the naval fire support group and the invading forces. Some last-minute aerial recon photos revealed a few newly discovered positions, but by the time they were dispatched from Hawaii and delivered to Banika Island, the amphibious convoy had sailed and was out of touch.

To their credit, despite the lack of enemy presence in the recon photos (or perhaps because of it), at least one or two of the Marine commanders sensed the danger they would be facing, including General Geiger and his superior, General Julian Smith. Colonel Puller himself had well sensed this aboard the USS *Crescent City* just before the landing. And of course, Admiral Halsey himself.

Naval Gunfire Support—The 3rd Day Controversy

One of the most debated issues of the operation centers around the naval gunfire bombardment sustained in the few days leading up to the landing. Some historians have concluded that it was adequate, while a whole host of others have claimed that it certainly was not.

Most historians do agree that the pre-invasion bombardment was a critical factor in the heavy resistance the Marines encountered. The details of this part of the operation though, have often been misrepresented or are inaccurate.

The original naval plan had called for a preliminary bombardment period of only three days, followed by an intensive pre-landing shelling during the early morning of D-Day. However, because the Navy was pressed in so many other areas of the Pacific and because of ammo shortages, they shortened this time period down from three days to two. When General Geiger, who had wanted at least four days of preliminary shelling, strongly objected to this, the Navy acquiesced and agreed to three days before the scheduled D-Day.

Unknown to the Marines though, this concession would not benefit them. Admirals Fort and Oldendorf had in their mind a finite amount of ammo that they could safely expend without jeopardizing the upcoming Philippines campaign. So all this compromise meant was that the same amount of ordnance would be fired over the course of three days, instead of the pre-planned two. Even so, the entire amount of shells to be expended in this effort would be far less than it had been in other operations. Indeed, the tonnage fired at Peleliu would be less than that fired at the shores of Tarawa in just three hours.

The Navy firmly believed that two days of intense shelling of this small island from a surface force that included four battleships and several cruisers, supplemented by attacks from carrier aircraft, would more than suffice. And true to that task, the shelling that began on September 12 was both thunderous and to many, impressive.

The four battleships and five cruisers of the fire support group began their shelling around sunrise of D-3 against various identified targets over the island. Tied in to the bombardment were occasional tactical bombing raids from Ofstie's escort carriers. The gunfire warships would zigzag around as they fired at previously identified targets for a couple hours. To maximize effectiveness, the larger warships used spotter planes to observe and direct the hits. Then naval tactical bombers would then fly in from the carriers and bomb other targets as the warships paused and regrouped for the next round. And so it went.

Apparent results after that first day's shelling seemed to confirm to senior naval officers that this one-two combination had been effective, and that there would not be too much trouble taking the island. Offshore observations and assessment of developed aerial recon photos seemed to show that substantial damage had been done to enemy positions near the landing area and the airfield. In addition, large areas of jungle had been destroyed on the lower slopes of the ridges rising to the center of the island. One observation described the effect as turning the area "into a barren wasteland." One report stated that "[the island's] tropical growth ... by Dog Day ... had been systematically destroyed, and only charred tree stumps and scarred rocks remained. Numerous caves were then visible on the slopes of the high land."

Many of the above-ground defense positions that had been previously identified and documented on the maps (nearly 300 of them) seemed to show indications of heavy damage or destruction. As expected, there was some concern that almost all of the enemy artillery pieces that had been photographed weeks before on island overflights had been curiously silent during the shelling. What Japanese gun crews there were on the ridges had simply remained in their sheltered positions. Moreover, in the photos taken that day, these guns had still not been spotted. No doubt, those few that had not been in caves, tunnels, or bunkers must have been moved underground beforehand, and so it was a safe bet that most of the enemy artillery had been barely damaged by the shelling.

The observations and recon photos of the second day's shelling on D-2, coupled to the total lack of enemy response in any way, in the minds of the naval observers seemed to reaffirm their estimates on the damage that had been inflicted, and on their confidence that this would be a quick operation. By that evening, all the registered positions for the naval bombardment, many having been targeted several times, appeared to have been seriously pummeled or outright destroyed. All of the above-ground positions—those spotted, that is—had been hit. No more targets appeared to be present. Indeed, in many respects, the island seemed all but deserted. To that effect, Oldendorf sent a progress message off to Halsey and Nimitz, who recorded the following in his operations daily summary for September 14: "CTG 32.5 [fire support group] reported operation 14 September proceeded on schedule. Unable to uncover any heavy defenses ... Found no mines."

It is here that the controversy comes in. Several sources document that after completing the second day's shelling of the island, Oldendorf decided that evening of September 13 to reduce the Peleliu pre-invasion shelling to the original number of only two days instead of the three that had been promised to the Marines. Supposedly, in a momentous decision, Oldendorf decided to save ammo and to cancel that third day's shelling. The claim was that Oldendorf signaled his change of plan to Nimitz back at Pearl Harbor, his justification being that he had "run out of profitable targets."

It has been documented that Oldendorf indeed sent some sort of message to that effect, and the key phrase that he had "run out of targets," was in the message. However, whether he sent the message on the 13th (D-2) and whether he added that very critical adjunct that the third day's shelling was going to be canceled is highly improbable.

Nimitz did not respond to Oldendorf's message. Those sources claiming that the third day's shelling was canceled cite this as Nimitz essentially sanctioning Oldendorf's cancellation decision. Nimitz in his CinCPac war diary, did not mention the cancellation message. It did though, have the following entry: "CTG 32.5 [fire support group] reported operation 14 September proceeded on schedule. Unable to uncover any heavy defenses."

Admiral Oldendorf then supposedly sent a message to that effect to the senior Marine commanders—some sources indicate that it was by ship-to-ship voice communication—involved in the operation on that same evening, adding that he was now waiting for their attack transports to arrive on scene. The Marine commanders were of course at that time en route and under strict radio silence, so they could not object to this fateful decision.

One source claims that after the two days' shelling, the larger fire support ships actually had then sailed from the area and were nowhere to be seen on the third day (D-1). Their confirmed departure from the immediate area was a plausible conclusion, although certainly temporary, based on the fact that each night, the vessels moved away from the island to avoid attack from enemy submarines and torpedo boats, which was expected, and second, to rearm or to refuel, either from tankers (which they did at one or more times in the campaign), or to provide fuel to the smaller warships, such as the destroyers. Another source makes the incredible claim that, "By the morning of 15 September, no new targets had been found, and Oldendorf departed to link up with MacArthur's Philippine invasion force."

This is impossible (unless the admiral left his task group behind). Oldendorf, his battleships, and his cruisers were definitely present in the dawn hours of D-Day to conduct the pre-landing bombardment. They remained for the subsequent days to provide additional naval gunfire support to the Marines ashore. Even as late as September 27 (D+12), the USS *Mississippi*, two cruisers, and six destroyers were on hand to provide naval support to the operation. Oldendorf himself on the USS *Louisville* did not depart the area until September 24.

When the commander of the 1st Marines, "Chesty" Puller, aboard his attack transport USS *Crescent City* (APA-21), was given this message with its key phrase "run out of targets," he immediately realized the implications of this order to his landing and became angry. He growled to his transport's commanding officer that if he knew Admiral Nimitz at all, when he received word of Oldendorf's "asinine" decision, there would be, "an order from Pearl Harbor to that admiral, ordering him to turn over his command to his next senior officer and continue the bombing and shelling for three days as ordered. If we don't keep up the fire, they'll be loaded and waiting for us."

Puller was probably basing his comment on his assessment of Nimitz's character. He had actually worked under the admiral for a while: their acquaintance went back to the mid-thirties, when Lieutenant Puller had been put in command of the Marine contingent on the heavy cruiser USS *Augusta* on China Station. His commanding officer had been none other than Captain Chester Nimitz, and they had worked well together. While Puller's hunch on what Nimitz's reaction to the message was, in the end, incorrect, his guess on the enemy's preparedness would turn out to be spot on, especially if the Japanese would have this third day to somewhat recover from Oldendorf's two-day bombardment.

All the Marine officers were furious at Oldendorf's message (especially after the campaign was over), feeling betrayed. They would later point out that various registered targets clearly shown on the maps (to say nothing of dozens that were never identified in the photos) had not been destroyed. Indeed many of them, especially that deadly, formidable blockhouse on The Point, which on D-Day had poured merciless enfilade fire onto the beaches, had not even been touched. The bombardment had left critically intact, enemy positions that enfiladed the beachhead on both flanks and that wrought serious havoc to the initial waves.

After the war, Oldendorf in a letter of March 25, 1950 to the Director of Marine Corps History, Major Frank Hough, wrote that in all the time leading up to the invasion, this particular blockhouse had never been identified on his maps. Perhaps offered as a partial reason, he in addition cited that he had been hampered in that first week of operations by widespread illness among his staff. In his letter, he wrote:

> [during] the preliminary bombardment and until several days after the landing, my entire staff was on the sick list; only my flag lieutenant remaining on his feet. This threw a heavy load on me, as I not only had to supervise the details of the daytime operations but also operate tactically at night during withdrawals.

If indeed the third day's shelling and bombing had been cancelled for D-1, this would have been a key factor disastrous to the amphibious operation. The Japanese would have had a lengthy period of time to recover from the bombardment and better prepare for the landing that was sure to come. With the shelling temporarily ceased, they would have spent most of the 14th shoring up any damaged positions and realigning their defenses. It was now obvious that from the position of the American fleet and the areas that had been shelled and bombed for the last two days, the landing was clearly going to take place along the western beaches of the island.

This conclusion was made even more obvious by the UDT teams that took out obstacles along the shoreline that evening. Thus, the Japanese would have been able to feverishly (but covertly) spend the afternoon and night of September 14 quietly moving units southward, while they carefully trained their artillery and mortars on the likely beach areas and rechecked their grid coordinates. In addition, they would have had the opportunity that night to bring some reinforcements down by barge from the nearby island of Babelthuap.

Many historians purporting that the third day shelling was canceled argue in addition that even if Peleliu had been shelled that third day, the effect would probably not have taken out too many more Japanese positions, fortified, entrenched and hidden as they were. Also, the Navy correctly concluded that enemy tanks hidden in fortified positions proved difficult to destroy by NGS alone. Still, that third day of shelling did damage a number of positions on each flank of the intended landing area, positions that would exact a deadly toll on the first few waves hitting the beach. No doubt, if the scheduled bombardment of the third day had been canceled, it would have definitely been a boon to the enemy. One source claims:

> General Murai and Colonel Nakagawa must have been bewildered, if not thoroughly amazed, by the next morning's eerie stillness. Not a solitary ship could be seen in the calm seas off Peleliu, nor was there a single plane in the cloudless skies.
>
> The Japanese commanders hadn't the vaguest idea why the Americans had broken off the engagement and sailed somewhere beyond the horizon. They were certain, however, that they would be back with a bigger armada—one determined to conquer Peleliu—very soon.

In all fairness to the Navy, two observations must be stated. First, the NGS did not leave the area for days. The OBBs stayed until D+7, at which time they began sailing for Kossol Passage to the north to refuel and then head southeast for Seaadler Harbor, about 950 miles away in the Admiralty Islands off New Guinea.

Most importantly though, the third day's bombardment was in fact not canceled. Oldendorf message notwithstanding, it was documented by some to have been sent on the evening of the 13th. In all probability though, the message was actually sent (as other sources claim) instead on the evening of the 14th. And it might very well have been by voice communications instead of by conventional means, that this was a voice message sent the evening of the 14th from Oldendorf on the *Louisville* to Fort on the *Mount McKinley*. Oldendorf in his own action report on Peleliu, stated the following in his log for September 14:

0505 – CTU 32.5.1 ordered Commander Battleship Division FOUR to have MARYLAND AND PENNSYLVANIA fire on areas on the eastern shore of PELELIU from 0545 to 0630 while Fire Support Unit BAKER bombarded the western side.

0545 – By this time all the heavy units had launched spotting planes and commenced scheduled bombardment.

0900 – Fire Support Unit ABLE launched spotting planes.

0930 – Fire Support Unit ABLE relieved Fire Support Unit BAKER continuing the bombardment.*

1230 – Fire Support Unit BAKER launched planes and proceeded to take station relieving Fire Support Unit ABLE of bombardment and close support (UDT No. 6) mission.

1630 – Fire Support Unit ABLE relieved Fire Support Unit BAKER of the bombardment duties.

1800 – Fire Support Unit ABLE ceased scheduled bombardment and recovered planes.

This was supported by Rear Admiral Theodore D. Ruddock, commanding Battleship Division 4 (a part of TU 32.5.2) on the *West Virginia*. He stated in his bombardment report of September 14:

Weather:
Wind – WSW, 8 knots.
Swells – WSW, 1 foot high.
Visibility – Good – hazy overhead.
Temperatures – Dry 83°F, Wet 77 1/2°F

0505 – (TBS) CBD-4 from CTU 32.5.1.At 0540 or as soon thereafter as practicable until 0630 from positions generally to the eastward of shoal spot in south of objective conduct bombardment in areas 131, 137, and the east side of valleys of high ground in 133 and 141.

0845 – Aircraft were launched and ships of TU 32.5.2 proceeded to bombardment stations.

---

* Fire Support Unit Able consisted of the battleships *Maryland* and *Pennsylvania*, heavy cruiser *Indianapolis*, light cruiser *Honolulu*, and destroyers *Newcomb, Bennion, Heywood L. Edwards*, and *Leutze*. Fire Support Unit Baker consisted of battleships *Idaho* and *Mississippi*, heavy cruisers *Louisville* and *Portland*, and destroyers *Richard P. Leary, Robinson, Ross, Albert W. Grant*, and *Bryant*.

0930 – Commenced firing scheduled bombardment.
1254 – TU 32.5.2 ceased bombardment and proceeded to form fueling disposition.
1600 – Commenced scheduled bombardment.
1800 – TU 32.5.2 ceased bombardment and proceeded to rendezvous with CTU 32.5.1 at a point bearing 300°T, 6 miles from Point Princeton.

The war diaries of the various major warships that comprised the Naval Gunfire Support Task Group 32.5, confirmed that all of the vessels did indeed shell the island on D-1, using both their main batteries and their secondary batteries, and the intensity of fire and amount of explosives hurled onto the island was very similar to that fired over the previous two days.

The log of the heavy cruiser *Portland*, for instance, shows a total of 189 8-inch shells that were fired on the 12th, another 189 on the 13th, and then another 131 on the 14th. The battleship USS *Idaho* records having fired 250 14-inch shells on each of the three days, and so on for the battleships *Mississippi* and the *Maryland* (this vessel's war diary indicates that the vessel began its shelling Peleliu on D-1 around sunrise at 0546 hours and finally ended for

Estimated ship shell expenditures at Peleliu.

Vessel	DATE			
	Sep 12	Sep 13	Sep 14	Sep 15
Pennsylvania BB-38 MB: 14" SB: 5"	MB: 175 SB: 644	MB: 114 SB: 712	MB: 158 SB: 797	MB: 215 SB: 1294
Mississippi BB-41 MB: 14" SB: 5"	MB: 175 SB:	MB: 250 SB:	MB: 250 SB:	MB: 250 SB:
Idaho BB-42 MB: 14" SB: 5"	MB: 250 SB: 310	MB: 250 SB: 300	MB: 250 SB: 300	MB: 273 SB: 585
Maryland BB-46 MB: 16" SB: 5"	MB: 170 SB: 655	MB: 148 SB: 470	MB: 165 SB: 238	MB: 331 SB: 2,038
Louisville CA-28 MB: 8" SB: 5"	MB: 222 SB: 200	MB: 213 SB: 159	MB: 187 SB: 238	MB: 285 SB: 465
Portland CA-33 MB: 8" SB: 5"	MB: 189 SB: 188	MB: 189 SB: 188	MB: 131 SB: 186	MB: 288 SB: 375
Indianapolis CA-35 MB: 8" SB: 5"	MB: 190 SB: 194	MB: 163 SB: 179	MB: 168 SB: 187	MB: 183 SB: 370
Honolulu CL-48 MB: 6" SB: 5"	MB: 348 SB: 328	MB: 321 SB: 311	MB: 331 SB: 149	MB: 1,028 SB: 572

Main Battery (MB) and Secondary Battery (SB) shells fired.

the evening at 1742 hours) The heavy cruisers *Indianapolis* and *Louisville* (Oldendorf's flagship), and the light cruiser *Honolulu* all record substantial fire missions during that day as well (see tables).

The other major warships in the area, the battleship *Tennessee*, the heavy cruiser *Minneapolis*, and the light cruisers *Cleveland*, *Columbia*, and *Denver* were on the 14th in the process of shelling Angaur Island for its own landing, projected for September 16.

Several additional sources support these figures. The COMINCH Bulletin 23 states that the bombardment went on for all three days before the landing. Then on D-Day, in the few hours before the amphibious landing actually began, the Naval Support Group did shell once again, and periodic airstrikes battered the island as well.

The chart below was taken from the war diaries of the various major warships present. However, their D-Day shell expenditure figures vary significantly from General Geiger's report. According to that report, the ammo fired at Peleliu—Admiral Fort's ammo expenditure report listed in his war diary for September, 1944 is nearly identical to these numbers—is as follows:

Estimated total preliminary bombardment expenditures at Peleliu

Size & Caliber	Shell Type	D-3	D-2	D-1	D-Day	Total
16"/45	HC	173	173	173	295	814
14"/50	HC	615	615	615	917	2,762
8"/55	HC	476	475	476	932	2,359
6"/47	HC	340	340	340	1,004	2,024
5"/51	Com	200	200	200	420	1,020
5"/51	HC	510	510	510	599	2,089
5"/38	Com	56	15	6	79	156
5"/38	AA	2,195	2,195	1,795	4,878	11,063
5"/38	Ill	-	-	75	325	400
5"/38	WP	-	-	-	1,362	1,362
5"/38	RV	-	-	-	1,200	1,200
5"/25	AA	1,490	1,490	1,490	3,554	
5"/25	Com	255	177	155	633	1,220
5"/25	Ill	15	21	27	43	96

Includes HC (high capacity, for lightly-armored targets), Com (common, for general purpose), RV (Reduced Velocity), Ill (Illuminating/star shell) and WP (white phosphorus)).

Geiger's report further states though, that a total of 1,406 tons of ammo was fired at Peleliu on D-Day, in the following breakdown:

- 16-inch shells: 240   *Maryland*
- 14-inch shells: 960   *Pennsylvania, Mississippi. Idaho*
- 8-inch shells: 480   *Louisville, Portland, Indianapolis*
- 6-inch shells: 1,220   *Honolulu*
- 5-inch shells   8,800   all

The shelling of the island was considered by some to have been somewhat lackadaisical, the amount of shells fired notwithstanding. Typically, the shelling would begin around sunrise at 0530 and would end just after sunset at 1830. However, the firing was not what one today might consider steady. The warships for the most part used spotter planes to observe the fall of shot and then radio corrections to the ship. These planes took time to launch and later to recover. During this down time, the shelling would always be suspended. The action reports of each of the eight major warships show several periods each day of no firing, sometimes for a few hours. On D-1 for instance, the *Maryland* and the *Pennsylvania* ceased firing at 1254 and did not begin again until 1600.

Furthermore, the war diaries support this. They indicate that the old battleships fired in tandem teams. Fire Team Able (*Maryland* and *Pennsylvania*) would shell the island for a few hours, and then Fire Team Baker (*Idaho* and *Mississippi*) would take over for a few more.

This would suggest that Oldendorf's decision to disburse the two days of scheduled ordnance over the preliminary three days that the Navy had agreed upon was carried out. A more telling bit of evidence to that effect though, is in two log entries that Rear Admiral Ruddock (commander, Battleship Division 4) made on September 14:

> 0606 – (Visual) PENNSYLVANIA and MARYLAND from CBD-4. Ammunition allowance this phase—remnants from previous schedule plus 25% D-1 Day allowance.
> 0630 – (TBS) CBD 4, MARYLAND, PENNSYLVANIA from CTG 32.5. Your prompt and efficient action on my bombardment request appreciated.

In each of the three preliminary days, after darkness fell, sporadic fire from a few destroyers would harass some of the enemy positions, but this for the most part was light and targeted against only several areas on the island. Thus every evening, the Japanese would have time to assess the intentions of the Americans, to repair or cover positions that had been hit, and to continue constructing or expanding hidden positions in anticipation of the upcoming landing.

So while the shelling did go on for all three days, the intensity of the fire was understandably considered by the Marines to be less than stellar. This is again because the Navy, while it had given in to a three-day bombardment period, did not resolve to fire a full three days of shells. Oldendorf evidently had decided all along on this decision, mostly because of the shortage of ordnance. Ruddock mentioned this factor in his after-action report:

> Perhaps, if more ships and more ammunition had been available, areas more remote from the landing beaches might have been neutralized, and thus all enemy gun and mortar fire directed on the landing beaches from the hills might have been prevented.

Because of the upcoming Philippines invasion and the issue of wear and tear on the larger guns, the amount of shells fired was to a substantial degree determined beforehand by these restricting factors. Added to that was the generally accepted belief by most senior officers that this operation would be quick and that the casualties would not be heavy. This view was furthered (and in some minds confirmed) when the pre-invasion shelling took place. The seeming lack of enemy presence, (despite the intelligence reports of some 10,000 Japanese troops on the island), the relatively few identified defensive positions, and the absence of enemy counterfire seemed to substantiate this common estimation (and, no doubt, fervent hope).

Another factor here might perhaps have played a crucial role in the sequence of events that was triggered by Halsey's message two days before to Nimitz recommending that the Peleliu invasion be canceled. Nimitz in his response had ultimately decided to continue with the landing, but in a series of messages between CinCPac and MacArthur the next day, it was agreed that Halsey's assessment of the Philippines was valid. The Leyte invasion would therefore be moved up two months, from December 20 to October 20. If Admiral Fort and/or Admiral Oldendorf were copied on these messages, it is logical that Oldendorf, no doubt surprised by the change, would have concluded that he now had two fewer months to prepare for the huge Leyte invasion. Instead of about 13 weeks to replenish his ordnance and to undertake whatever maintenance was needed on his warships, he would have less than a month after the Peleliu operation to be ready for MacArthur's big push, and to have enough ammo for whatever response would come from the Imperial Japanese Fleet. Taking into account the concerns about wear and tear on the guns, Oldendorf would have realized that from now on, every shot fired by his battleships and cruisers would have to count. Seemingly needlessly firing at unseen (and perhaps unlikely) targets that might be hidden deep in foliage would not be useful to the overall war effort in this theater.

One last factor that came to Oldendorf's attention was regarding a number of reports of large numbers of dud ricochets of the heavier caliber shells which had been observed. The *Pennsylvania* reported one every two or three salvos. One heavy cruiser reported as many as 80 percent were ricochets. Admiral Ainsworth later wrote in his report of the NGS planning:

> The Task Unit Commander again recommends that the pro-assault bombardment phase be as long as practicable, commensurate with the other elements of surprise, *enemy opposition in the objective area*, and *other essential considerations* [my emphasis]. This does not necessarily mean that the total ammunition expended in the pre-assault bombardment be increased. It does mean, however, that ammunition can be expended to better advantage, and that enemy guns and installations can be definitely checked off as destroyed.
>
> The procedure for accomplishing this should be by successive observations of the same targets, both by aerial reconnaissance and aerial photography on successive days ...

General Geiger was probably not made aware of the ordnance compromise until just before the landing. In the naval gunfire section of the general's action report on the operation, dated October 24, 1944, Major W. M. Gilliam, his naval gunfire officer, commented on his behalf: "A longer period for preliminary operations against both objectives [Peleliu and Angaur], especially PELELIU, would have been highly profitable." His recommendation for subsequent operations was: "That a period of at least a week or ten days be allowed for preliminary operations against an island as heavily defended as PELELIU."

Another point was that although the warships were using spotter aircraft for the shellings, and despite the fact that there was no counterfire from the enemy ashore, the larger vessels themselves were firing from appreciable distances. None of them fired any closer than 3¾ miles out, and a good part of the shelling from the heavy cruisers and battleships was as far out as eight miles.

Still, regardless of the Navy's shelling procedures and times, many targets were never hit or even fired upon, simply because they were never identified. And since the enemy refused to return fire at the warships, it seemed to the Americans that most of the island's defenders had either escaped to one of the northern islands or had been killed.

One of these undamaged, critical positions was the jutting promontory land just to the left of Beach White-1. Colonel Puller had of course, realized before the invasion the tremendous significance of The Point's position to his landing area. In a final conference aboard Oldendorf's flagship just before D-Day, he had expressly requested that the Navy specifically saturate the entire position with heavy fire, even though no enemy positions there had been detected. However, the shelling there as it turned out was viewed by the Marine officers as being wholly inadequate, which resulted in heavy Marine casualties that first morning. Sadly, so many of them could have been avoided, because when the Marines finally (and urgently) requested that the Navy target another blockhouse on D+1, the 14-inch guns of the old USS *Mississippi* and a supporting cruiser, having been given accurate grid referencing by the Marines, within an hour took out the blockhouse and the surrounding pillbox positions.

Thus, as the first wave of Marines chugged toward the beaches on D-Day, even though the Navy that morning had given them another two hours or so of preliminary shelling and was now giving them cover fire, the senior naval officers were wholly unaware that a good many of the enemy positions, most of them never spotted or identified, were never affected by the naval shelling or the air attacks. Even Oldendorf was stunned when he saw on the morning of D-Day sudden, concentrated fire commence from many concealed and undamaged enemy batteries; in his same letter of March 1950, he wrote:

> The preliminary bombardment was, I thought at the time, one of the most thorough that could be devised considering the lack of intelligence concerning enemy strong points. The pre-landing gunfire support was, I thought, superior to anything which had been put on heretofore. My surprise and chagrin when concealed batteries opened up on the LVTS can be imagined.

Admiral Ainsworth in his action report stated something similar:

> During the movement of the assault waves to the beaches, a tremendous bombardment by ships and aircraft was laid down. This was so heavy that it was hard to conceive that anyone in the vicinity of the beaches could live through it. Nevertheless, when our first waves reached

---

* According to one report, the Navy for all three days fired 519 rounds of 16-inch, 1,845 14-inch, 1,427 rounds of 8-inch, 1,020 rounds of 6-inch, and 12,937 rounds of 5-inch shells, making a total of 17,745 shells, about 2,255 tons of ammunition. (Garand & Strobridge p.103)

the beaches, they were met by small arms fire from enemy personnel who had returned to the beach areas when the bombardment was lifted.

Even a couple days after D-Day, Rear Admiral John W. Reeves, who would lead the development in future base development in the Western Caroline Islands, was also shocked at what he saw when he came ashore. The carnage that the Japanese had managed to wreak on the Marines would leave a lasting impression on his mind.

Oldendorf though, considered that he had done his job. In his letter, he added:

> Under these circumstances, no matter how many shells you fire, or their caliber, you cannot destroy enemy gun emplacements on an island the size of Peleliu, unless the enemy will oblige by disclosing the position of his guns … The best that can be done is to blast away at suspected positions and hope for the best.

In support of Oldendorf's actions, Admiral Fort, in a letter to Marine Corps historian Major Hough, written about the same time as Oldendorf's letter of 1950, completely agreed with and justified any decision Oldendorf might have made to either curtail the intensity of the bombardment, or to cancel that third day's shelling altogether. He claimed that the identified targets seemed to them to have been destroyed, and that:

> The original plan was for two days' bombardment at Peleliu, which was subsequently increased to three. Whereas this increase permitted somewhat more deliberate bombardment, it did not increase the weight of metal in the slightest. The same amount of ammunition was to have been used in the originally scheduled two days as was subsequently used in three.

Still, although Fort supported Oldendorf in his actions, he does not seem sure about the suspension of the third day's shelling, because he adds:

> If Admiral Oldendorf broke off fire before he had used up his allowed ammunition on the grounds that there were no more targets, he was entirely correct. The idea which some people seem to have of just firing at an island is an inexcusable waste of ammunition.

At least one of the Marine senior officers agreed with him. Colonel William Harrison, commanding the 11th Marines, later wrote that he doubted "whether 10 times the gunfire would have helped. No doubt, nearly all of the rest of the experienced Marines that landed there strongly disagreed. Also, various U.S. Army artillery techniques revolving around the concepts of indirect fire and fire for effect tactics that were developed around this time would argue against Fort's claims. Needless to say that the role and tactics used in pre-landing bombardments for amphibious warfare, based upon experiences such as Peleliu, Normandy, Iwo Jima, and Okinawa, have been argued for decades since.

The Marines eventually had to destroy all these positions individually, taking heavy casualties in doing so. This was to become even more difficult after some of Oldendorf's ships eventually departed to join MacArthur's force for the moved-up invasion of the Philippines (though at least one battleship, four cruisers, five destroyers, and 12 LCIs remained through the Angaur operation).

General Geiger, in his operations report of the invasion, dated October 24, 1944, in his summary of the naval bombardment, wrote:

> It seems no longer questionable that naval gunfire is capable of making the beach areas selected for a landing practically untenable for the defense. However, it still remains a fact that naval guns cannot search defiladed areas, nor can they effectively destroy or neutralize mobile artillery or mortars. Therefore, one must guard against the overenthusiasm of naval gunfire advocates who believe that nothing can survive the heavy preliminary bombardments.

Two historians of amphibious warfare, Isely and Crowl, concurred, later writing that:

> the conclusion cannot be avoided that preliminary naval gunfire on Peleliu was inadequate, and that the lessons learned at Guam were overlooked. Guam had demonstrated without shadow of doubt that slow, prolonged, and deliberate naval bombardment could accomplish amazing results even against a strong, well-equipped, and determined enemy force. Peleliu, like Tarawa and to a lesser extent Saipan, demonstrated that the only substitute for such prolonged bombardment was the costly expenditure of the lives of the assault troops.

Even afterwards, the Navy did not at first see the implications of the inadequacies of the shorter preliminary bombardment. In his review of the operation in COMINCH bulletin #23, Nimitz's chief of staff, Admiral C. M. Cooke Jr., acknowledged:

> During the short time allowed for these preliminary operations, only the more obvious targets could be covered, and by DOG Day and FOX Day, many of the enemy installations remained intact." However, he then goes on to state that: "The initial bombardments succeeded in their primary purposes, which were to reduce coastal defense guns and beach installations and to make possible the landings themselves without serious casualties.

At least one admiral though, had a different opinion. Rear Admiral T. D. Ruddock in his after action report, although he reported that the bombardment had been effective (despite all the main battery ricochets), added:

> Perhaps, if more ships and more ammunition had been available, areas more remote from the landing beaches might have been neutralized, and thus all enemy gun and mortar fire directed on the landing beaches from the hills might have been prevented.

NGS—Lessons Learned

Among the many lessons that the Navy did learn from this operation, two critical ones stand out. First, for a number of reasons already discussed, their pre-invasion bombardments and tactical air bombings were not nearly as effective as predicted they would be, especially when undertaken over just a few days. Second, in keeping with a rudimentary tenet of warfare, a naval force that is stretched too thin could invite failure in one or more locations, as this one did.

The action report of the First Marine Division written after the campaign, thoroughly (as one might imagine) examined the shortcomings of the bombardment, and subsequent call fire missions, which sometimes went unanswered or were never undertaken, usually because the support vessels could not be reached by radio. In the report, several recommendations were given.

1. **Longer preliminaries.** A much longer pre-invasion bombardment period would need to be assigned for future, similar amphibious operations, along with much larger amounts of tonnage in ordnance to be fired. Ngesebus Island in comparison to Peleliu, was worked over for five days before the 5th Marines landed, and when they did, resistance was minimal (although of course, there were few high ridges from which the enemy could hunker down in).

2. **Better Preliminary Bombardment Planning.** Several naval reports detailed the difficulty the warships had throughout the operation in identifying or even spotting the enemy targets. This of course was because of the enemy's excellent use of camouflage or intervening foliage. Another factor was the position of the target relative to that of the warship. All the naval officers realized that the ability to pinpoint the enemy positions was critical to the success of the shelling. The reports that were submitted therefore included four specific recommendations:
   – Increased use of low-altitude spotting planes in communication with the warship, and that they be on the same radio frequency as shore fire control parties. Radio coordination on call fire missions was often a problem. Only on rare occasions did a spotter plane for a warship and a fire control party operate on the same frequency.
   – Each warship be given the same regularly assigned target area from one day to the next. This would better allow both the gunnery team and the spotting aircraft crew to become better familiar with the area being shot

at, especially on subsequent fire missions. It was also pointed out that valuable target information and geographical characteristics be passed on from one warship to the one relieving it, so long as the information was not too voluminous or confusing.

– Improved, closer shelling patterns for each warship. This would minimize each having to fire at grids that were far apart from each other.

– For preliminary bombardments or selection for call fire missions, that the warship have improved firing positions as close to the target as possible, to still be "consistent with navigational safety."

3. **Longer ranges for main batteries**. Balanced against the advantage of the last bullet point was the effectiveness of naval gunfire against the enemy's well-prepared tunnel network. The flat trajectory of the naval shells, especially when fired from under 7,000 yards, simply had little effect on anything except a cave's entrance, and even then the damage was usually minimal. Too many times, because of the angle of descent and the wet foliage from the occasional showers, the shell would simply ricochet off the ground and go careening off in another direction. The only clue to such an occurrence was the lack of explosion at the target. It was only on D-1 that the ground became dry enough for the observers to see a dust cloud at the spot where the shell impacted the ground.

The report of Rear Admiral Ruddock recommended that longer ranges be given for large-caliber shells. The many ricochets, he reasoned, were the result of the wet ground and the relatively short distances the shells traveled (which of course, made for flatter trajectories). At one time, it was observed that 80 percent of the shells being fired by one of the heavy cruisers were ricocheting off the ground. Longer ranges with higher-angle trajectories seemed to be the answer. This would minimize the number of duds hitting the target areas.

4. **Closer NGS fire to the first wave**. Admiral Ainsworth felt that the reason the first waves were met with such intense enemy fire was because in the time that the Marines negotiated the barrier reef and traveled to the shore, there was no naval gunfire support, in order for the ships to not accidently hit one of the incoming craft. This, Ainsworth felt, gave the Japanese plenty of time to come out of their caves and move into forward defensive positions. He therefore recommended that: "in planning for future assault operations on beaches protected by an outlying reef such as this one, naval gunfire be continued until the troops approach the actual beach itself. This

recommendation is made with full knowledge that the heavy smoke over the beach areas makes accurate control of fire difficult in the extreme."

This recommendation though, was turned down by Ainsworth's superiors. Oldendorf (CTG-32.5) did not comment on the recommendation, but Fort (CTF-32) wrote that the practice was based upon his own attack order (A502–44). It stated that main batteries over 5-inches would cease shelling when the first wave was a thousand yards from the shore, and 5-inch or below would cease when the first waves were 300 yards off. Admiral Wilkinson (CTF-31) concurred, adding: "The plan for lifting gunfire upon the approach of the first boat wave to the beach is in practice and is considered doctrine."

5. **Marine Naval Gunfire Liaison Officer (NGLO).** While each Marine rifle regiment and battalion had a naval officer assigned to it as its designated NGLO, the Marines had no NGLO of their own in the division to better coordinate call fire missions between the battalions and the warships. The report recommended that select artillery officers in the division be trained in the naval gunfire process and assigned to division headquarters.

6. **Navy NGLOs.** It was recommended that additional NGLOs should also be assigned to each Joint Assault Signal Company (JASCO).

7. **Radio reliability.** Each JASCO team should be given a better, more reliable radio. The divisional and regimental teams on Peleliu used the large TBX—Navy code designator for "semi-portable radio equipment of low power"—ship-to-shore radios. With a range of 15 miles, it was reliable, and ideal to operate in larger command posts. It could be used for both CW (Morse code) messages at 9 watts, and for voice communications at 3 watts. It was though, classified as a semi-portable radio, and its size limited where it could be taken and used. It required at least three men to carry the entire assembly: one for the 29lb transceiver, one to carry the 25lb hand-cranked 500-volt portable generator and the antenna, and one to carry the 31lb battery and accessory box. The entire assembly also needed at least 15 minutes to set up. Furthermore, the TBX was found to be more susceptible to water and weather, and the batteries had a short life.

It was recommended that the SCR-694 model (set complete radio, model 694) replace the TBX. The SCR-694 was more of a field radio. Much lighter at only about 20 pounds, although it was usually set on the ground to be used, it was more versatile that the larger TBX, and could be used closer to the requesting unit. Some three dozen sets were delivered to the Marines as they left for Peleliu as spares, and fortunately, with so many dozens of radios lost or inoperable during the earlier days of the landing, they became a godsend.

Most of the battalion and company units used the SCR-536, the traditional infantry "walkie-talkie." It was a hand-held radio, and, at only five pounds, it was convenient and easier to carry around. Its range though, was under a mile, and it was more unreliable in the jungle. Thus, making contact with vessels offshore or even units close by was often difficult. It was recommended that the SCR-300 model replace the SCR-536, which was found by the men to be unreliable. By comparison, the SCR-300 was carried as a backpack, and though it weighed about 35lb, it had a reliable range of three miles and was more dependable in tropical warfare, partly because it was an FM transceiver, as opposed to the other's lower-quality AM transmissions.

8. **NGS Marine coordinators**. The report stressed that Marine liaison officers must be assigned to the NGS forces during the shelling periods.

9. **Pre-invasion coordination conferences**. One or more pre-invasion conferences should be held between NGS gunnery officers and Marine forward observers.

10. **NGS replacement plan**. It had been previously decided that if an NGS warship on station for call fire missions had to withdraw to replenish ammo, that another vessel come on station to take its place before it left. Several times in the operation this did not transpire, when the fire warship withdrew without being replaced.

11. **Naval gunfire during air sorties**. NGS during the operation was always suspended whenever an airstrike began, so that the attacking aircraft would not be hit by shells. It was recommended that this practice "be the exception rather than the general rule."

12. **Patrol firing discretion**. Whenever picket vessels spotted any enemy barges coming in at night from Ngesebus and Kongauru islands to the northeast, they would have to radio the command ship and request permission to fire on them. A few times, by the time the permission to fire came, the barges had all but landed the enemy reinforcements. It was recommended that such picket vessels be allowed to commence firing independently, and without obtaining prior permission.

13. **Call fire missions.** The issue of call fire missions was addressed as well, a problem that had occurred on previous landings. For instance, Holland Smith after the war wrote of the Tarawa invasion: "If the Marines had received better cooperation from the Navy, our casualties would have been lower. More naval gunfire would have saved many lives. I had to beg for gunfire, and I rarely received what the situation called for." Although this issue was better handled for the Peleliu operation, there were nevertheless many instance where call fire missions were desperately needed, but the Marines had no way to contact the appropriate warships for the task.

14. **Improved starshell patterns.** Another important lesson learned was the value of starshells at night. Many a Marine gave thanks to the occasional (although spotty due to a lack of such ammo) night illumination given to them by the Navy, for even in the dark, it often allowed them to see their enemy stealthily approaching. General Geiger wrote: "One of the greatest factors in support of the ground forces after a foothold has been obtained ashore is adequate night illumination. Naval vessels are admirably equipped for this and proved invaluable on this operation. However, too frequently illumination must be curtailed to conserve the available stars. It is recommended that the allowance of stars for vessels supporting amphibious operations be increased."

15. **Better, more timely bomb-damage assessment.** Admiral Ainsworth recommended that assessing damage on a target would be improved by more timely observation using photos. That way "the bombardment group may well expend a limited amount of ammunition on a given objective, then shift to another target, pending receipt of photographs as to the results obtained. Should the target not then be destroyed, the ship could return the next day and ensure destruction, rather than expend a large amount the first day without being certain of the results achieved."

Fort in his endorsement of Ainsworth's report concurred. He also added the recommendation that each battleship and cruiser in the bombardment have its own portable cameras and developing/printing equipment onboard. That way, the spotting planes could take on the spot photos of the damage incurred and have the images immediately developed, so that the gunnery officers could determine how effectively the target had been hit.

Other valuable naval lessons were observed as well. Geiger's report on the operation stressed the importance of the role the DUKWs played in the operation, despite the fact that they too, like the LVTs, had to negotiate the wide barrier reef:

> These amphibious vehicles were of equal importance with the LVTs in successfully prosecuting the operation. They are astonishingly seaworthy and, when under a competent driver, are exceptionally well adapted to landing through the surf. There were days when these vehicles were the only ones available and capable of moving supplies ashore or of evacuating casualties to ships.

The Marines also realized that, regarding the mines at Peleliu, they had been lucky. Most had either not been properly armed or installed, were defective, had been rendered inoperable because of the weather or surf, or had been cleared by minesweepers or UDTs. For that reason alone, most were not destroyed, defused, or cleared for days. Which was just as well, because there many had been laid, and Geiger wisely concluded that in future operations they would encounter such large concentrations. To that end, he recommended that strong minesweeping operations be factored into the plan.

Unfortunately, some issues were fogged in the after reports of the senior officers. Fort's war diary has quite a number of contradictions and inaccuracies. For instance, he stated that the operation was carried out under "prevailing excellent weather" that remained so for the first two weeks of the operation. Yet in another section of his report, where he listed the daily weather conditions from September 14, only four of the entries did not list showers or rain in the summary. And, in still another section, he described heavy rain on September 22, and from September 28 to 30.

Another discrepancy in his report was about the controversial NGS preliminary bombardment. He summarized:

> The bombardments prior to DOG and FOX Days were well handled and thorough. Those on DOG Day and FOX Days were devastating. The naval gunfire support and air support both at PELELIU and ANGAUR were to the satisfaction of all commands ... All existing structures were shelled and completely destroyed beyond any use to the enemy.

Perhaps the last word though, comes from Oldendorf himself, who wrote five years after the war:

> if military leaders (including naval) were gifted with the same accuracy of foresight that they are with hindsight, undoubtedly the assault and capture of the Palaus would never have been attempted.

Airpower

The Navy's preliminary tactical airstrikes were not nearly as effective as originally thought. They had first raided the airfields in early March when Mitscher's TF-58 had pursued the Japanese fleet fleeting out of Truk and down to the Palaus. There, Mitscher's carrier planes had for two days also devastated and taken out the airfields on Peleliu and Angaur islands, as well as many Japanese support vessels in the area. Later that month, carrier raids were conducted against the Palaus to support MacArthur's operations in New Guinea. Peleliu was hit again in June and July in support of the Marianas invasions. Three days of intensive air raids prefaced the Peleliu invasion starting on September 6, and four days later, Task Group 38.4, consisting of two carriers and two light carriers, hit the island again on September 10 and 11 (D-5 and D-6). Then arriving with Admiral Oldendorf's gunfire support fleet was Rear Admiral Ralph Ofstie's Escort Carrier Group, TG-31.2, consisting of 11 escort carriers,* 13 destroyers, and four destroyer escorts.

From D-3 through D-Day, the naval air sorties totaled 916: 330 fighters (F6F Hellcats and F4U Corsairs rockets, strafing), 264 dive-bombers (SB2C Helldivers), and 322 tactical bombers (modified TBF Avengers with rockets, strafing, bombing). A total of 507.6 tons of bombs and rockets were released in that time, including some 25 tons of napalm.

Although the tactical bombings had the potential of doing extensive damage to the enemy, they failed to do so. One reason was many of the inland defensive positions were not visible from the air. They were too well hidden and camouflaged. In fact, the bombs and napalm dropped by the Navy planes nearly benefited the enemy as much as it did the assaulting forces, because the explosions and burning did a good deal of clearing away trees and other jungle foliage obstructing the defenders' views. The Marines coming ashore would be easier to target.

Another problem was that in many instances, the strafing runs were conducted at too high an altitude and at too steep an attack angle (mostly by the naval aviators). The main reason for this was because the Navy pilots had been so trained. Another reason though, was because a significant portion of

---

* Escort carriers (CVE), also called jeep carriers, were smaller versions of the fleet carriers (CV) that normally conducted battle against the Japanese Navy. An escort carrier typically was about half the length and a third the displacement of a fleet carrier and carried about 26 aircraft instead of the latter's complement of 90. While escort carriers were typically much slower than the fleet carriers or the mid-sized light carriers (CVL), they were easy to construct in quantity and could fill the gap between the front and rear areas. Thus, they were typically tasked with convoy escort, air support for amphibious landings, and ferrying aircraft from rear areas to the front. About 150 were constructed during the war.

the ordnance had a high detonation factor, making a low-level strafe risky. General Geiger, himself formerly a Marine aviator, recommended that the pilots be trained in jungle attacks, and that strafing runs

> should be delivered ... from a shallow dive. Also, bombs should be dropped in sticks from a glide in similar direction; the bombs to be so fused as to permit their release at a low altitude without endangering the plane.

He also recommended that the bomb fuses, which for the Navy had been set at instantaneous or one-second delay, be set in such conditions at between three and five seconds.

It is worth noting that the Navy also learned from Peleliu that the tactical air support given in the first phase of the landing was not as effective as in the second phase. In Phase 1, conducted by the Marines, the tactical bombings were undertaken by naval aviators from offshore carriers, trained at their jobs of hitting land targets, but not nearly as much so as their successors. In Phase 2, Marine aviators provided the ground units with air support right off the captured airfield. These airmen had been specifically trained in taking out fortified Japanese bunkers and were more qualified in that field that their naval counterparts. In addition, flying from the island itself, their mission times were substantially shorter, sometimes no longer than a couple minutes.

While air sorties from both naval and Marine tactical aircraft proved to be effective against the enemy on relatively level ground, most of the airstrikes were found to be largely ineffective against deeply dug tunnels and caves, which nearly always had a sharp turn just past the entrance, making even a direct-hit explosion mostly ineffective. Napalm though, often proved successful, and the flames and intensive heat from thousands of gallons dropped on the enemy helped to take out dozens of positions.

Perhaps as troubling as ineffective airstrikes were against the dug-in positions was the lack of accuracy they had compared to direct fire weapons from short distances. As trained as the pilots might be in such sorties, whether the ordnance landed exactly on target was often a matter of speculation, especially for napalm drops. At such times, even the Marines would hunker down whenever a bomber flew in for a drop, especially in a tight boxed-in area, because they worried (often legitimately) that the death from the skies might very well find them instead of the Japanese.

A Different Enemy Strategy

The new Japanese strategy implemented for island defense was an unsettling development to U.S. planners and caught them all by surprise. Unrestrained frontal *banzai* suicide attacks against the beachhead, which had been seen at Guadalcanal and Tarawa, had been determined by the Japanese to be too costly and through sheer need, this type of proactive defense had to be replaced by a different style—one of hunkered-down resistance. Instead of mass charges, enemy counterattacks were now mostly limited to small nightly infiltration attacks; instead, the Japanese had developed more improved methods of using the terrain for defensive position, especially around the mountains. This also was a direct result of their resolution to minimize their losses from direct and by now omnipresent and overwhelming preliminary U.S. naval gunfire. Only a little over 2,000 Japanese and conscripted islanders were tasked with directly repulsing the landing and defending the airstrip. The other 12,000 or so were ordered to stay in the caves and bunkers on the rest of the island and conduct a vigorous, stubborn defense.

The enemy's new style of defense was the major reason the Peleliu operation was drawn out for so long. In this less proactive type of come-get-us defense, the Japanese, lacking command of the sea and the air, made excellent use of well-entrenched positions, natural barriers, and a large number of interconnected caves and other such developed underground positions that honeycombed the island. The entrances were reinforced and supported by blast walls and oil drums filled with coral and stone. Some entrances even had reinforced plate doors that could be opened and closed to allow the Japanese to wheel out an artillery piece, fire a few rounds, and then wheel it back into the cave.

This new type of defensive strategy was termed *fukkakku* tactics by the Japanese; a defensive term that refers to "underground, honeycombed defensive positions," it is based on the predominant translation interpretation, "using multi-connected castle walls." This strategy had first proven successful on Tarawa. It would later be used even more effectively at Iwo Jima and Okinawa.

There were several exceptions to the new strategy on a tactical level. Many times, the Japanese ventured from their caves, especially at night, to harass or counterattack locally. There were many instances on Peleliu where they made frontal counterattacks on the Marines, but these were nearly all at night, and on a limited scale. The most notable exception to this was on D-Day, when elements of the Japanese 1st Battalion, 2nd Infantry Regiment and the light tank company of the 14th Division made that coordinated though ill-fated armor–infantry counterattack in the late afternoon against the 1st Marines and 5th Marines across the northern part of the airfield. Even this counterattack though, had not been carried out in the traditional *banzai* style so common in the past. Rather, it was planned, coordinated, and executed more methodically than previous-style, all-out charges, although it was improperly timed and for various reasons met with failure. These types of counterattacks, although infrequent and on a smaller scale than in previous operations, would typify the enemy's new strategy. Colonel Nakagawa, who commanded the Japanese crack 2nd Infantry Regiment on the island, was following the new plan. They were going to make their last-stand defense in well-protected, heavily fortified, concealed caves and tunnels located on the high, sharp ridges, and not at the shoreline.

Strategically, the Japanese stuck to the plan. They remained in sheltered pillboxes, tunnels, and caves, especially in the Umurbrogol ridges. These positions were well constructed, with entrances sloping upward and blast walls and sharp turns just inside the opening to thwart direct fire, grenades, and flamethrowers. Nearly all of them were amply provisioned and most had some sort of emergency exit. The enemy remained in these protected positions—some estimates put the number of Japanese caves and bunkers at over 500—and later might emerge, take up other entrenched positions, and conduct hit-and-run assaults.

General Geiger addressed this in his after action report. He recommended that for future operations, the Marines should be given stronger educational classes on this new type of enemy defense. He stressed the importance of giving classes and hands-on training in demolitions and bomb disposal, especially to the combat engineers and even to the infantry. He even suggested that a special panel of experts be created to study in detail this new enemy strategy, and how it had been used in the last few amphibious operations in the Marianas, and especially at Peleliu.

Communications

Communication failure between units became another critical drawback for the Marines. Almost half the problems arose simply due to enemy fire. Underway and headed toward the beachhead on D-Day, all five amtracs that were carrying the entire headquarters unit of the 1st Marines, including radio operators and equipment, took direct hits while crossing the coral reef and were all destroyed. The LVT that carried the communications equipment for the 3rd Battalion, 5th Marines suffered a similar fate. To complicate the 1st Marines' communications problem further, their command post took a direct hit from an artillery shell soon after it had been set up (Fortunately, Colonel Puller had already departed, headed for the front line). Also, late in the day, around 1830, an accurately fired shell took out a number of senior officers and communications at the 3/5 headquarters.

On the morning of September 16, communication problems were to continue, as the networks suffered damage from indirect enemy fire. A lucky hit by a Japanese artillery shell took out the 5th Marines field telephone switchboard, compounded by another hit a short time later on the regiment's command post.

Further communications problems stemmed from the mobile radios that the infantry units carried. Those that made it ashore without getting hit or waterlogged were difficult to use in the first few hours because of the incessant, high level of surrounding noise from both incoming and outgoing fire. This was probably irrelevant, because many of these radios often failed to work at all.

This breakdown was exemplified by the problems that the unit commanders and FiST* communicators experienced with the SR-536 walkie-talkie (cynically dubbed a "spam can"). The main form of communication used on the Marine front lines, it not only had a short range, but was also notoriously unreliable, especially in thick jungle. Thus getting in touch with even a nearby unit was at times impossible, especially if there was any type of foliage in between. Units were therefore forced to use runners, who of course, would have to dart back and forth under enemy fire. One company commander, under constant heavy crossfire, became increasingly frustrated, as he could not get his walkie-talkie to work. Finally, he angrily grabbed it and pitched it onto the coral rocks below. Many still were not calibrated correctly, although that problem had mostly been corrected during the August 27 dress rehearsal.

Those that did work well were used steadily all day, and as a result, by evening, some of the radio batteries had already gone dead. Unfortunately, many of the replacement batteries had either been lost at sea on the way to the beachhead, were already spent, or were lying in stacked crates on the shoreline.

There were a number of problems experienced with the landline field telephone communications as well. Typically used by Marine units in the Pacific were the EE-8-A and TBX field telephones. Range varied with the size as well as the type of wire used. While the use of field phones substantially improved command coordination with forward units and with fire support from artillery batteries or with the warships offshore, this contact tool was cumbersome and too fragile a setup to be consistently reliable. Phone units taking a direct hit aside, the network had a weak link: the phone wires

---

* Fire Support Team, a component of a rifle company or battalion used to coordinate heavy weapons support to the unit. Examples included artillery forward observer (Arty FO) or 81mm mortar forward observer (81s FO).

The SR-536 walkie-talkie, unreliable in a jungle environment.

themselves. The act of laying down the wires, especially while getting shot at, was a challenge in itself, and the wires usually had to be strung along the ground. Worse though was that once these lines had been strung or laid, they then became vulnerable to damage by a multitude of causes: vehicles running over them in congested beach areas, men tripping over them as they rushed forward, incoming artillery or mortar fire, and in forward areas quietly getting cut at night by infiltrating Japanese.

Another communications innovation that did not perform as well as hoped was an experimental communications center. An LVT(A) was set up with radio equipment and was to function as a mobile radio station ashore. Sardonically christened the USS *Fubar*—"F**ked up beyond all recognition"—it worked well enough for emergency transmissions, and ADO Smith was able to use it to a degree on D-Day to communicate with several units ashore and afloat. Again, a good part of the failure was the inability of the wiremen to set up and maintain wires to the unit, especially since the entire area was under fire, and because the wires themselves were too vulnerable to work effectively in combat.

Communication difficulty was one factor that contributed to another basic problem: preliminary organization after the landing. Even when enemy fire onto the beachhead finally diminished, creating coherency among the units was difficult, even after the fighting had shifted inland. One source referred to the landing area as a "battlefield junkyard," strewn with the debris of broken tree stumps, shattered trunks and branches, burning hulks of wrecked amtracs, piles of supplies, ammunition crates, dead bodies and body parts, vehicles moving back and forth, and medics evacuating the wounded. Just getting around the narrow beach was not easy, especially since the area was under intermittent indirect fire from enemy mortars and artillery. Because of this and the thick underbrush, platoons spreading out inland often became separated from each other because of enemy fire, the hilly terrain and jungle growth. Isolated, they became vulnerable to enemy counterfire and infiltration attacks.

Command Failure

Many historians have argued that one of the largest contributing factors to the high numbers of casualties in this campaign should be directly attributed to the Marine division's commanding officer himself, General Rupertus. His generally conceded command errors throughout the entire operation were numerous. His release of the RCT reserve before Peleliu was secured was one. Again, Rupertus's stubborn insistence that his division could quickly take the island, coupled to his disdain for the Army, was a considerable part to blame for his poor performance. Indeed, late on the afternoon of September 16, the Army's 323rd RCT, slated as a backup to the Marines, was released by him and given the okay to go ahead and take part in the Angaur landing the next morning.

It should be mentioned that opposing the original 17 September date for the Angaur landing had been General Julian Smith, Geiger's superior and predecessor as the III Amphibious Corps' operational commander. Smith argued that releasing the RCT before the Peleliu operation was more developed would be premature. His advice though was ignored by Vice Admiral Theodore S. Wilkinson, commander of Task Force 31, and the entire joint expeditionary force. Wilkinson instead approved the release of the 323rd.

Another critical tactical mistake was Rupertus's decision of sending the remaining elements of the 1st Tank Battalion home, along with the battered 1st Marines at the beginning of October (remember, only a portion of the battalion had taken part in the operation due to transport constraints). One Marine later wrote:

> My guess is that the 1st Tank battalion was relieved not because the men were "badly depleted and debilitated"—the official reason given—but because the machines were wore out or needed overhauling and maintenance, but men were expected to keep going. Tanks, amtracs, trucks, aircraft, and ships were considered valuable and difficult to replace way out in the Pacific. They were maintained carefully and not exposed needlessly to wear or destruction. Men, infantrymen in particular, were simply expected to keep going beyond the limits of human endurance until they got killed or wounded or dropped from exhaustion.

A substantial part of Rupertus's reasoning was the nature of the island's terrain. The right side had been secured, and what remained were the spines and ridges of the Umurbrogol range. It seemed to him that the Shermans would probably not be able to maneuver there, or be of much used to the riflemen. He evidently still did not appreciate how valuable an asset the tanks had become to the riflemen in ferreting out the enemy and in neutralizing the caves and tunnels. Their firepower was also useful in moving up to the ridges and blasting away some of the thick foliage, and openings to fortifications. Their powerful 75mm guns were sorely missed, and so the 81st Division's Company A, 710th Tank Battalion, along with a couple M10 tank destroyers and a mortar platoon, had to be brought over from Angaur Island to help the Marines.

Doing so though, presented some other issues. The riflemen were used to working with their own Marine armored unit, and they found that fighting with the Army tankers forced them to make a few adjustments. For one thing, a fourth of the tank battalion (Company D) was made up of M5A1 Stuart light tanks. These vehicles were a big improvement over riflemen advancing in the open, but with their 37mm gun, they were not nearly as effective against the caves and tunnels as the Shermans with their 75mm guns. Of more concern was the unit's combat experience. The 710th, like the rest of the 81st Infantry Division, was a green outfit, and their entire wartime experience up until that point had been limited to a few days of action on Angaur.

Another difference was in each unit's fighting style. The 710th was an Army unit, and, as such, it had been well-indoctrinated in the U.S. Army's style of waging war. Their tactics were therefore different than those of the Marines. The 710th had mostly been trained for mobile, open, tank warfare against the Germans on large land masses. They had not practiced much fighting on small, hilly, tropical islands. While they were trained to work with in conjunction with infantry around them, their radios and tactics were somewhat inadequate for effective teamwork, as the Marine tanks had been. ADO Smith later wrote that evacuating the Marine tank battalion was "a bad mistake and the tanks were sorely missed when heavy mobile firepower was so important."

Part of Rupertus's failure in this operation also stemmed from his inability to often not understand the current tactical situations. When he hobbled ashore on the morning of D+1, limped over to O.P. Smith's command post and had taken over, one of the first things that he did was to look over the heavy casualties that the 1st Marines had suffered on D-Day, a wise thing to do. Understandably, he became upset. However, he then strangely and erroneously concluded (or at least alluded to the fact) that his men were not fighting vigorously enough. Convinced that an explosive advance would break the back of the enemy's defense and send them reeling across the island, he became frustrated that his men could not give it just a little more to push the battle over the edge into victory.

Worried about this loss of momentum, when he eventually got in contact with Colonel Puller by field phone and heard Puller's report that the 1st Marines battalions were struggling to advance forward, Rupertus reacted angrily, snapping, "Can't they move any faster! Gawddammit Lewie, you've gotta kick ass to get results. You know that, gawddammit!"

Nor did it end there. As the days went on and the 1st Marines kept getting bogged down during their advance into the Umurbrogols, taking heavy casualties in the process, Rupertus kept on at Puller, pushing him to keep attacking, no matter what, even though it had to be by direct assault against the well dug-in Japanese. Add to this Puller's natural reluctance to admit that his men could not take the next objective and then the next, the result became an onslaught of Marine carnage and death.

One big reason that General Rupertus was often in the dark tactically was that he did not get around much, mostly because he was recovering from an ankle injury. His injury had occurred during an earlier landing rehearsal on June 30. Returning to his amtrac, he had started to climb on when the metal handle he was holding suddenly broke. Rupertus slipped backwards onto the coral, shattering his ankle. His injury though, had not been made known to his superior officer, General Geiger, until the division began dress rehearsals for the invasion in late August. Geiger, who incidentally disliked Rupertus to begin with, had finally been able to detach himself from the Guam campaign and had flown out to where the division was undergoing a set of dress rehearsal exercises on Guadalcanal for the upcoming operation. Going over to the divisional command post as the exercise began, he was surprised to find that the division's only senior officer present was the ADO, Brigadier General O. P. Smith. Rupertus could not come ashore because his broken ankle prevented him from being able to get into a boat. Geiger asked Smith where the division commander was. Smith, who had forgone informing Geiger of Rupertus's injury up until that point, was now forced to tell him of it. Geiger was and remarked "If I'd known that, I'd have relieved him."[*]

---

[*] One unreliable account (Moran & Rottman, p. 24) indicates that it was General Julian Smith, Geiger's predecessor, who made the remark. A few reliable accounts (Ross, pp. 107 & 176–7, Wright, p. 223) state that Geiger made the remark on D-Day, when he came ashore in the afternoon to assess the situation and asked Smith the whereabouts of Rupertus. Most other sources (Hallas, p. 22, Camp, p. 101, Gailey, p. 61, Hough, p. 30 fn, La Bree, p. 54, and Shisler, p.75, based on Smith's own personal narrative) correctly maintain that Geiger found out from O. P. Smith about Rupertus's condition and made this remark during the division's first dress rehearsal on August 27. Based on the reliability of the sources, it can probably be concluded that Geiger made the remark both times.

General Smith had already been in consultation with the division doctor about the injury and had indicated his concern: "I said, 'Look doctor, frankly, is this general going to be able to make it for Peleliu?' He told me he thought he would, but would have to use a cane. I said okay. And I never said anything."

Smith did keep the injury quiet and had never told General Geiger, who he felt did not like him. Smith had advised Rupertus to let the corps commander know. Now at this rehearsal he had no choice. In his own words: "He had not realized that General Rupertus was unable to make the trip ashore and was somewhat concerned about him going on the operation. I assured General Geiger that in the two weeks remaining before the landing, I felt General Rupertus's ankle would mend sufficiently to permit him to carry on."

While some historians have questioned General Smith's failure to notify any higher authority of Rupertus's injury, most Marines agree that to have done so would have been a breach of proper etiquette. Smith knew this, and having a strict sense of duty to the chain of command, felt that it was not his responsibility to do so. Additionally, one of the battalion surgeons had certified the division commander fit to make the landing. Besides, who would Smith have reported the injury to? The division had been training on isolated Pavuvu, and none of the III Amphibious Corps officers had visited the island before the landing. So there was no opportunity to tell anyone privately, And Smith would have had some explaining to do if he had flown to Guam to see Geiger specifically for that purpose.

Partly because of his injury, all during D-Day, Rupertus had remained aboard his floating headquarters, the USS *DuPage*, and did not come ashore until 0930 on September 16 (D+1). By then, the ADO had spent over 24 hours on the beach, directing the regiments.

After coming ashore, Rupertus hobbled his way over to Smith's divisional CP and immediately took over without any kind of thorough briefing. It was clear to say that neither Rupertus nor the admirals had a good handle on how severe the day had been for the Marines. This is evidenced by some of the messages that they sent. One example was:

CINPAC COMMUNIQUE NO. 117, SEPTEMBER 15, 1944.
OUR CASUALTIES DURING THE FIRST DAY OF THE ASSAULT WERE LIGHT, ALTHOUGH THE LANDING BEACHES HAVE BEEN UNDER SPORADIC MORTAR AND ARTILLERY FIRE.

Clearly, Rupertus was not aware of the situation.

His leadership style on Peleliu is also a critical point that must now be taken into account. There was no denying that Rupertus had a consistently moody nature. A 30-year career Marine, he was considered a micromanager and was not well liked, either by his superior General Geiger, by O. P. Smith his ADO, or by the division's other officers. He was considered opinionated, which sometimes stemmed from idiosyncratic quirks in his nature.

He absolutely did not allow his ADO to assist him in commanding the division, even though Smith had done the bulk of the division's planning for the operation before Rupertus had returned from Washington D.C. to resume command. In support of that belief, he often thwarted Smith's attempts to simply do his job In Rupertus's opinion, ADOs should not be "under foot," and he told Smith so in no uncertain terms.

Worse, Rupertus did not hide this disdain for his ADO. On September 14, the night before the landing, with the division's senior officers gathered ton Rupertus's command ship, the USS *DuPage*, the general strode into the compartment with a no-nonsense attitude. According to Colonel Lewis Puller:

> Rupertus came in and told us: "You have your orders. I will not be ashore on D-Day, and may not be there on D-Plus-One. It depends on the course of the action. But I want you to understand now that there will be no change in the orders, regardless. Even if General Smith attempts to change my plans or orders, you regimental commanders will refuse to obey.

He then turned to his ADO and asked, "Do you understand, General Smith?"

The ADO hesitated and replied, "Yessir."

Then Rupertus similarly asked each of the regimental commanders in turn, to get verbal acknowledgement that each of them understood the order.

Originally, Rupertus only planned on O. P. Smith going ashore on D-Day and setting up a beachhead message center, and that was it, as General Shepherd had done at Cape Gloucester. Smith had objected to this though, pointing out that his staff was a part of the division's headquarters, and if he were ashore, logic would dictate that he coordinate the assault of the three regiments until the main staff arrived the next day. When Rupertus told him that he could manage that aboard his command ship, Smith became adamant.

> I told the General frankly that to send me ashore in advance of himself with no authority to control the situation ashore put me in a very anomalous situation; I could not escape responsibility for what transpired ashore.
>
> I suggested that he organize two command groups, a skeleton group with me, and the bulk of the staff with him. I would go in early and set up an advance command post … After considerable discussion, the general agreed.

It seems clear that Smith in using the phrase "considerable discussion" was being polite. Rupertus clearly wanted his ADO out of the command process for the operation.

Ironically though, on D-Day, O. P. Smith, as the senior officer ashore for the landing, did take an active part in directing the battle. He remained so for the entire first day, setting up the division command post in a Japanese antitank ditch. The next morning though, impatient for over 15 hours to get ashore, Rupertus finally did storm ashore with his staff, and, after reaching the command post and being briefed by Smith on the current situation, basically told Smith to "not hang around." Smith took the hint and moved his own men back to a draw between the antitank ditch and the beach. Thereafter, his only command function was to periodically get details from commanders at the front and then report his findings to Rupertus. "I never sat in on any conference on planning or anything like that," he later wrote.

Fortunately for the division, Smith was compelled to do what he could there. The day Rupertus came ashore (D+1) and took over, Smith set up his new post in the draw, while his staff fortified it with sandbags. Thereafter, Smith stayed on the island, snatching a few hours' sleep here and there every night on a litter. The men christened the post "Sleepy Hollow," because its position in the draw and the high banks around it had the effect of muffling the noise of combat, especially incoming enemy shells. In the weeks that followed, Smith's staff set up a small mess tent, an aid station, and a portable shower (fortunately, they found fresh water by digging down a few feet).

Although the tactical situation remained serious that first day and the next, Rupertus remained stubborn in his zeal to manage the whole operation alone. Even on September 24 (D+9), when Rupertus had been able to move his divisional headquarters off the beach to what had been the Japanese two-story headquarters building next to the airstrip (after the Seabees had cleared it out), he maintained his determination to direct operations himself. Before leaving for his new location, he walked over to O. P. Smith's post, which was still in the draw, and told him that he was moving his command center. When Smith asked if he wanted him to move as well, Rupertus brusquely told him, "I'll let you know when I need you. You stay here and do your job, and I'll do mine from the division HQ in the Jap building."

Many considered this behavior unfairly peculiar, since Rupertus himself had been the First Marine Division's ADO under General Alexander A. Vandegrift. He had held this position from the division's initial training in early 1942 throughout the Guadalcanal campaign, and until he took over as division commander on July 8, 1943.

Another underlying factor that several officers after the war revealed was that Rupertus was anxious to make sure the campaign went swiftly and triumphantly. His previous commander, General Vandegrift, had been promoted for his leadership at Guadalcanal to Commandant of the Marine Corps. Rupertus, considered an opportunist and who at Guadalcanal had been Vandegrift's Number 1 boy, had his sights on succeeding his old boss in that position. A glowing success at Peleliu would be his "ticket" to that spot.

Thus now, his remarkably quixotic optimism continued throughout Phase 1 of the operation, even after both the 1st Marines and the 7th Marines had been taken off the line. At that time, he still insisted that his division could finish the job. This was despite the fact that the units available in his division now consisted of one worn rifle regiment—the 5th Marines—the artillery of the 11th Marines, and some support units. Even the division's tank battalion had been evacuated.

Not realizing that the harder he pushed, the more determined the Japanese became in their defense, Rupertus, as he had with Puller's regiment earlier, kept mercilessly committing the 5th Marines, the remaining combat regiment, into one assault after another. It seemed to most that he clearly wanted them to take the entire island before he was forced to turn the operation over to the Army. As casualties mounted, Rupertus remained adamant that his men push ahead, no matter what. To the remaining Marines though, it was an "endless nightmare," just a matter of incessantly being pushed day in and day out from one frying pan into another, as casualties continued to mount.

Smith though, in his many visits to the front lines, saw what was happening and became increasingly alarmed. He knew something had to be done to support the Marines, but Rupertus, still hampered by his broken ankle, was in no mood to listen and seemed to be drifting farther and farther from reality. The stress of command and the slow progress his men were making, not to mention the high casualty list, began to take its toll. Day after day, as his four-day campaign stretched into weeks, he became depressed and seemed at a loss as to how to deal with the protracted enemy resistance.

Many historians have criticized the division's regimental commanders, especially Puller (1st Marines) and Harris (5th Marines), for blindly following Rupertus's directives and for continuing to push their men hard into pressing attacks that were more than likely to bring about heavy casualties. Puller after the war wrote privately: "Orders were to attack dead ahead, and that was the only thing we could do, to take ground regardless of losses ..."

It was clear to the senior Marine officers that Rupertus's command style and his insistence that his units get the "whole thing over with as soon as possible" left no room for negotiation. This attitude was consistently blinding him to the severe casualties his units were taking.

General Geiger, having seen this mindset in his general for days now, at last decided that action needed to be taken. He had been upset for a while over

Rupertus's callous disregard for his Marine casualties and his insistence that they continue to advance at full bore. Coupled to his dislike of the man and his methods, Geiger soon realized that he was going to have to take some authoritative action and make a grave command decision. He had already argued, or strongly recommended, his position to Rupertus several times in the last couple days.

Logically, he only had two options available: he could directly order Rupertus to relieve the shattered units and take them off the line before they were totally destroyed, in the hope that they could rebuild and recover in time for the Okinawa invasion next year; or he could take the unprecedented, drastic action of relieving Rupertus in the field, something that had never been done to any Marine general in combat in the history of the Marine Corps. Such an act would remain an ugly stain on the Corps' record for all time. In the media, this would appear a very awkward Marine embarrassment, and the action would of course, permanently and utterly ruin Rupertus's distinguished career, as well as any chance for advancement. It certainly would bar him as a future Commandant of the Marine Corps, which was what Vandegrift seemed to be grooming him for. Such a move would also of course by design damage Geiger's own career in the process. It would also have repercussions outside the Corps; it would raise a firestorm throughout the military, and the Army would no doubt seize the opportunity to further its case of absorbing the Marines into their service, to in their minds, better train the Marine commanders.

Still, something had to be done. Historians have nearly all agreed that, because of his nature, General Rupertus, while he commanded with a firm hand, did not to inspire loyalty in his men, who called him, behind his back, of course, "Rupe the Dupe" or "Rupe the Stupe." To his own ADO, he seemed to assign tremendous confidence in his own command abilities and hence, his own ideas, and he seldom consulted with his subordinate officers. This style, coupled to a strong optimism (which unfortunately often seemed to fly in the face of reality), made for a situation in which it was hard to share with him the burdens of commanding a division. Besides avoiding getting close to his officers and seeming as though he, as one of his officers put it, "didn't give a damn about the people under his command," Rupertus was parsimonious with compliments, recognition, and in awarding medals. He avoided socializing with his officers, and was not considered personable.

He did, however, have some powerful friends, including his old boss, General Vandegrift, who had commanded the First Marine Division before him. Vandegrift, by now the Commandant of the Marine Corps, had been his mentor, and those who knew the two understood that he had Rupertus in mind to someday succeed him as commandant. Rupertus himself was evidently well inclined to have the spot. Many felt that his grumpy, sometimes hostile nature was just his innate character, and that he had always been that way. Others felt that this was a character change that he had undergone, having been brought on when his entire family had succumbed to scarlet fever in China some 14 years before. The loss of his first wife Marguerite and his two children, daughter Ann Rodney and his son William Henry Jr., emotionally devastated him.[*]

Others recall his bombastic overconfidence, and the way he pushed his units, relentlessly and unrealistically in the face of tremendous resistance. His optimistic persistence at Peleliu was renewed after the second day, when the major objective, the Japanese airfield, was secured. He was now convinced that the entire island would be taken in just another few days. He had absolutely no idea that while the most savage and desperate combat was behind them, the longest and most arduous fighting still lay ahead in the cliffs and ravines of the Umurbrogols.

In the end, Geiger, again looking over the high and ever-mounting casualty lists, on September 21.finally chose the latter course of action.

By early October though, Rupertus was starting to get severely depressed by the protracted battle. On two different occasions, two of his senior officers saw clear evidence of this. About a week after the 1st Marines had been relieved, his divisional personnel officer, Lieutenant Colonel. Harold Deakin, found him sitting on his cot, head in hands, distraught, confessing, "This thing has about got me beat."

Although Deakin had never been popular with the general, he was moved by what he saw. He put his arm around his commanding officer and said gently, "Now, General, everything is going to work out."

Then on October 5, almost three weeks after the landing, Rupertus summoned 5th Marines commander Bucky Harris by phone to his headquarters immediately. Harris jumped in a jeep and drove over there, only to find the division commander distraught. With tears running down his cheeks, he confessed to Harris, "Harris, I'm at the end of my rope. Two of my fine regiments are in ruins." Pausing, he added, "You usually seem to know what to do and get it done. So I'm going to turn over to you everything we have left."

"Yessir," Harris replied.'

Rupertus looked at him and added, "This is strictly between us."

---

[*] Some sources (e.g., Hallas, p. 14) erroneously record that Rupertus lost two daughters. Rupertus eventually remarried his second wife Alice just before he left for the Pacific. Months later, she gave birth to a son, Patrick H., who was born in 1940 (Shisler, p. 72).

Needless to say, Bucky Harris returned to his unit deep in thought. The general could not have turned over command to Harris that easily, but it did show the younger man how stressed his commanding officer was by then.

Conditions on Peleliu

There were other considerable reasons that the Peleliu operation was so difficult for the Marines. An important factor was the abysmal combination of overall conditions the men suffered during the operation, and this was by no means limited to those inflicted by the enemy. The island, located just 7° above the equator, along the same latitude as Columbia, Venezuela, Central Africa, or Ethiopia, has a naturally tropical jungle climate. Daytime temperatures on the island around that time of year could soar to as high as 115°F (46°C) or more in the interior, where, with little breeze, heat exhaustion and heat stroke were common.

Seriously compounding the climate problem were those regarding water supplies. Military studies had concluded beforehand that in tropical climates, at least two gallons of fresh water were needed per man per day, infinitely more than the pair of one-pint canteens each man brought ashore. Because of the steamy environment and the fact that there were no natural lakes, rivers, or springs on the island, it was assumed that water supplies would be little or non-existent.

To make matters worse, salt tablets quickly became in short supply. As a result of these factors, most Marines would probably suffer some degree of sunstroke or dehydration.

The fresh water problem came on early. By noontime, the temperature had soared to over 110°F. The two pints of water each man carried had quickly been consumed, and by the afternoon, as the temperature continued to climb and the men sweated profusely, they began to suffer the onset of heat exhaustion. Weak and on the brink of unconsciousness, the Marines struggled to advance inland, let alone attack the enemy.

To alleviate the situation, because trailer tanks were in short supply and getting them over the barrier reef posed problems, the Navy decided to prepare a few thousand 50-gallon drums of water, which could more easily be brought ashore, rolled to wherever they were needed, tipped on their sides, and uncapped for easy access. Thus, a few hours after the landing, the amphibious tractor units began ferrying the drums ashore. As it turned out though, these all-metal drums had recently contained fuel or petroleum products, and in their haste to prepare them, the Navy had unfortunately not properly steam-cleaned them. Many had only been wiped clean, or in the case of gasoline, allowed simply to evaporate. Thus most still carried vestiges of petroleum distillates, and the water put into them was neither palatable nor potable, described as "a dark color, and tastes very much like crude oil, but it's water, and the doctors have okayed it for drinking."

Additional problems developed from the practice of not completely filling these drums. This in the tropical climate caused many of them to rust internally around the top, which further lent to the terrible taste (and color) of the water. Marines drinking this vile fluid became ill, subject to cramps and convulsions, some of them severe. Others were subject to violent coughing, vomiting, or acute diarrhea. Water-purifying tablets—chlorine-based halazone—helped some, but not much. As a result, many men had to be evacuated.

The Navy thought that the water problem would be alleviated when engineers got the opportunity to drill wells for fresh water. A few days after the landing, the 1st Engineer Battalion starting drilling, and did in fact reach water. They soon found out though, that this supply qualified under the loosest of interpretation of fresh: while the liquid was not saline, because of decomposing coconuts and foliage, it was brackish and difficult to swallow. According to one source:

> it was the most god-awful stuff you can imagine. Its unique flavor was not enhanced by the rotting coconuts which had seeped through the coral-streaked mud to the water supply, and one was forced to spike it with the lemonade component of K-rations which, in itself, was more like battery acid and more suitable for burnishing canteen cups and mess gear than for drinking.

Water-purification equipment was unloaded several days after the landing, which alleviated the situation somewhat. However, the water supply problem was not finally solved until engineers were able to set up distillation equipment at the beginning of October, long after the beachheads had been secured. Surprisingly, no mention of the polluted water drums was mentioned in the First Marine Division after action report. In fact, the water supply section outlined the water situation, the drums brought in, and the evaporators and wells. The report then stated that "sufficient water supplies were available for all personnel." The section then ended with one sentence: "There has been no illness attributable to the water supply." Furthermore, there was no mention of the water problem in the supply recommendations.

Another natural problem related to the island's tropical nature was the issue of pests. It was bad enough that the men had to deal with a determined enemy in well-protected positions, the tropical heat, and a lack of fresh water, without having to deal with a cornucopia of bug swarms that quickly arose in the days

An LST loaded with supplies. Note the drums of water in the center. The only water source for the Marines over the first few days, they had been improperly cleaned.

following the preliminary shelling and the landing. Millions of insects soon abounded, and with so many casualties arising on both sides, after the first couple days, thousands of huge blowflies, and other insects feasted on a variety of menu items, including the bloating, putrefying corpses, dumped food, open latrines, and exposed feces where men simply did not have the luxury of moving away from their foxhole to relieve themselves. It was infuriating to be lying on unyielding sandy coral, dodging not only bullets and shells, but also bugs that made their own relentless, determined strafing runs on any exposed skin, hell-bent on buzzing and biting the men.

As a consequence to the water and insect conditions, illness became an issue. Many suffered from heat stroke. Others came down with acute bacterial dysentery from unsanitary or polluted water, and others caught malaria, especially in the swampy areas north and south of the airfield. These illnesses were hard to fight because of the conditions on the island, the intensity of the combat, and the shortage of medicine.

Another fauna-related problem for the Marines was one that they had been subjected to back on Pavuvu. They again suffered constant infestation of land crabs that lived around the shoreline. These crustaceans came out after dark and while they fed on the corpses, feces, and ration remains, they were certainly willing to crawl over anything and everything in their quest for food. One Marine recalled with a scowl, "The crabs were all over the place. Them damn things at night would crawl right on top of you and crawl all around your shoulders and scare the hell out of you. I mean, you didn't know if it was a Jap or not."

Even when the pests and the enemy gave one a break, just being stationary on the island was usually an olfactory nightmare. Between the bodies, the rotting vegetation, the insects, and the man-made odors that came from explosives, fuel, fires, and the unbathed, sweating men, the stench was mostly terrible, especially when there was a lack of breeze.

Beneath the vegetation—although at this point, not much was left—was coral. Moving around was an effort. Struggling over that jagged coral was not easy, and it was quite the task to dig a foxhole in it, especially while under fire. In comparison, this problem hardly affected the Japanese at all, because they had had the time to blast their positions months before. Thus they were able to lay out holes not just to make a stand at, but to fall back on as well. After the war, the regimental narrative of the 1st Marines stated:

> The pockmarked surface offered no secure footing, even in the few level places. It was impossible to dig in: the best the men could do was pile a little coral or wood debris around their positions. The jagged rock slashed their shoes and clothes, and tore the bodies every time they hit the deck for safety ... Every blast hurled chunks of coral in all directions, multiplying many times the fragmentation effect of every shell.

One Marine later wrote:

> Picture an island completely made out of coral rock. That was Peleliu. I tell you, all that rock was tough on your skin. It bloodied your knees, your elbows. It just shredded your clothes apart. There was no place to sleep at night. You couldn't make a decent foxhole because you couldn't dig. If there was any loose coral around, you'd kind of pile it up around you. That was your foxhole.

Another later recalled:

> Around this place, there's nothin' but sharp coral. I mean, you get down on your hands and knees, you're getting cut. And grenades are going off. And each time, this coral is shattering

in small bits and it peppers you. I guess it would be as if somebody turned a sandblaster on you. It stung you all over.

Yet another wrote:

> The only place that you could dig a foxhole on that damn island was in the sand at the edge of the beach. I was there a week, and the only decent foxhole I got to dig was that first day in the sand.

The miserable conditions on Peleliu were perhaps best summed up by General Geiger's chief of staff, Colonel Merwin Silverthorn:

> The terrain was against us. The weather was against us. We were on the tail end of a typhoon. We ran short of rations. We were on two meals a day … The terrain was abominable … The sharp coral would cut the shoes and the clothing of the Marines. Then the island had been mined for many years for phosphate deposits. So there were many tunnels running through these ridges. And in addition many caves and tunnels had been dug by the defending forces.

The Umurbrogols

A significant factor that led to the high casualty rate were the Umurbrogols. Pre-invasion reconnaissance did little to describe the detailed problems the men would face just trying to navigate this range, much less suffering withering crossfire from the honeycomb of defensive positions that the Japanese had chiseled out of the coral peaks. One Marine, Robert Leckie, described it this way:

> it was neither ridge nor mountain, but an undersea coral reef thrown above the surface by a subterranean volcano. Sparse vegetation growing in the thin topsoil atop the bedrock had concealed the Umurbrogol's crazy contours from the aerial camera's eye.
>
> It was a place that might have been designed by a maniacal artist given to painting mathematical abstractions—all slants, jaggeds, straights, steeps, and sheers with no curve to soften or relieve. Its highest elevation was 300 feet in the extreme north, overlooking the airfield—islet of Ngesebus 1,000 yards off the coast there. But no height rose more than 50 feet before splitting apart in a maze of peaks and defiles, cluttered with boulders and machicolated with caves.
>
> For the Umurbrogol was also a monster Swiss cheese of hard coral limestone pocked beyond imagining with caves and crevices. They were to be found at every level, in every size, crevices small enough for a lonely sniper, eerie caverns big enough to station a battalion among its stalactites and stalagmites.

This image was later similarly described in General Geiger's after action report:

> A fanatical enemy has retired to a coraline hill mass comprised of many pinnacles, sharp ridges, sheer cliffs, and narrow ravines, honeycombed with caves. Many of these caves were on the sides of the cliffs or precipitous slopes. They faced in all directions, were on different levels, and were frequently reinforced with concrete and with steel doors covering entrances,

which were practically invisible. Often they were provided with many chambers and multiple entrances. They were so stocked and located as to be self-supporting, as well as mutually supporting and were almost inaccessible to an attacking force.

Every conceivable and practicable method of reducing these positions which was available was tried, but it might be said with truthfulness that the infantry was confronted with a defense against which no single supporting weapon at its disposal could be brought effectively to bear. This posed a problem, the only solution for which was a slow, methodical, and relatively costly operation for their final reduction.

It was obvious to most of the planners that next to the beach obstacles, this series of ridges and cliffs would be the key to the enemy's defenses on the island. They had however, grossly underestimated the extent to which the enemy had taken advantage of terrain, and had little idea about how coarse this terrain was, or how well suited it was for the enemy to be able to construct their last-ditch defensive positions in it. From the recon photos, the entire area looked like an endless sea of broccoli. It was impossible to tell that the Japanese had created an underground defensive network, first by utilizing existing caves, and second by improving these and creating new ones, and third by connecting them by a series of tunnels, often supplying the larger ones with electrical power. These positions not only offered refuge from offshore shelling, but also from air attack. Their only vulnerabilities were their immobility and potential communication problems with their other positions.

Do We Have to Fight Next To THEM?

Just like today, inter-service rivalry between the three military departments— the Army Air Corps was of course, still part of the Army—had always been a factor, and this was especially true in wartime.

The struggle between the Navy and the Marine Corps, which had been classically intense for decades, was still alive and well, although through several operations an effective, grudging working relationship had been forged. Still, even though they worked closely together with the Marines in combat, the Navy it seemed frequently took pleasure in letting the Marines know that they were in charge. The Peleliu operation was no different. The Navy had originally outlined and scheduled the operation, and they well knew that they would oversee its entire execution.

This command control element in amphibious operations was never lost on the Marines, and, no doubt, the resentment worsened the Navy's image appreciably when Marines embarking to landing craft to storm the beaches noted sailors and naval officers calmly standing around watching them.

Peleliu was no different. As the men of the First Marine Division gathered their equipment to pile down into their amtracs, they spied naval officers and sailors casually standing around on the decks, smoking cigarettes, calmly watching the Marines go into battle. One Marine later wrote: "I caught a glimpse of several sailors on board the LST drinking from coffee mugs and watching us depart. I thought then, maybe I was in the wrong service."

He was not alone. Another later recalled: "As soon as we were in the water, I looked up and I saw those sailors standing up on the bow, and I cursed myself for not joining the Navy."

Their contempt understandably grew even more so when struggling up the beaches they found themselves in a hornets' nest. Clearly the damn swabbies had not done even a mediocre job of clearing the enemy positions in the bombardment.

As much as the Marines did not get along with the Navy though, animosity toward the Army was far worse. Nimitz knew that the Marines could take and hold a beachhead. However, he often liked to augment them with Army units, and the difference in their styles of fighting frequently led to clashes in command.

Marines were trained to land and secure their coastal objectives, no matter what. They usually operated with just as much efficiency in a battalion, regimental, or divisional size operation. They had honed to a fine skill the ability to approach a beach in force, take and hold a beachhead, and advance swiftly, aggressively.

In contrast, Army units were trained to operate as part of a larger fighting force, usually in corps- or army-sized operations. As such, they were used to fighting in a more systemic, deliberate manor. Army units were used to making assaults with full support from established artillery and mortar positions. Their attacks were punctuated with regular pause periods so that they could dig in to support their advance and cover their flanks, as well as to allow slower elements and supplies to catch up to them.

The dissimilarity between these two styles had flared up earlier in the Saipan operation, which was under the command of the Marine Amphibious V Corps. Two Marine divisions had landed on the designated beachhead on June 15, and it was only on the night of June 16, after the beachhead had been secured and the Marines had moved inland, that the reserve unit, the Army 27th Infantry Division, had come ashore.

The 27th was a New York National Guard unit, commanded by 50-year-old Major General Ralph C. Smith, an affable, easygoing leader who got along with his men. In comparison, the on-location corps commander was Lieutenant General Holland M. Smith, a 60-year-old diehard Marine, nicknamed

"Howlin' Mad" because of his blistering temper and short fuse (especially on any obvious issue that made the Marine Corps look bad). His combative nature was the total opposite of Ralph Smith's calmness. The two had clashed over styles once before during the Tarawa operation back in November, 1943, and working together again on Saipan was not a prospect either one looked forward to.

On June 23 (D+8), over a week after the landing, all three divisions were once again ordered to conduct an all-out attack and to move forward aggressively. The Second Marine Division forcefully advanced along the coastline on the left flank, while Fourth Marine Division attacked and began moving forward on the right. In the center though, the 27th Infantry Division, faced stiff Japanese resistance from what the men had dubbed "Purple Heart Ridge," beset by enemy positions on ridges that flanked the division. They therefore set out to assault the enemy positions on the flanking ridges and then advance carefully forward in a methodical fashion, despite Holland Smith's insistence that they charge forward. The G.I.s though, instead were probing the enemy lines, using their artillery to soften them up. This was typical of the Army doctrine of deliberation that they had been taught back at Fort Benning, Georgia. To make matters worse, the Army began its attack an hour after the ordered start time, which force the Marines on each flank to slow their advance until the Army units in the center could catch up and cover the Marine flanks. As a result, with the Army units lagging behind, the line took on a sort of U-shape, with the 27th at the bottom of the U.

Holland Smith by now thought he was witnessing what was in his opinion an "infuriatingly slow" performance by the 27th. Angered over the Army's morning attack delay, their lack of aggression, and, with a chip on his shoulder, he decided that enough was enough. Fuming, he went to his superior officer, Vice Admiral Richmond Turner, commanding the Fifth Amphibious Force. Holland Smith told him in no uncertain terms that he wanted to relieve Ralph Smith immediately. Turner reluctantly agreed with his assessment, and the two of them went to confer with the senior naval commander in the area, Admiral Spruance aboard his flagship, the USS *Indianapolis*. Spruance reluctantly agreed, and Holland Smith immediately sent out to the 27th's commanding officer a message to that effect. A following order went out instructing the Army general to pack up his gear and be off the island by June 25.

As expected, the action stirred up a firestorm of words and temperament. Lieutenant General Robert Richardson, the senior Army commander in the Central Pacific, was a strong advocate for keeping Marine operations to a minimum, and for the Army to oversee any land operations. He was outraged when Smith showed up and reported to him in Hawaii. Richardson reported the issue to Chief of Staff George C. Marshall, who became upset as well, because Ralph Smith was a good friend of his, and because this made the Army look bad. Richardson immediately scheduled a board of inquiry to investigate the matter, and then flew out to Saipan. About a week after the island had been secured, he put on an elaborate review of the 27th, complete with awarding medals and citations, a flagrant breach of military etiquette.

General Holland Smith, surprised when he heard of the event, reacted angrily, and the two had it out.

Richardson at one point roared, "I want you to know that you can't push the Army around the way you have been doing. You and your corps commanders aren't as well qualified to lead large bodies of troops as general officers in the Army. Yet you dare to remove one of my generals." He paused and quipped, "You Marines are nothing but a bunch of beach runners anyway. What do you know about land warfare?"

Holland Smith, livid and frustrated, stormed out of the meeting and immediately went to Turner's command flagship, the USS *Rocky Mount*, to complain. Turner, ready to defend the Marine, confronted Richardson and asked him bluntly what command rights he had in a battle area not assigned to him, and, for that matter, what the hell right he had to even come to Saipan. Richardson argued that Nimitz no less had given him permission. Turner wanted to see the proof.

Richardson went over Turner's head to Spruance, who gave Richardson a "what do you expect from Turner" shrug.*

*

The Peleliu operation three months later perhaps brought out the worst in this rivalry. In the weeks leading up to the invasion, the Marines stuck to themselves, and the Army, sensing their animosity, did so as well. Both sides

---

* While Ralph Smith's relief of command stood, a board of inquiry later exonerated him. The incident, which boiled over into the media, also strained Holland Smith's relationship with Nimitz to the point where the Marine general was eventually transferred out of the combat area of the Pacific and back to Hawaii. As a placating gesture, Nimitz assigned him the task of creating a new command, the Fleet Marine Force, Pacific (FMFPAC), but the position was purely administrative in nature. And probably as payback, MacArthur, when he accepted the Japanese surrender on the USS *Missouri* in Tokyo Bay in August, 1945, made sure that Holland Smith was not there to attend the ceremony.

concentrated instead on their own part of the operation: the Marines landing on Peleliu, and the Army landing on nearby Angaur Island.

The First Marine Division, proudly calling themselves the "Old Breed," resented the G.I.s in the 81st Infantry Division for three main reasons. First of all, they looked down upon them just because they were Army, and to Marines, therefore wholly inferior warriors. Marines considered themselves the best of the best, volunteers every one, warriors of the highest caliber, audacious and brave. Soldiers, with their stereotyped minds, were all draftees, inferior in their attitudes, with little stomach for war. The Marines believed that they were doing most of the fighting in the Pacific because the job had to be done by someone. To them, the Army was there because they had been ordered to be there, and because there just were not enough Marines to go around.

Bombastic, career-Marine General Rupertus in particular had an intense dislike of the Army. After the Cape Gloucester operation, the First Marine Division had been transferred back to the Navy's control. While the division had been moved to Pavuvu to recover, Rupertus instead had accepted a personal invitation from General MacArthur to travel to Brisbane and stay at his headquarter there as his guest. To Rupertus's chagrin though, MacArthur's main reason was to try and persuade Rupertus to support him in reverting the division back to the control of the Army.

Rupertus's disdain for the Army of course, simply exacerbated the operational situation, especially since the 81st's commander, General Mueller, knew of Rupertus's dislike for his unit. Even in the early planning stages, Rupertus had objected to the 81st Division taking any part in the Peleliu operation and had requested that the Fifth Marine Division, still in training in Hawaii, participate instead.

The second reason for the disdain toward the G.I.s was that the Marines were now seasoned fighters who had already gone through several hard-fought Pacific invasions, including the Guadalcanal and New Britain campaigns. The 81st in comparison had yet to see action. Their commanding officer, 51-year-old General Paul J. Mueller, had seen action in World War I as a battalion commander, and had won the Silver Star. He had not been in combat since, and what they all were facing here was a new type of warfare.

To make matters worse, that summer, the still-green 81st Infantry had thoroughly enjoyed partaking of the many, luxurious pleasures of Hawaii while it underwent over a year of training. The almost nightly liberties included the beautiful beaches of Oahu, the many bars and entertainment centers, air-conditioned theaters, fantastic restaurants, and, of course, the countless beautiful women ...

In contrast, the men of the First Marine Division had suffered wretched conditions in sweltering, jungle-ridden, primitive, bug- and rat-infested conditions on the remote island of Pavuvu, supposedly recuperating from the ferocious experience of Guadalcanal. Thus, when the Army units finally arrived in the Solomons, they would only have to endure the primitive conditions of Guadalcanal for a few weeks before sailing off with the Marines.

The difference between the two divisions was actually visibly, physically obvious. The smiling G.I.s were tanned, physically fit, fresh, and well fed. The dour Marines in contrast were gaunt, ragged, their skin a ghoulish yellow from all the anti-malarial atabrine they had been taking.

A third point, every bit as important as the first two, was that the aggressive combat methods of the Marines differed significantly from the more methodical ones employed by the Army, which often caused further resentment and, worse, at times, confusion in combat. The Marines prided themselves on being an élite fighting force, proud, well-trained volunteers to the man. Army G.I.s to them were seen as civilians-turned soldiers, a good half of them having been reluctant draftees (although as it turned out, a few draftees did indeed wind up in the Marines).

The hard-hitting, hard-charging Marines had been trained over and over to use a direct, vigorous, proactive attack pattern, to maneuver overwhelming assaults against the Japanese, and then to tenaciously hold their ground until relieved. Their doctrine was to overwhelm a position by sheer determination and then to defend that position at all costs, sometimes down to the last man. They were stubbornly unwilling to yield ground, and thus often found themselves holding a hill or ridge to the point where they faced annihilation.

In comparison, the Army's methods of attack were more systematic, usually preceding their assaults with heavy barrages and preliminary recon patrols. This was borne out on Peleliu, where the Army resorted to more standardized siege-and-root-out techniques. Army units usually did not readily charge into heavy firestorms, but tended rather to pull back, regroup, and call in air, artillery, or any available naval fire support.

On Peleliu, one rifleman in the 5th Marines in mid-October quipped a sentiment common to all Marines: "Hell, they don't send in the Army guys until the tough fighting's over, and the Marines have the situation well in hand."

The dissimilarity between these two techniques naturally caused a high degree of hostility whenever G.I.s fought alongside Marines. If the two attacked together and met the same resistance, the Marines would usually in the end take their objective and cling to it, while Army units would tend to fall back and wait for artillery and air support, which of course, infuriated the Marines fighting next to them.

Naturally, General Rupertus used these differences to criticize the Army. At one point, just after units of the 81st had relieved several of his Marine units, employing their ponderous technique in taking the Umurbrogol heights, he smirked, "Now I can tell General Geiger, 'I told you so. That's why I didn't want the Army involved in this in the first place.'"

To underline the differences in the two styles, on the afternoon of September 23, when the Army's 321st RCT was in the process of relieving the battered 1st Marines in front of Bloody Nose Ridge, the 321st's regimental commander, Colonel Robert Dark, approached the line to see how the takeover was progressing. Very near the front and subject to occasional sniper fire, he came upon Colonel Puller's command tent. Greeting the Marine, he asked him where his CP was located.

Sweating and shirtless, Puller in his gravelly voice growled, "Right here."

Looking around and convinced that Puller had thought he meant OP (observation post, which is typically near the front) instead of CP, Dark replied with emphasis, "No, I mean your command post."

Puller glared, spat at the ground, and barked, "Right HERE!"

Later that day, word went up and down the lines that Dark had subsequently located his own CP a thousand yards to the rear of Puller's.

This antagonism inevitably persisted even after the turnover to the Army began, and the remaining senior Marine commander, General Smith, had a number of run-ins with the Army commander, General Mueller. The animosity came out into the open at the onset of the turnover, when Mueller openly questioned the combat efficiency of the Marines. Smith, by nature a relatively non-confrontational officer, looked at him and told him in no uncertain terms that these men by God were MARINES, and that in itself vouched for their combat efficiency. He then added that those Marine units being relieved would not be used offensively anymore: they had done their job on Peleliu. Smith of course was referring to their fatigue from prolonged exposure to intensive combat, and to the casualties that they had sustained, but his response nevertheless did nothing to improve their image in Mueller's mind.

Mueller then asked Smith for a map overlay showing the positions of all the Marine machine-gun positions on the island.

Again, Smith defended his men. He looked at Mueller and remarked acerbically, "We have been attacking every day. We don't make overlays for machine guns when we are attacking. We keep them moving."

Finally, Mueller shook his head and remarked that he was going to have to start a whole new campaign, since, up until now, the Marines had not done much to take out the Japanese on the island. Smith, despite the memories of the savage fighting of the last couple weeks or so, remained silent and just glared ahead.

One last clash between the two generals bears mention. A simple, tasteful makeshift cemetery had by now been built on the island for the fallen, laid out with plain walks and simple crosses. Smith's thought was that it was a pity that the cemetery had to be so big. However, Mueller in contrast responded by insisting that the Army graves be moved to their own section, so as not to be alongside fallen Marines. Smith pointed out that this was not just a Marine Corps cemetery, but rather an Armed Forces cemetery, because men of all branches rested there. Mueller though contended that the G.I.s had to be dug up and moved, since the preponderance of the graves were, of course, of fallen Marines. Smith was forced to take the matter up the chain of command, and, luckily for him, overall command of the operation was the Navy, which sided with Smith.

The Army's animus toward the Marines would intensify after they had taken the island and the operation was over. It would continue thereafter, with the Army complaining that for what they had accomplished, the Marines had taken far too much credit for victory.

Back in Washington D.C., the inter-service struggle between the three services was more rudimentary and, because of the ranks involved, more serious, with each service fighting for control of operations in the Pacific. As the war continued, the tussle for operational control intensified: the Army wanted the commander-in-chief to be a ground commander from their service—specifically, MacArthur—to lead the invasion of the Japanese home islands. The Navy's strategy differed: they saw no reason to invade the islands, and felt that the enemy could be brought down through blockade, bombing, and general siege. Therefore, they argued, the overall commander should be a Navy admiral—specifically, Nimitz—the man who had led them across the Pacific so far.

The Army wanted to oversee all ground campaigns, including amphibious operations. As a—doubtlessly logical to them—corollary to this, they especially favored combining all Marine units into their service. On the other side of the argument, the Navy wanted to oversee their own amphibious operations, including command of any Army units participating in them. The Marines were naturally caught in the middle, wanting to at least oversee their own landings. Because they were ultimately a part of the Navy, and relied on not just them, but Army air and infantry components to achieve success, theirs was the weakest position.

One of the Army advocates for assimilating the Marines into their branch was MacArthur himself. The First Marine Division had been under his command at Cape Gloucester in late December, 1943, and perhaps, surprisingly, the general had retained a great respect for them throughout his career. With the Cape Gloucester campaign ending in late April, 1944, and the Marines moving off to the Russell Islands to recuperate, MacArthur, along with other senior Army officers, had argued for them to not only be kept under him for the upcoming campaigns to liberate the Philippines, but to be incorporated into the Army itself.

He had broached this plan at his headquarters in Brisbane, Australia to General Rupertus himself. As an enticement, the general had said with a smile, "You know, in the Central Pacific, the First Marine Division will just be another one of six Marine divisions, [but] if it stayed here, it would be MY Marine Division." Rupertus, clearly uncomfortable with the idea, knew what sort of explosive reaction to this would come from senior Marine and Navy commanders.

He was right. General Vandegrift, his mentor and now Commandant of the Marine Corps, railed at the idea, but had no power to do anything about it. The problem would have to be resolved between the Navy and the Army, specifically between Nimitz and MacArthur.

As expected, Nimitz, normally a soft-spoken, calm man, was enraged at the idea. As later revealed by his public affairs officer, Captain Waldo Drake, a few months later: "He really blew his stack, cussing like an old sea dog. 'The First Marine Division was part of the United States Navy,' he yelled, and by God, he was the Navy's top enchilada in the Pacific, and he wanted the First Division back under his command, now that Cape Gloucester was over!"

In the summer months leading up to the invasion, senior officers of all three services in this campaign had done little to dispel the animosity between the services. The Army and Marine Corps units avoided each other with a passion. To make matters worse, the press became involved. When the Second Marine Division took excessive casualties of nearly 20 percent when it landed at Tarawa in late November 1943, a good part of the press was quick in its criticism of so many lost for such a small island. One source compared the assault to Pickett's bloody charge at Gettysburg. Another pro-MacArthur paper labeled the Marine action as "reckless and excessively costly," comparing it to the Charge of the Light Brigade at Balaclava in 1854.

Planning the operation had been no different. Even after the 81st had landed on Pavuvu, they stayed as far away as possible from the Marines, and it was only a few weeks before the scheduled D-Day that senior divisional officers actually met to begin final planning and coordination for the landings. The meetings were terse and frosty, with open hostility and distrust obvious.

Coupled to the Navy's haughty control of the planning, the Marines were understandably convinced that they occupied the low spot on the totem pole. And yet, they would be expected to take on the hardest task of the operation. In many respects, the Marines once again somewhat felt totally isolated.

Other Lessons Learned: New Stuff

There had been a number of innovations that had been implemented as a result of the Peleliu operation, and their effectiveness was carefully analyzed. One was a better assessment and improvement of the new method to negotiate offshore reefs with amphibious tractors, the second time in the war that this was done.

One transport commander recommended that negotiating the reef with supplies and replacements going in, and evacuating the wounded going out, would be expedited by creating bridging structures across the reef at key spots. These structures would consist of steel pilings secured into the coral and then stringers and planked platforms running between them, and all covered by steel matting and better secured with cross bracing. A ramp on the open sea end could allow LVTs and DUKWs, to cross over.

Practical solutions in tactics were improved as well, especially for the new type of cave and tunnel warfare encountered on the Umurbrogol ridges. In that regard, the Marines learned to hone to a fine edge coordinating, by necessity, their constricted assaults against these fortified positions, manned by fanatic enemy soldiers ready to die for the Emperor. This was especially true in using the tanks. There were few if any instances in the Pacific war where such inter-cooperation was used as effectively, including in difficult, rough spots where no armored vehicle conceivably could go. Because of the tactics employed and their effective results, the Shermans operated very much on a tactical level; thus, while the battalion retained its battalion and company command HQ functions, platoons and sometimes even individual tanks were freely shifted from one rifle platoon to another, depending on the tactical situation.

One new tactic involved moving a tank or if necessary, an LVT-A with a 75mm gun, up to a suspected entrance to entice the Japanese to fire at it.

If the enemy took the bait, the vehicle would then fire at the entrance to pulverize it. Then the infantry would move up and take out the position with flamethrowers and bazookas. This technique ended up saving many lives. Or the infantry would stay close to the tank to prevent the enemy from crawling up to it and taking it out by grenade or explosive, and then move in and destroy the rest of the cave.

There were other techniques used to protect the tanks, since their presence made a big difference in taking out enemy positions. Borrowing a lesson learned from the Germans earlier in the war, spare treads were affixed or even welded onto the tanks's turret or front sloping plate to prevent any armor-piercing or HE shell from destroying the tanks. It had worked well for the Germans and now did for the Americans as well; this technique was officially documented as saving at least three tanks in the operation.

Unfortunately, General Rupertus relieved the Shermans at the end of September, so these techniques were not utilized for the latter part of the campaign; at least, not until some Shermans from the Army's 710th Tank Battalion, sent over in late September, were deployed to assist the Marines, and the Army, and even then, an "educational" period was needed.

This operation was also the first time the newly developed insecticide DDT was used to address the populous insect problem. On the island, this complex insecticide was mixed with diesel oil for application. It was also mixed with lighter oils to be sprayed on nets, jungle hammocks and the exteriors and interiors of tents. While this seemed to work well on the insects, it was not effective in killing the larvae.

Still, the Marines persisted. On the line, three-man squads would follow the advance of the infantry, spraying from portable knapsacks onto spoiled food, decaying corpses, and puddles. There was on the island at least one truck with a large sprayer. It would travel about, spraying anything that insects might feed on. Around mid-October, an aircraft sometimes would be tasked with dousing an area. Strangely, fire would lessen during these runs, almost an unspoken agreement between the two sides. As one Marine later recalled: "Everybody just kind of let it go, including the Japanese."

Another innovation combat tested was a shoulder-fired mortar, the 60mm Garrett Model T20. Developed by the U.S. Army, the American weapon was a direct response to the effective Japanese 50mm Type 89 mortar. Nicknamed the "knee mortar," this enemy weapon technically was the Japanese Type 89 Grenade Discharger. This short-range weapon, having been in production since 1932, saw extensive service by the Japanese. The 10lb assembly was only two feet long, with a 9½-inch rifled barrel and a small base plate. Trigger fired, it was designed to be braced against a tree trunk, a log, or the ground and be fired at a 45° angle, with trajectory eyeballed and controlled by hand). In emergency situations though, it could be horizontally braced and thus fired. It was considered versatile, because it could be carried by one man (including several rounds), had a relatively high rate of fire, and could be used with standard Japanese grenades, firing a Type 91 fragmentation grenade or a Type 89 HE mortar shell. The Type 89 shell was 50mm wide, weighed about two pounds, and, with an eight-second delay, had a range of about 500 yards. Shell types included high explosive (HE), flare, and smoke.

The moniker "knee mortar" evolved from the fact that American intelligence initially translated from the weapon's classification in the manual: *Hachikyu shiki jutekidanto* (Year 89 heavy grenade launcher). An improper translation of segments in the manual were references to it being a "leg mortar." This was because the weapon was carried strapped to one's leg. Intelligence though, also initially critically mistook this as a means of using the weapon, concluding that it could be fired by bracing the end against one's leg. The slightly curved base—so designed that it could dig into whatever it was leaned against, be it wood or soil—lent credence to this idea. However, the recoil was too severe for this. Early on, a soldier tried to fire a captured one that way on Guadalcanal. It broke his leg.

The much bigger T20 fired a standard HE mortar shell. The Army rated the weapon with an effective range of about 600 yards, although the Marines found that its effective range was not more than about 125 yards. The weapon consisted of a regular 60mm M2 mortar barrel featuring a powerful recoil spring. The weapon was fitted with a pistol grip and trigger below the tube in the middle, so the operator could fire it without using the base plate and tripod.

The T20 was used on Peleliu together with flamethrowers and small arms to take out cave and tunnel entrances. Unfortunately, despite the fact that this new weapon was somewhat effective against enemy positions, overall it did not perform successfully for several reasons. First, the T20 was about three times as heavy as the preferable, standard 13lb M9 bazooka. Carrying around the heavy weapon and ammo was a burden for the light riflemen, who were used to moving fast. Getting it into position often proved difficult, which defeated the purpose of having a compact, portable mortar. Second, the T20 broke down frequently—sometimes at critical moments in combat—because several key components were too weak for their purpose and not durable enough for sustained firing. Third, the weapon was muzzle loaded, which meant that it could not be fired downhill.

The T20 shoulder-fired mortar. Its recoil proved to be too powerful for a rifleman to fire more than a couple rounds.

Most importantly though, was its performance in actual use. The weapon's recoil was tremendous, and the impact of firing it was so hard that even an experienced gunner had to be replaced after only firing a few rounds, or worse, sent to the medics for treatment. Most of the T20s issued were returned to supply within a week after the landing. Several were eventually used later in the campaign, but only fired with its tripod and thick rubber base pad sturdied against a wall or frame.

Another new weapon that was tried in the Peleliu campaign was a long-range flamethrower mounted on an LVT-4. Three of these were given to the division before the landing, and assigned to the 1st Amphibian Tractor Battalion. A fourth amtrac was used to carry supplies for the other three. These flamethrowers had a much longer range than the more portable ones: 75 yards with a gasoline and oil mixture for a total 55-second burn, and twice the range if using napalm for an 80-second burn. Clearly napalm was the better mixture to use, but it was in shorter supply.

While this technique was next to useless in open combat, in close, tropical island situations, it proved invaluable, and many enemy positions were taken out with them. Such usage nevertheless did have some drawbacks. Because the flamethrower was somewhat clumsy to position, and ready, the lightly armored vehicle was itself rendered vulnerable to attack. To maximize the vehicle's safety, the amtrac coordinated its approach with a Sherman. The tank would move up to the enemy defensive position and pulverize the entrance with its 75mm gun. Then the LVT would move up as the Sherman covered it, and take out the position with its flamethrower. Unfortunately, many of the LVT-A4 crews found that if a flamethrower was mounted on their vehicle, the sacrifice of carrying less 75mm ammunition outweighed the advantage of carrying the flamethrower.

In addition, the flamethrower components were somewhat fragile in construction, and not designed to be carried about in a bumpy, roughshod, fashion, a ride that was typical of an LVT over rough coral terrain. When not used, the gun was laid loose inside the LVT well or turret, which, when en route, was jostled about. Several times in doing so, they were damaged and had to be repaired. Thus, while the combination had proved a deadly duo at Peleliu, it was recommended that for future operations, such flamethrowers be mounted onto the Shermans instead, making for a smoother ride for the weapon. This was tried on a couple of Shermans, but the flamethrower mounted was a short-range, handheld model, and because of that, and the fact that it was mounted where the tank's bow machine gun normally was, it rendered the Sherman vulnerable to close-in enemy attacks. The recommendation was eventually taken up though, and long-range, flamethrowing M4s were used effectively on Iwo Jima, Okinawa, and later during the Korean War.

Another weapon considered not as effective as its counterpart was the Mk III concussion or "offensive grenade." Its main purpose was to take out the enemy with the blast. The Marines though, found it unsatisfactory. It had a small radius and had no fragmentation effect, like the Mk II fragmentation "pineapple," which the riflemen swore by. Worse, although it was designed to explode on impact, the mechanism was unreliable, and in at least two incidents, the grenade exploded in the hand of the rifleman throwing it.

There were many other innovations or improvisations worked out as well, some critically important, some not. For instance, the end of the ramp on an LCT was found to have had the annoying habit of flying up the moment that the tank's treads cleared it. This reaction had the effect of swiping up the rear of the tank, often ripping off waterproofing material or rear attachments. A simple remedy was to affix a half-inch-thick steel plate four feet long and one and a half feet wide to each end of the ramp. Together they acted as an extension of the ramp, so that when the treads cleared the extensions and the ramp flew up—which was not as high with the added weight of the plates bolted on—it would clear the end of the tank.

The Japanese too had a couple new weapons innovations that they first employed on Peleliu. One was a 150mm mortar, a large, high-trajectory weapon, with a tube over six feet tall and a base plate that was so heavy the mortar could not effectively be considered mobile. Four of these mortars were captured. Another was an oversized, ad hoc rocket made out of a 200mm (8-inch) naval shell. There was no aiming device: it was simply pointed at the American lines and fired electrically. Its range was less than 1,500 yards, its trajectory was wild (there were no stabilizing fins), and the shell traveled so slowly that men in the impact area could see it coming and flee accordingly. The explosion though, was ground-shaking, the concussion devastating, and the crater it made tremendous.

The very makeup of the island had been an important consideration in the way the campaign unfolded. Unlike islands taken earlier in the war, those invaded later on were mostly composed of volcanic rock or coral, hard to forge into defensive positions, but formidable when they were. As a result, better bombardment techniques were developed, and more extensive air support was brought into the planning. Newer weapons such as flamethrowers and napalm were used more effectively and played a bigger tactical role in reducing dug-in enemy resistance.

The new style of Japanese defense was a hard lesson for the Marines to learn, but, as always, they took to solutions with a methodical, if not savage style. As they struggled to take the enemy positions on the Umurbrogol ridges, they created a relatively new standard of assault. Seeking out any cave or tunnel opening became number one priority in their short, careful advances. Any opening that even remotely resembled an entrance of any sort was, if possible and appropriate, first assaulted with grenades, flamethrowers, and explosives. In any event though, the opening was sealed, one way or another, while other Marines carefully watched for any escapes from another or back entrance. Considerable quantities of explosives were used for this technique, but the results seemed to be effective, and risk to the men became minimal. It was hard to judge how many of the enemy were actually killed this way, but that statistic was certainly not relevant to the mission.

As for going over the entire battle itself, for over ten years after the island had been taken, a mandatory study course on Peleliu, which featured a mockup of The Point, was used at the Marine Corps College at Quantico, Virginia. It became a primary teaching tool in amphibious warfare for young Marine officers.

The lessons of Peleliu would not be forgotten.

CHAPTER FIVE

After the Battle

The Commanders

The fate of the American commanders after Peleliu vary. As mentioned, General Rupertus had for a while been earmarked by his former commanding officer and mentor, General Vandegrift, to someday succeed him as the Commandant of the Marine Corps. Rupertus himself had expected the appointment.

It was not to be, though. After the Peleliu operation, Rupertus, when he landed at Guadalcanal, was again recalled to Washington, and ordered to report to Marine Corps Headquarters. He arrived on October 29.

General Vandegrift later wrote:

> I decided now to bring Bill Rupertus home ... Bill was already tired when I saw him in the Pacific, and I let him stay on only because of the personal request of Admiral Halsey. I knew the Peleliu Campaign must have nearly exhausted him ...

The initial conversation between the two went unrecorded, but was no doubt intense. Vandegrift years later told one of his close aides that he told Rupertus that "he had no choice but to relieve Rupertus of his command, and expressed his sorrowful displeasure and regrets over the way things turned out, and the heavy losses suffered in the Palaus." The official reason given for Rupertus's relief of command was ostensibly because of his health. He was though, given a new command: the Marine Corps schools. And possibly as a placating gesture, Vandegrift saw to it that Rupertus received the Distinguished Service Medal for his part on Peleliu.

Perhaps not so surprising, some five months later, his health did fail him. On Sunday evening, March 25, 1945, just a week before his division was scheduled to go into battle on another contentious island—Okinawa—Rupertus, after attending a small dinner party, suffered a massive heart attack in his quarters and collapsed. He was rushed to Bethesda Naval Hospital, where he was pronounced dead. Two days later, he was buried with full military honors in Arlington National Cemetery.

Sadly, General Geiger's fate was not far behind. After Peleliu, he was flown back to the States for a short leave, before returning to Honolulu to assess plans to reorganize the armed forces and help in planning the invasion of Okinawa. Ultimately, he was again given charge of III Amphibious Corps under the command of the operation's ground commander, 59-year-old Army general Bolivar Buckner, commanding the Tenth Army for that operation.

The invasion, started on Easter Sunday, April 1, 1945, stretched on into mid-June, with the Marines and the Army relentless in their offensive, and the Japanese fanatic in their defense. Geiger led his men in that campaign the same way he had at Peleliu, often up at the front, assessing the situation.

Then in the early afternoon of June 18, as Buckner was inspecting advance units at an 8th Marines frontline observation post, the Japanese, who had spotted his presence, fired a salvo of 150mm artillery shells at the position. One of them hit a coral outcrop near the general. No one else was hurt, but the explosion from the shell rammed a few lethal fragments of coral into the general's chest. He was taken to an aid station where he died on the table a few minutes later. Buckner became the highest-ranking U.S. officer to be killed by enemy fire during World War II.

Succeeding him in command was General Geiger, who immediately took command of the Tenth Army. With Geiger's new command came his third star, promoting him to lieutenant general. The Army though, was upset by this, and resented having a Marine take over command of what they considered their operation. With the antagonism between the two services still alive and well, the Army moved swiftly to remedy the embarrassment. Reliable, although also controversial, four-star Army general Joe Stillwell (who had originally been chosen to later take over from Buckner) was quickly ordered to Okinawa and to take command. In the meantime, on June 21, General Geiger declared that the island had been taken and hostile resistance had ceased.

Two days later, on the morning of June 23, Stillwell arrived on the island, and the next day he assumed command of the entire operation. Still, for a brief few days, Geiger had commanded the Tenth Army. He would go down in U.S. military history as the only Marine Corps general to ever command an entire army in a war, the operation resulting in his being awarded his fourth Distinguished Service Medal.

Geiger survived the war, witnessing the official surrender of the Japanese on the USS *Missouri*, the only senior Marine officer present. He returned to the States a hero, and decided to retire in mid-November, 1946. Unfortunately, he died from complications due to lung cancer on January 23, 1947, also at the Bethesda Naval Hospital. He is buried at Arlington, and was later posthumously promoted to four-star general.

General O. P. Smith and all the division's regimental commanders were repatriated to the States in early November for long overdue rest. Smith later participated as Buckner's deputy chief of staff in the Okinawa invasion, and also fought in Korea (including the historic Inchon invasion) as the First Marine Division's commanding officer. Under him in Korea was again Colonel Puller, who first commanded the 1st Marines, advanced to the division's ADO, and later took over commanding the division when Smith took over command of IX Corps after its commander, Major General Bryant Moore, was killed in a helicopter crash. Smith was eventually appointed Commanding General Fleet Marine Force, Atlantic. He died on Christmas Day, 1977, in Los Altos, California.

Colonel Puller stayed in the Marines and once again saw combat with the First Marine Division in Korea. There he earned his fifth Navy Cross, as well as an Army Distinguished Service Cross. Colonel Hanneken, promoted to brigadier general, became the chief of staff of the Troop Training Unit, Pacific Amphibious Forces. He retired in 1948. Colonel Harold "Bucky" Harris after the war became an instructor at the Army and Navy Staff College in Washington D.C. until the spring of 1946, when he was transferred to the staff of the of CinCMed, and then back to the Marine Corps headquarters in Washington. He retired from the Corps on New Year's Day, 1950.

After most of the 81st Infantry Division was taken off Peleliu in January of 1945, General Mueller flew to New Caledonia on January 13 to rest and reorganize. The division was later sent to Leyte Island in May, 1945 to end enemy resistance. There Mueller began training his men for the anticipated invasion of Japan. When the atomic bomb put an end to the war in August, 1945, the division was sent to Japan in mid-September as part of the occupation force. Mueller himself, while he retained command of the 81st, was ordered to Tokyo to become part of General MacArthur's occupational high command as its chief of staff.

Continued Resistance: The Raid

Peleliu was declared taken at the end of November, 1944. Long after that day though, there still remained several Japanese holed up in caves, and enemy resistance continued to be a nuisance to the island for months. Nearly all of the Japanese holdouts refused to give up, and despite the eventual methodical sweep of the American infantry units, they were able to evade capture. This trait was actually common on numerous Pacific islands until long the after war had ended. In the instance of Peleliu, a good number of the enemy soldiers who had survived or gone undetected during the battle were able to hide for many weeks, with one group holding out for as long as eight months. A few of them, having been buried alive when their caves or tunnel entrances were sealed by explosives, managed to dig their way out and persisted. They were able to subsist by living off residual supplies or by foraging, occasionally venturing out to ambush lone Americans who out and about looking for souvenirs, or occasionally ambush a U.S. patrol.

To make matters worse, the Japanese forces still in the northern islands refused to give up on losing Peleliu, and the senior commanders felt that with the American invasion of the Philippines and their efforts to take them, an opportunity to strike might present itself. To that end, raiding parties from other Palau islands to the north occasionally tried to cross over by barge or small boat from nearby Babelthuap or Koror Island. Most of the time, as they attempted the crossing, normally at night, they would get spotted or electronically detected by American gunboats. Sometimes in the morning hours, Marine Corsairs from Peleliu's restored airfield would spot some and strafe them. If a raiding party made it to shore, they would then be dispatched either by more aircraft or by a 381st RCT response team dispatched to intercept them.

As late as January 18, 1945, one such Japanese raid of some 75 soldiers came across to Peleliu.* Around 0200 hours, the two barges stealthily approached the island, the men carrying an odd assortment of weapons: different types of rifles, grenades, some incendiaries, packs of demolitions, and, of all things, spears. Nearly all these men had originally been part of the defending forces on Peleliu, but had escaped, crossing over to Ngesebus or Garakayo Island, slowly working their way northward to Japanese lines. Unfortunately for them, because of the strict Bushido code, they were arrested and held in disgrace for abandoning their posts. Contemptibly seen as deserters, they were isolated in a detention compound on Arakabesan Island and held there as prisoners.

Finally in mid-January, they were taken out of the compound, armed with that odd assortment of weapons, and put onto the two barges. In what was to essentially be a suicide attack, they were ordered to infiltrate onto Peleliu. They were to destroy whatever aircraft they could, conduct raids, kill whomever they encountered, blow up supplies, and wreak whatever damage they could.

---

* One source (Hallas) put the number at 64.

Expected to either take the island or die trying as Japanese warriors, they were curtly told NOT to return.

The barges worked their way southward. One group actually circled Peleliu from the west and finally came ashore, ironically at what had once been Beach White-1. The other putted around the other side of the island and landed at what had been Purple Beach. Both barges were spotted as they passed alongside the island, and the entire Peleliu garrison, the 381st RCT, was immediately put on alert. The raiders at White Beach were easily found and by 1030 hours, they had been eliminated. Those who landed on Purple Beach though, managed to infiltrate as far as the airfield, where they spread panic among the Marine pilots before they too were finally eliminated.

All but two of the enemy were killed; the dead included two Japanese dressed in American uniforms. Evidently they had come out of hiding in the hills to join the attackers. After the war, the Japanese commander, General Inoue Sadao, and his chief of staff, Colonel Tada, were both very reluctant to talk about this raid. In Inoue's mind, these men had truly shamed themselves, their honor, and their country, but he nevertheless did not want to bring dishonor to the units or the branch of service that they had served. In the little he ever said about the subject, he made known that this type of action was made to atone for their disgrace by dying honorably.

The Last Surrender

Even by early 1945, occasional reports of Japanese survivors on Peleliu continued, and supplies were sometimes found to have been broken into by unknown individuals. Living miserably in various hidden caves and tunnels, first on their own provisions, and then on supplies stolen from the small U.S. occupying force of just a hundred men, these few Japanese survivors stubbornly refused to surrender. They occasionally came out to take a few shots at Americans here and there, and from time to time, whether from necessity, discovered opportunity, or sheer frustration, they would venture forth at night to scavenge for food and fuel, sometimes ambushing an American patrol in the dark. Eventually, many more of the cave and tunnel entrances were simply sealed shut by the Americans. Others that were found to harbor holdouts or were under suspicion of such were periodically assaulted. The rest of the Japanese leftovers were thus slowly flushed out.

On Sunday, September 2, 1945, while General MacArthur aboard the USS *Missouri* in Tokyo Bay was accepting the surrender of the Japanese Empire from their government delegates, another ceremony, much simpler, was taking place in the Northern Palaus. After a couple days of conferences with the Americans, the Japanese area commander for the Palau Island District Group formerly surrendered all his forces aboard the USS *Amick*.* Lieutenant General Inoue Sadao signed the article of surrender of 24,900 soldiers, sailors, and airmen, as well as 9,750 Japanese civilians over to the Peleliu Island commander, Marine Corps Brigadier General F. P. Rogers.

In the spring of 1947, incredibly over two years and a half years after Peleliu had been declared secure, and over a year and a half since the war's end, it was rumored that there was a last group of holdouts on the island. Reportedly they were lurking in one specific area of the Umurbrogol ridges. Patrols were again sent out to try and find these men.

On April 3, a Japanese straggler from that group was caught by a Marine patrol, though some accounts suggest he actually walked up to the patrol and surrendered. He was spotted sitting on the side of a road next to a section of what had once been referred to by the Marines as Bloody Nose Ridge. Seeing the Marines approaching him, he raised his arms in surrender. The Marines came up to him and noted beside him a sawed-off carbine with a primitively fashioned stock, a few clips of ammunition, and a grenade. The man identified himself as a Japanese sailor, 24-year-old Superior Seaman Kiyokazu Tsuchida.

The seaman was taken to the island's brig and interrogated. He told his captors that he had been a part of a small renegade group. Questioned at length, he revealed that they were a mixed batch of 20 soldiers, seven sailors, and four Okinawan workers, all under the command of a strict career Army officer, a Lieutenant Ei Yamaguchi. Tsuchida told the Americans that Yamaguchi would never surrender, and it would be almost impossible to convince the others to give up without his consent. Ever since Peleliu had fallen to the Americans back in November, 1944, the group had survived together in one of the island's elaborate tunnel systems that the Japanese had prepared before the invasion and that somehow had thus far remained undetected.

---

* USS *Amick* (DE-168) was launched May 27, 1943. A 1,620-ton Cannon-class destroyer escort, she was 306 feet long, 36½ feet wide, and had a draft of 11 foot 8 inches. Armed with three 3-inch guns, four 40mm mounts, and ten 20mm AA guns, the ship was named after Eugene Earle Amick, communications officer aboard the USS *Astoria* (CA-34), killed in the Savo Island engagement, August 9, 1942. After the war, she served for 20 years as the JDS *Asahi* (DDE-262), before being returned to the U.S. Navy in 1975. Finally retired from service on June 15 of that year, she was sold to the Philippine Republic in September, 1976, before finally being scrapped in 1989.

While the renegade group had never mounted any sort of direct threat to the American occupying force, they had often been able to harass personnel on the island with occasional pot-shots from a distance. These ambushes though, were few, since the group had needed to conserve ammo. Yamaguchi, a veteran who had served with the 2nd Infantry Regiment in China for several years, was a strict disciplinarian, Surrender, he had told the men, was not an option, since their warrior code condemned it and the Japanese Military Field Code prohibited it. So as the months went by and they watched the vegetation slowly beginning to return to the island, the holdouts had just barely survived. They often wondered how the war was progressing, all the while waiting, either for some choice moment to take advantage of the Yankees and seize the island, or else be rescued by a Japanese counter-invasion.

Convinced by the Americans that the war was indeed over and his group could come out of hiding, Tsuchida went back to the cave with a small Marine detachment and pleaded for the holdouts to give up. Still the Japanese refused, and the Americans finally returned to base.

In further talks with the Americans, Tsuchida confided in greater depth the reasons the group was reluctant to surrender: it was their duty to the Empire to continue to resist. The captured sailor told them at length about the Bushido code, and what it meant to the Japanese soldier. He himself expressed some apprehension about what the group would do, something the group had discussed many times. Things he felt, could very well come to a head now that they knew that they had been found. If these men sensed that the Americans were closing in on them or that they could no longer hold out, they might resort to their final plan of going out in a blaze of glory, some sort of last-ditch *banzai* attack.

Moreover, tensions were continuing to mount among the group. One of them had a few months before become antagonistic to the point where the Lieutenant Yamaguchi had summarily shot him. Another, in one of their recent raids, had been wounded by a Marine sentry and, seeing no other choice available, had committed suicide. Things were getting desperate.

The concern was serious enough that the island's garrison was put on alert. The Navy contingent of 110 personnel stationed there, along with their dependents, were moved to a safe area. The island commander, Captain Leonard Fox, in the interest of trying to resolve the matter peacefully, took additional steps to try and persuade the men to surrender. He radioed Guam to send over a high-ranking Japanese officer to talk the holdouts into surrendering. The man was Rear Admiral Michio Sumikawa. He had been participating as a witness to Japanese war crimes committed during the war. Having served on several aircraft carriers during the war, he had ended up at the war's end as chief of staff for the Japanese Fourth Fleet.

On April 21, the Japanese admiral, 26 Marines and Seaman Tsuchida rode in jeeps to the cave where the renegades were holed up. Using a megaphone, the admiral told the men that the war was over, and they could come out with their honor intact. Still, nothing.

Determined, Seaman Tsuchida cautiously entered the cave. This time though, he had an edge. In a bag slung over his shoulder he carried letters for the men from back home. After disbursing the mail, Tsuchida had a number of conversations with them. He promised them several times that despite what they feared, they would not be shot, but rather they would be well treated and soon be repatriated back to Japan. Finally, he was able to persuade most of them, including Lieutenant Yamaguchi himself, to come out of their hideout and surrender.

At length, after some cautious preparations (on both sides), Lieutenant Yamaguchi advanced out of the tunnel with 25 of his men. Amazed that they had actually lost the war, they all marched smartly down the road in formation and over to what had once been the Japanese headquarters at the northern edge of the airfield. As 80 Marines in full gear stood in formation and saluted, Yamaguchi bowed low, then offered his sword and his battle flag in surrender to the Marine detachment commander.

Yamaguchi returned to the cave in 1994 on a tour. In an interview, he related that on several occasions, over a weekend, he and a couple of his men would creep onto the American base at night and calmly watch the outdoor movie from the shadows just a few feet from the enemy. In a 1995 television interview, he confessed: "We couldn't believe that we had lost. We were always instructed that we could never lose. It is the Japanese tradition that we must fight until we die; until the end."

The next day, April 22, 1947, the final holdouts in the cave, the last seven men in stained, tattered uniforms, came out and also surrendered.

The war on Peleliu was finally, really over.

Amazingly, there were even more holdouts on other islands in the Pacific. One of the very last to give up was Second Lieutenant Hiroo Onoda, who had been in Japanese intelligence on Lubang Island, about 90 miles southwest of Manila. After the Americans retook the Philippines, he had gone into hiding with three others. Although the other three were finally caught or shot, Onoda, who had been trained in guerrilla tactics and evasion, stubbornly continued to hold out for an astonishing 29 years, until 1974. That February, a Japanese student adventurer, a Norio Suzuki, set out to look for him to see if the phantom holdout that had been rumored over the years was true. Suzuki finally found him hiding in the woods. He tried to tell Onoda that the war was long over, but Onoda refused to give up, telling him that it was all enemy propaganda. In any event, he would never surrender, unless he was specifically ordered to by a superior officer.

The word went out, and in early March, Onoda's previous commanding officer, Major Yoshimi Taniguchi, now a bookseller, himself flew to the island to try to get Onoda to surrender. The major's last orders to him in 1945 had been to hold out and continue to resist the Americans. His last words to Onoda had been, "It may take three years, it may take five, but whatever happens, we'll come back for you."

Now he returned to the Philippines and traveled to his former lieutenant's hideout on March 9. After an emotional reunion, Taniguchi told Onoda that he was officially relieved of duty, actually presenting orders that their unit had been commanded to "cease military activities and operations immediately and place themselves under the command of the nearest superior officer. When no officer can be found, they are to communicate with the American or Philippine forces and follow their directives."

Just nine days shy of his 52nd birthday, Lieutenant Hiroo Onoda finally surrendered to the Americans, turning over his battle sword, his rifle, several hundred rounds of ammo, and a few hand grenades. With him, he also carried a dagger that his mother had given him in back in 1944 to kill himself with if he was ever captured. Onoda returned to modernized Japan as a national hero. His war was finally over. (He would years later document his stubborn resistance in a book entitled *No Surrender: My Thirty-Year War*.)

Conclusion

In terms of the number of infantrymen committed to battle, the length of the campaign, and taking into account the number of enemy awaiting them, the Peleliu invasion, with the ironic title of Operation *Stalemate II*, went on record as the most costly amphibious invasion in American history. U.S. casualties totaled 9,615 men (over two-thirds of them Marines), with about 1,600 killed and another 8,000 wounded. Nor do the casualty numbers take into account those who were incapacitated by heat or combat fatigue, today known as Post-Traumatic Stress Disorder (PTSD).

In comparison, about 11,000 Japanese and forced laborers were killed and only 200 to 300 taken prisoner. Again, numbers vary with sources. One source puts the number of enemy dead as high as 14,000 and adds that many more escaped to some of the Palau islands to the northeast. Of the few hundred enemy prisoners taken, only a few dozen were actually Japanese soldiers, and only about a third of them were Japanese sailors. The rest were mostly Korean or Okinawan forced labor civilians.

It is sad to point out that Peleliu did not receive the claim to fame in history that other Pacific amphibious battles were given, such as Wake Island, Bataan, Guadalcanal, Leyte Gulf, Tarawa, Iwo Jima, or Okinawa. Back home (just like today), the name Peleliu was barely known. To the average American, Peleliu seemed another distant island that was being secured. And what few reports there were focused on the heavy casualties.

Another critical reason that the battle is rarely mentioned in American history of the war is the matter of timing. That fall of 1944, the news at home concentrated heavily on the war in Europe, which was then at its height. Germany was reeling on all fronts. Only two days after the Peleliu landings, the massive American–British airborne operation *Market Garden* began in the Netherlands. In the East, the Germans had been bled dry, and the Russians were ruthlessly driving forward across Eastern Europe, with Operation *Bagration* resulting in the destruction of German Army Group Centre and over 400,000 German casualties. In the West, the Americans were racing across France, the British were liberating the Low Countries, and in Italy, their combined armies had taken Rome and Florence and were moving northward. The Reich was being bombed round the clock, the Americans by day, and the British by night. The battle of the Atlantic was all but won.

On top of all these developments, even while Peleliu was still being secured, MacArthur's epic invasion of the Philippines began, dwarfing the Peleliu invasion and essentially turning it into a needless, backwater operation.

The Peleliu invasion also suffered from poor media coverage. Only a half dozen of the three dozen reporters assigned to the division actually went ashore with the Marines (Damien Parer, an Australian war photographer for Paramount News, was killed the morning of September 17 while filming the 2nd Battalion, 1st Marines begin their attack). This was mostly because they thought that the operation would not last long. Remember, Rupertus had stated it would all be over in four to five days, although the correspondents were skeptical of his initial predictions before the landing. Still, because of his predictions of a quick operation, most correspondents decided to forego covering the Peleliu operation because it did not seem worthwhile. They waited to go in on the Philippines invasion.

It also did not help that Rupertus detested the media and avoided them whenever he could. Then, as the Marine casualties quickly became excessive and the operation stalled, this naturally made for bad press, the news that came out sorely dampening morale back home. People naturally turned to the better news coming from Europe. In contrast though, Japanese radio propaganda made good use of the Americans' struggle and boasted of their heavy casualties.

Perhaps, in the end, the Marine Corps itself might have preferred the battle be downplayed, because they had previously taken criticism from both the Army and the press over high casualties at Tarawa and Saipan, and then again weeks later when it became clear that Peleliu was not turning into a big success.

Peleliu had indeed been a difficult mission for the Marines. Almost every senior Marine officer who had taken part of the operation wrote after the war that Peleliu was one of the hardest fought battles in the history of the Marine Corps, and the battle left a vivid, indelible memory to all who had been there. General Geiger later referred to the operation as "the toughest fight of the war." General Harold O. Deakin, the division's planning officer at Peleliu and later its D-1, wrote after the war:

> Here [Peleliu] is the worst campaign in the history of warfare, and Peleliu—I am sure the historians ought to be able to have found by now—was far worse than Iwo Jima, or the others. I think you'd find statistically that the ferocity of Peleliu was worse.

General Hough in his history of the operation referred to Peleliu as "one of the most vicious and stubbornly contested, and nowhere was the fighting efficiency of the U.S. Marine more convincingly demonstrated."

Brigadier General O. P. Smith never forgot this operation. After his retirement in the fall of 1955, although in his office at home there were many maps and memorabilia from all of his campaigns, there were only three pictures on his dresser: his wedding on Guam, a picture of his sister Marguerite, and that photograph of him crouching down in a foxhole on Peleliu with a field phone in his ear, a look of intensity on his face as he directs his men, who at that moment are locked in savage combat.

Historians George Garand and Truman Strobridge in their account of the battle perhaps put it best:

> Except for those who participated in it, Peleliu largely remains a forgotten battle, its location unknown, its name calling forth no patriotic remembrance of self-sacrifice or gallant deeds, as do the battles of Guadalcanal, Tarawa, and Iwo Jima. For the Marines who stormed ashore on Peleliu, however, the strategic value of the island may not have been clear, but duty was. They had been given a job to do, and they went ahead and did it.

The War Department did recognize the bravery of the Marines who took part in the invasion. The First Marine Division, along with the units that reinforced it, received the Presidential Unit Citation for Peleliu. In that one month the First Marine Division fought there, no less than eight Marines, seven of whom were part of the First Marine Division, were awarded the Congressional Medal of Honor:

- Corporal Lewis K. Bausell, USMC, 1/5 (awarded posthumously)
- Private First Class Arthur J. Jackson, USMC, 3/7
- Private First Class Richard E. Kraus, USMCR, 8th Amphibian Tractor Battalion (awarded posthumously)
- Private First Class John D. New, USMC, 2/7 (awarded posthumously)
- Private First Class Wesley Phelps, USMCR, 3/7 (awarded posthumously)
- Captain Everett P. Pope, USMC, 1/1
- Private First Class Charles H. Roan, USMCR, 2/7 (awarded posthumously)
- First Lieutenant Carlton R. Rouh, USMCR, 1/5

In addition, another 69 Marines were awarded the Navy Cross, the U.S. Navy's second highest decoration, and yet another 330 received the Silver Star, all for their actions on Peleliu.

Although Peleliu had been a costly campaign, lessons learned there would eventually profoundly change American strategy. Out of the savagery of the battle, key elements came forth that ultimately, dramatically, and permanently shaped U.S. amphibious warfare, not just through the rest of World War II, but even unto today. Unfortunately, many of the bitter lessons the First Marine Division had learned on Peleliu did not seem to immediately filter over much to the Third, Fourth, and Fifth Marine Divisions, who would sadly have to learn them on their own at considerable cost when they landed at Iwo Jima in mid-February, 1945. And the First Marine Division would have to refine what they had learned on Peleliu and teach it all to the new Sixth Marine Division when the two units landed on Okinawa on April 1, 1945.

Peleliu—Present

The natives on Peleliu suffered greatly throughout the war. Nearly all of the males who were not killed by their oppressors were forced into hard labor and worked relentlessly on defensive positions. Most of of the population were taken off the island and resettled on the northernmost islands of Babelthuap or Koror.

After the war, these dispossessed islanders were allowed to return to Peleliu. They found that most of the southernmost areas of the island had been destroyed, including their villages. The airfield and surrounding zones were for years occupied by the American military. So the people tended to resettle in the northeastern parts of the island. Over time, even though the Americans finally left, the residents, which only numbered about 500, tended to remain in the north, as the southern sections have reverted to the jungle, sometimes remaining undeveloped (*chutem buai*) or used for agriculture (*chutem beluu*). There are a number of cemeteries on the island located it areas designated as sacred land (*chetemel chelid*), as well as war memorials. If a man is affluent, he might have been able to have built on private land (*chetemel a blai*) a fancy meeting house called a *bai*.

Exactly two years after VJ Day, on August 15, 1947, the General Assembly of the newly created United Nations passed by unanimous vote a resolution making the Palau Islands a U.S. mandate, along with another 2,000 islands in the Pacific that had been captured and occupied by the Japanese.

The Palaus became self-governing in 1981. Peleliu is now referred to as the Palau state of Bliliou, with nearby Angaur Island now referred to as Ngeaur.

A couple years later, the U.S. National Park System Advisory Board made a study of making the island a national landmark, and on February 4, 1985, the Peleliu Battlefield National Historic Landmark was approved by the outgoing Secretary of the Interior, William P. Clark.

Today, Bliliou—or Peleliu, depending on who you talk to—is considered by many as a vacation spot in the Pacific. It is a popular location for those wanting an unusual Pacific getaway experience. In addition, over time, it has become a favorite choice for a number of scuba enthusiasts, and periodically, a few U.S. veteran groups. What had once been Purple Beach on the southeastern side of the island, where the 1st Marines had regrouped before being evacuated, is now known as "Honeymoon Beach."

The scars of war on Peleliu, while still plentiful, are today to some extent difficult to find. While there are many markers and plaques in the area, they must be sought out. Souvenir hunting and scavenging is now illegal, since the Palau Republic has established Peleliu as a historic landmark in 1985. For those sturdy enough to brave the risk and explore the jungles in tropical heat, even finding a specific location is difficult, because the jungle has grown back to its primeval thickest. Just navigating over or through the areas, especially on the Umurbrogol ridges, is difficult at best. Artifacts and memento items can still be found though, although usually in some level of decay or decomposition. This is especially true in the caves where the Japanese held out. Explorers might find decaying weapons, boxes, perhaps some empty sake bottles, and, who knows, maybe even the bones of a Japanese holdout.

Almost all the wartime buildings—those not destroyed—have been removed, and the caves and tunnels that the dug-in Japanese had so vigorously defended have over the years gone to ruin, and most of them are either fully or partially collapsed. Those in the open have long been reclaimed by the jungle.

The war and its consequences though, have not been forgotten by the local populace. Many families on the island carry souvenirs from the battlefield. Their homes often contain remnants of the thousands of pieces of gear and equipment that the invaders of both sides left behind. Domestic items include mess trays, silverware, canteens, pots, containers, spades, and coffee cups. The runway that was put up by the Seabees over the old Japanese airfield was eventually carved up and its surfaces used to make fencing structures for the natives. Other more obvious items such as empty shells, aircraft parts, helmets, are sometimes used as front-yard decorations. The U.S. cemeteries in which the bodies of those killed in combat once lay are now empty, the remains having been exhumed and sent back years ago to the large veteran cemeteries,

Hawaii or to the service member's home state. The grounds though, are still properly kept by the islanders.

Japanese veterans and their families have returned to the island on numerous occasions, usually to try to locate the remains of a lost relative, to commemorate their loved ones by paying their respects, or to hold memorial services.

Not many surviving Marine veterans who fought in that battle have ever returned to the island. Of the few who have, reasons have mostly been either for some type of cathartic emotional quest or else to establish memorials. Obviously, unlike for the Japanese, the extra thousands of miles to get there is also a considerable factor.

Quite a number of Marine veterans though, have felt a strong sense of reluctance in returning to the scene of the crime, so to speak. One Marine, Sergeant George Peto, explained it this way:

> Many times in the last few decades I have been asked why I never returned. I wouldn't go back, not even to pay homage to my buddies who had died there. I mean, what for?
>
> Why would I want to go back? In the years since, Peleliu has gone back to being a tropical island. And I hear it's real nice now, a type of tourist resort. Purple Beach is a good example. It's now called "Honeymoon Beach." You'd probably see couples vacationing, walking along the sand holding hands, sitting under some umbrella sipping tropical rum drinks. There would be a few native girls dancing in their lavalava skirts with pretty smiles, swinging their arms to the music with the gentle waves behind them, and looking at you with those dreamy eyes.
>
> Me, I figure that I would stare right next to where the tourists were sitting and imagine seeing bodies lying in the sand, or rolling in the surf. Tourists would hear soft Polynesian music. Me, I'd hear mortar shells and tracers echoing in my head. The vacationers would see the beauty of a tropical paradise, and I would just see shattered mangroves, burnt amtracs, craters, and corpses—lifeless friends of mine lying face down in the wet sand.

For those who fought there, Peleliu would never be forgotten.

Bibliography

Ainsworth, 1st Sgt. Jack R., USMC, *Among Heroes: A Marine Corps Rifle Company on Peleliu*, CreateSpace Independent Publishing Platform, 2015.

Alexander, Joseph H., USMC, *Storm Landings: Epic Amphibious Battles in the Central Pacific*, Naval Institute Press, Annapolis, MD., 1997, & USNI *Proceedings*, Vol. 124/11/1,149, November 1998.

_____, "What Was Nimitz Thinking?" *Proceedings*, U.S. Naval Institute, Vol. 124/11/1,149, November 1998.

Blair, Bobby C., & DeCioccio, John Peter, *Victory at Peleliu: The 81st Infantry Division's Pacific Campaign*, University of Oklahoma Press, Norman, OK, 2011.

Burgin, R. V., & Marvel, Bill, *Islands of the Damned: A Marine at War in the Pacific*, New American Library Division of Penguin Group, NY, NY, 2010.

Cameron, Craig, M, *American Samurai: Myth, Imagination, and the Conduct of Battle in the First Marine Division, 1941–1951*, Cambridge University Press, Cambridge, UK, 1994.

Camp, Dick, *Last Man Standing: The 1st Marine Regiment on Peleliu*, Zenith Press Division of MBI Publishing, Minneapolis, MN, 2008.

Chen, C. Peter, "Pacific Strategy Conference: 16 July 1944–27 July, 1944," World War II Database, www.ww2db.com.

Davis, Burke, *Marine! The Life of Chesty Puller*, Bantam Books, NY, NY, 1962.

Gailey, Harry A., *Peleliu 1944*, The Nautical & Aviation Publishing Company of America, Annapolis, MD, 1983.

_____., *War in the Pacific: From Pearl Harbor to Tokyo Bay*, Presidion Press Division of Random House, NY, NY, 1997.

Generous, William Thomas Jr., *Sweet Pea at War: A History of USS Portland (CA-33)*, University Press of Kentucky, Lexington, KY, 2003.

Gypton, Jeremy, *Bloody Peleliu: Unavoidable Yet Unnecessary*, www.militaryhistoryonline.com/wwii/peleliu/default.aspx, Military History Online, 2004.

Hallas, James H., *The Devil's Anvil: The Assault on Peleliu*, Praeger Publishers, Westport, CT, 1994.

Heinrichs, Waldo, & Gallicchio, Marc, *Implacable Foes: War in the Pacific, 1944–1945*, Oxford University Press, NY, NY, 2017.

Hoffman, Lt. Col. Jon T., USMCR, *Chesty: The Story of Lieutenant General Lewis B. Puller, USMC*, Random House, NY, NY, 2001.

Hoyt, Edwin P., *How They Won the War in the Pacific: Nimitz and His Admirals*, Lyons Press, Guileford, CT, 2000.

Hunt, Capt. George P., *Coral Comes High: U.S. Marines and the Battle for The Point on Peleliu*, Harper & Brothers, NY, NY, 1946.

Isely, Jeter A. & Crowl, Philip A., *The U.S. Marines and Amphibious War*, Princeton University Press, Princeton, NJ, 1951.

Kilmer, David, *Daughters of Infamy: The stories of the Ships That Survived Pearl Harbor*, iUniverse, Inc., Bloomington, IN, 2011.

La Bree, Clifton, *The Gentle Warrior: General Oliver Prince Smith, USMC*, Kent State University Press, Kent, OH, 2001.

Leckie, Robert, *Helmet for My Pillow*, Random House, NY, NY, 1957.

Lippman, David, "The War Between the Smiths: High Command Feud at Saipan," Warfare History Network, Sovereign Media, McLean, VA, 2017.

Luzinas, Edward C., *Tanker: Boys, Men, and Cowards*, Athena Press, UK, 2004,

Makos, Adam, *Voices of the Pacific: Untold Stories From the Marine Heroes of World War II*, The Berkeley Publishing Group, London, UK, 2013.

Manchester, William, *American Caesar: Douglas MacArthur 1880–1964*, Little, Brown & Co., NY, NY, 1978.

McEnery, Jim, & Sloan, Bill, *Hell in the Pacific: A Marine Rifleman's Journey From Guadalcanal to Peleliu*, Simon & Schuster, NY, NY, 2012.

McMillan, George, *The Old Breed*, Infantry Journal Press, Washington, D.C., 1949.

Medeiros Jr., Maj. John L., "Strategic and Operational Importance of Peleliu During the Pacific War," (master's thesis), U.S. Marine Corps Command & Staff College, Marine Corps University, Quantico, VA, 2010.

Moran, Jim, & Rottman, Gordon L., *Peleliu 1944: The Forgotten Corner of Hell*, Osprey Publishing, Oxford, UK, 2002.

Morison, Samuel Eliot, *History of United States Operations in World War II: Leyte June 1944–January 1945*, University of Illinois Press, Chicago, IL, 1958.

Murray, Stephen C., *The Battle over Peleliu: Islander, Japanese, and American Memories of War*, University of Alabama Press, Tuscaloosa, AL, 2016.

North, Oliver L. & Musser, Joe, *War Stories II: Heroism in the Pacific*, Regnery Publishing, Inc., Washington, DC, 2004.

O'Reilly, Bill, & Dugard, Martin, *Killing the Rising Sun: How America Vanquished World War II Japan*, Henry Holt & Co., NY, NY, 2016.

Peto, George, & Margaritis, Peter, *Twenty-Two on Peleliu—Four Pacific Campaigns with the Corps: The Memoirs of an Old Breed Marine*, Casemate Publishers, Havertown, PA, 2017.

Peto Jr., Sgt. George, USMC, interviews on June 17, June 24, June 30, July 22, & July 31, 2015.

Polmar, Norman, *Aircraft Carriers: A History of Carrier Aviation and Its Influence on World Events, Volume 1: 1909–1945*, Potomac Books, Inc, Washington, D.C., 2006.

Potter, E.B., *Nimitz*, U.S. Naval Institute Press, Annapolis, MD, 1976.

_____, *Bull Halsey: A Biography*, U.S. Naval Institute Press, 1985.

Rielly, Robin L., *American Amphibious Gunboats in World War II: A History of LCI and LCLS (L) Ships in the Pacific*, McFarland & Company, Inc., Jefferson, NC, 2013.

Robinson, C. Snelling, *200,000 Miles Aboard the Destroyer Cotton*, Kent State University Press, Kent, OH, 2000.

Ross, Bill D., *Peleliu: Tragic Triumph*, Random House, NY, NY, 1991.

Rottman, Gordon L., *The Big Book of Gun Trivia: Everything you want to know, don't want to know, and don't know you need to know*, Osprey Publishing, Oxford, UK, 2013.

Shisler, Gail P., *For Country and Corps: The Life of General Oliver P. Smith*, U.S. Naval Institute Press, Annapolis, MD, 2009.

Sledge, E. B., *With the Old Breed: At Peleliu and Okinawa*, Presidio Press Division of Random House, NY, NY, 1981.

Sloan, Bill, *Brotherhood of Heroes: The Marines at Peleliu, 1944*, Simon & Schuster, NY, NY, 2005.

Smith, Gen. Holland M, & Finch, Percy, *Coral and Brass*, Dept. of the Navy Headquarters, U.S. Marine Corps, Washington, D.C., 1949.

Snead, David Lindsey, *Obscure but Important: The United States and the Russell Islands in World War II*, Liberty University Press, Lynchburg, VA, 2003.

Tillman, Barrett, *US Marine Corps Fighter Squadrons of World War II*, Osprey Publishing, Oxford, UK, 2014.

Tully, Grace, Appointment Diary of Franklin D. Roosevelt, Pare Lorentz Center, FDR Presidential Library, Hyde Park, NY, 2011.

Wellons, Maj. James B, USMC (2007), *General Roy S. Geiger, USMC: Marine Aviator, Joint Force Commander* (master's thesis), School of Advanced Air & Space Studies, Maxwell Air Force Base, AL, 2007.

Wright, Derrick, *Pacific Victory: Tarawa to Okinawa, 1943–1945*, The History Press, Gloucestershire, UK, 2005.

(unknown author), *History of the USS Crescent City (APA-21): From October 10, 1941 to December 1, 1945*, U.S.S. Crescent City Association and Reunion Group, Ashland, OR, 1945.

U.S. Government Sources*

Crowl, Phillip A., *U.S. Army in World War II: War in the Pacific – Campaign in the Marianas*, Office of the Chief of Military History, Dept. of the Army, Washington, D.C., 1960.

Frank, Benis M. & Shaw Jr., Henry I., *History of U.S. Marine Corps Operations in World War II. Vol. V. Victory & Occupation*, Historical Branch, G-3 Division Headquarters, U.S. Marine Corps, Washington, DC, 1968.

Garand, George W., & Strobridge, Truman R., *History of the U.S. Marine Corps Operations in World War II, Vol. IV: Western Pacific Operations*, Historical Division, Headquarters, U.S. Marine Corps, Washington, D.C., 1971.

Gayle, Brig. Gen. Gordon D., USMC, *Bloody Beaches: The Marines at Peleliu*, Marine Corps Historical Center, Washington, DC, 1996.

Hough, Maj. Frank O, USMC, *The Seizure of Peleliu* (also printed as *The Assault on Peleliu*), Historical Branch, G-3 Division, Headquarters, U.S. Marine Corps, 1950.

Nimitz, Chester, *Gray Book*, Naval War College, Naval Historical Center, Washington, D.C., 2012.

Silverthorn, Lt. General Merwin H., USMC (Ret.), *Oral History*. History & Museums Division, Headquarters U.S. Marine Corps, Washington, DC, 1973.

Smith, Robert Ross, *United States Army in WWII: The Pacific—The Approach to the Philippines*, Center Of Military History, United States Army, Washington, D.C., 1996.

U.S. Army & Marine Infantry Battalions Table of Organization & Equipment File #3, General Headquarters, United States Army, Pentagon, Washington, DC, 1994.

U.S. Army Commanding Officer, 81st Infantry Division, Operation On Peleliu Island, 23 Sept.–27 Nov., 1944, U.S. Army Historical Branch, Washington, D.C.

U.S. Marine Corps

Commander, III Amphibious Corps Operations Report, Palaus Operation, October 24, 1944.

First Marine Division, Palau Operation Action Report, January 8, 1945.

Official Ledger, September, 1944, 1st Battalion, 1st Marines, First Marine Division, Historical Branch, G-3 Division, Headquarters, U.S. Marine Corps.

---

* All government sources are either unclassified or have been declassified.

U.S. Navy

Commander, Battleship Division 3, Action Report – Bombardment and Capture of Peleliu Island, Palau Islands, 10 September, 1944.

Commander, Battleship Division 4, Action Report of Bombardment and Fire Support for the Assault and Capture of Peleliu Island, Palau Islands, 12 September to 25 September, 1944, 2 October, 1944.

Commander, Carrier Division 26 (CTU-32.7.3), War Diary, September, 1944.

Commander, Cruiser Division 4 (CTG-32.5), Peleliu Action Report, 26 September, 1944.

Commander, Cruiser Division 9 (CTU 32.5.2) Action Report, 5 October, 1945.

Commander, Destroyer Squadron 19, War Diary, September, 1944.

Commander, Destroyer Squadron 56, War Diary, September, 1944.

Commander, Task Group 32 War Diary, September, 1944.

Commander, Task Group 32.5 Action Report – Bombardment and Capture of Peleliu Island, Palau Group, 12 September to 24 September, 1944.

Commander, Task Group 32.5.2, Action Report, Seizure and Occupation of Peleliu Island, Palau Group, 05 October, 1944.

Commander, Task Group 38.4 Action Report, December 12, 1945.

Commander, Third Fleet, Bulletin, Palaus Operation, December 28, 1944.

Commander, Third Fleet, War Diary, October 24, 1944.

Commander-in-Chief, Pacific, War Diary, September, 1944, October 4, 1944.

Commander-in-Chief, Pacific, Operations in the Pacific Ocean Areas during the Month of October, 1944, March 7, 1945.

Commander-in-Chief, United States Fleet (COMINCH), Battle Experience Bulletin #21, Supporting Operations for the Occupation of Palau and Ulithi, January 5, 1945.

War Diaries for September, 1944, for the following vessels:

LST 227

USS *Albert W. Grant*, DD-649

USS *Bennion*, DD-662

USS *California*, BB-44

USS *Centaurus*, AKA-17

USS *Cleveland*, CL-55

USS *Columbia*, CL-56

USS *Crescent City*, APA-21

USS *Denver*, CL-58

USS *DuPage*, APA-41

USS *Elmore*, APA-42

USS *Honolulu*, CL-48

USS *Houston*, CL-81

USS *Hunt*, DD674

USS *Idaho*, BB-42

USS *Indianapolis*, CA-35

USS *Iowa*, BB-61

USS *Leutze*, DD-481

USS *Louisville*, CA-28

USS *Maryland*, BB-46

USS *Minneapolis*, CA-36

USS *Mississippi*, BB-41

USS *Mount McKinley*, AGC-7

USS *New Jersey*, BB-62

USS *Pennsylvania*, BB-48

USS *Portland*, CA-33

USS *Pullam*, DD-474

USS *Richard P. Leary*, DD-664

USS *Robinson*, DD-562

USS *Tennessee*, BB-43

Index